The Poetics of Prose

Also by Tzvetan Todorov and available in English

The Fantastic: A Structural Approach to a Literary Genre
(translated by Richard Howard)

TZVETAN TODOROV

The Poetics of Prose

Translated from the French by
RICHARD HOWARD

With a new Foreword by
JONATHAN CULLER

Cornell University Press ITHACA, NEW YORK

Originally published in French under the title *La Poétique de la prose*. © 1971 by Editions du Seuil.

Copyright © 1977 by Cornell University

All rights reserved. Except for brief quotations in a review, this book, or parts thereof, must not be reproduced in any form without permission in writing from the publisher. For information address Cornell University Press, 124 Roberts Place, Ithaca, New York, 14850.

First published 1977 by Cornell University Press.

First printing, Cornell Paperbacks, 1977.
Third printing 1984.

Printed in the United States of America

The paper in this book is acid-free and meets the guidelines for permanence and durability of the Committee on Production Guidelines for Book Longevity of the Council on Library Resources.

Library of Congress Cataloging in Publication Data
(For library cataloging purposes only)

Todorov, Tzvetan.
   The poetics of prose.

   (Cornell paperbacks)
   Translation of Poétique de la prose.
   Includes index.
   1. Narration (Rhetoric)—Addresses, essays, lectures. 2. Criticism—Addresses, essays, lectures. I. Title.
PN218.T613   808.3   76-28024
ISBN 0-8014-0857-1
ISBN 0-8014-9165-7 pbk.

Contents

Foreword

"One proof that a systematic comprehension of a subject exists," writes Northrop Frye in his *Anatomy of Criticism,* "is the ability to write an elementary textbook expounding its fundamental principles." By this test, literary criticism is in a sad state indeed—"a mystery-religion without a gospel," Frye calls it. Critics perform their acts of devotion. They interpret individual poems, novels, or the complete works of a particular author; but for criticism to become a proper intellectual discipline it must, Frye says, return to the task first undertaken by Aristotle in his *Poetics:* the task of developing a systematic theory of literature. Literary critics should assume, as Frye says, that "there is a totally intelligible structure of knowledge attainable about poetry, which is not poetry itself, or the experience of it, but poetics."

When Frye wrote these words in 1957, he noted, sadly, that poetics had scarcely advanced since Aristotle's day. But since 1957 there has been an astonishing revival of poetics—not in America, nor among Frye's followers, but in France, among critics who have approached literature from a radically different perspective. Taking as their model not the Jungian archetypes which guide Frye's *Anatomy* but the concepts and analytical techniques of modern linguistics, these "structuralists," as they have generally been labeled, have begun to fill the need which Frye authoritatively described.

The poetics which emerges from their work, and of which *The Poetics of Prose* is an important example, aims to be a systematic theory of literature, an account of the modes of literary discourse and of the various conventions and types of organization which produce meaning in literature. But to speak of poetics simply as theory or as a systematization of theoretical insights is to miss what for Anglo-American criticism must be its most radical claim. We have been accustomed to assume that the purpose of theory is to enrich and illuminate critical practice, to make possible subtler and more accurate interpretations of particular literary works. But poetics asserts that interpretation is not the goal of literary study. Though the interpretation of works may be fascinating and personally fulfilling, the goal of literary study is to understand literature as a human institution, a mode of signification. When poetics studies individual works, it seeks not to interpret them but to discover the structures and conventions of literary discourse which enable them to have the meanings they do.

This crucial reversal of the customary relation between theory and interpretation is admirably illustrated and justified by the comparison with linguistics. The task of linguistics is not to interpret sentences, not to tell us what they mean, but to make explicit the rules and conventions which we have assimilated in learning our language and which make it possible for the sentences of our language to have the meanings they do. Speakers of a language are, of course, primarily concerned with the meanings of the sentences which they hear or utter, just as readers are primarily concerned with the meanings of literary works; but poetics, the systematic study of literature, attempts to specify the codes and conventions which make these meanings possible, just as linguistics, the systematic study of language, makes explicit the rules and conventions of a language.

Todorov's *Poetics of Prose* is an excellent introduction to this enterprise, for a variety of reasons. First of all, French structuralism has acquired a certain reputation for obscurity. Its predilection for technical terms and neologisms, the foreignness of its concerns and goals, and its pursuit of theoretical abstraction make many of its writings initially forbidding. But Todorov writes with an awareness of the Anglo-American critical tradition, and he consistently seeks the most economical formulation of important ideas. The clarity of his writing makes him, of all those working in the French tradition, the most immediately accessible and attractive to the nonspecialist reader.

Second, Todorov can speak with authority about poetics because he has himself been a central figure in its revival. His anthology of Russian Formalist criticism, *Théorie de la littérature* (Seuil, 1965), had considerable impact and made available in a Western language early twentieth-century work in poetics which had until then been generally ignored. His *Littérature et signification* (Larousse, 1967) introduced a series of distinctions and categories which were to be important for later research, and he made central contributions to genre theory with his *Introduction à la littérature fantastique* (Seuil, 1970) [1] and to the formal analysis of plot structure in his *Grammaire du Décaméron* (Mouton, 1969). Finally, as editor of the journal *Poétique* he has encouraged the consolidation of poetics as an academic discipline, and his long essay on poetics in *Qu'est-ce que le structuralisme?* (Seuil, 1968) [2] is an authoritative account of the discipline. The essays in *The Poetics of Prose* explore a range of topics which he has addressed at greater length elsewhere and draw upon his unusually diversified expertise.

Finally, the very heterogeneity of *The Poetics of Prose* makes it an excellent guide to the variety of projects which can be pursued under the banner of poetics. Although the chronological arrangement of the essays obscures their relations with one another, they can be organized into four groups according to their central concerns.

The first group—"Language and Literature," "Poetics and Criticism," "An Introduction to Verisimilitude," and "How to Read?"—deals with the general nature of poetics, its relation to other critical activities, and its basic concepts. Poetics, at least as it has developed in France, is based on linguistics but is not

[1] An English translation has been published: *The Fantastic: A Structural Approach to a Literary Genre* (The Press of Case Western Reserve University, 1973; Cornell Paperbacks, 1975).

[2] A revised and much improved version of this essay was published separately by Editions du Seuil in their Collection Points in 1974.

simply an application of linguistic categories to the language of literature. Description of that kind might tell us something about the organization of literary works and their predilection for particular linguistic constructions or effects, but it would miss the central fact with which poetics is concerned: that in literature perfectly ordinary linguistic constructions combine, according to conventions which are not linguistic but literary, to produce literary meanings. The move from linguistics to poetics thus involves a shift of level. Linguistics defines the units of a language and the way they combine to form meaningful sentences; poetics moves up to a second level and studies how phrases and sentences form literary units which combine to produce characters, plots, thematic structures. And just as linguistics is concerned with those norms of linguistic usage in a speech-community which make linguistic communication possible, so poetics is concerned with the norms of particular genres and of verisimilitude which make possible a variety of effects at a literary level.

Defining poetics in this way, Todorov locates it within the full range of potential critical activities through a series of distinctions. On the one hand, poetics is not concerned with extraliterary causes or referents and can thus be distinguished from what he calls "projection." Projection is criticism which treats literary works as the record of experiences (which may be defined biographically, socially, historically, thematically) which the analyst seeks to recover. On the other hand, since poetics aims at a general theory and not at the interpretation of individual texts, it may be distinguished both from "commentary," which sticks close to a given text and elucidates its individual elements, and from "interpretation," which attempts an integrated reading of a given work by translating the text into another set of terms which represent its meaning. This first group of essays distinguishes poetics from these and other interpretive activities.

The second project to which *The Poetics of Prose* contributes is the formal analysis of plot structure. Plot is obviously a central feature of narrative, and many of our traditional literary categories—comedy, tragedy, the picaresque, the *Bildungs-*

roman—seem based on loosely defined types of plot; but we still lack a systematic typology of plots and a rigorous method for the analysis of plot. Todorov has taken linguistics as a model in his attempt to work out a "grammar" of plots, and his essay "The Grammar of Narrative" is a summary of conclusions reached in his longer study, *Grammaire du Décaméron*. His essay "Narrative Transformations" addresses another and very important aspect of the topic. As readers we are able to distinguish between a complete and an incomplete narrative sequence, but what is it that makes a sequence seem to us complete or incomplete? The various narrative transformations which Todorov defines are hypotheses about the nature of such sequences and thus about the basic forms of plot structure. This approach marks an advance over his earlier work and should further our understanding of narrative structure.

A third project, central to any conception of poetics, is the analysis of genre. Prior to its recent revival, the notion of genre had fallen into disrepute because it seemed as though genres had to be treated either as sets of prescriptive norms (every tragedy, ode, and so forth must obey certain rules of the genre if it is to be a good tragedy, ode, and so forth) or as purely descriptive categories (any group of works which have common features could be treated as a genre). The first approach leads to incorrect normative judgments and the second makes the notion of genre trivial (for example, works in which the heroes ride horses could be treated as a genre). But once genres are treated as sets of norms or conventions which make possible the production of meaning, much as linguistic norms do, then the notion of genre is restored to a central place in literary theory. Generic conventions account for the meaning that is produced when a work violates or evades these conventions, and generic codes are postulated in order to explain the way we treat details in different sorts of works. Todorov's best work on genre comes in his book *The Fantastic*, but here he offers an essay on structural forms of the detective story, and his "Narrative-Men" and "Primitive Narrative" provide categories for the description of a narrative genre.

Finally, there is a large group of essays which seem to call into question the distinction, on which Todorov has insisted, between poetics and criticism or interpretation: "Speech according to Constant," "The Ghosts of Henry James," "Art according to Artaud," "The Quest of Narrative," "The Secret of Narrative," and "Number, Letter, Word." As some of their titles suggest, these essays focus on particular authors or works, and one is certainly justified in asking how they relate to poetics.

The answer is perhaps to be found in Todorov's discussion of "reading" in his concluding essay. Reading, as he describes it, involves "superposition" and "figuration": comparing works or passages from a single work with one another in order to discover common figures or configurations. Reading, he says, presupposes poetics, in that the reader must have a sense of what he is looking for, but on the other hand the reader does not simply apply the categories of poetics to a text; he does not simply note the presence or absence of attested literary devices and procedures. Reading involves, rather, the discovery of how a given work employs, modifies, parodies, and implicitly comments upon the signifying procedures defined by poetics. What Todorov calls reading is in fact a criticism guided and informed by poetics.

To many readers this sort of criticism may not appear highly distinctive. The two essays on Henry James attempt to discover common features of a group of short stories, and the essays on Constant and Artaud pursue a particular theme through one or several works. But there are two qualities of Todorov's criticism which do stand out. First, one might speak of the prominence, in these essays, of a "formal imagination." Though his conclusions do have thematic implications, he is interested less in the meanings of the works discussed than in the various formal structures or figures which are repeated either in different works or at different levels of a single work.

Second, and this is the more important point for someone like Todorov who is accustomed to looking at individual works as examples of literary conventions and techniques, criticism becomes an investigation of how a particular work resists, complies with, and implicitly comments upon the general signifying practices of literary discourse. The most interesting aspect of a literary work will be what it tells us about literary signification, and how it illuminates for us the problems which literature encounters as it tries to organize and give meaning to human experience.

These essays involve a return from poetics to criticism, a blurring of distinctions. That this return should take place does not diminish the importance of making an initial distinction between poetics and interpretation. This distinction remains crucial because only in that way can poetics be established. But we must also note that the literary theorist can always become a critic again; he can return to the interpretation of literary works, though this is neither the goal nor the justification of his theoretical projects. Structuralism is not a method of interpretation, but it can lead to an interpretive activity, and much of the interest of present-day criticism, especially of American criticism inspired by European example, is focused precisely here: in a subtle reflection on what individual works have to tell us about our attempts, in and through literature, to make things signify. Here, as in the other projects which belong to poetics itself, Todorov's *The Poetics of Prose* is a clear and informed introduction to the work of modern criticism.

JONATHAN CULLER

Oxford, England

□

Translator's Note

For the American edition of his work, the author has omitted references concerning some of the articles in their periodical form, and has occasionally emended the text by additions and deletions. The first chapter of the French edition appears in the present volume as an Appendix.

R. H.

New York

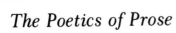

The Poetics of Prose

Introductory Note

The texts collected here were written between 1964 and 1969; some are published for the first time. They have not been altered; I have merely revised certain references and corrected occasional details of style. A more thoroughgoing correction would have resulted in the disappearance of the book, for each of these studies is, as I see it, no more than a new version of its predecessor or predecessors (rather than explore new subjects, one always returns, like a murderer to the scene of his crime, to traces already left behind). These texts figure here precisely for what is *incorrigible* about them.

According to Pascal's adage, the outcome of an inquiry leads to a knowledge of its basis. These texts constitute a series of attempts (if not two series) which I could not replace by a systematic exposition, an organizing synthesis. We shall not regret this if we accept in all investigation, hence in poetics, the law which Schiller formulated for epic poetry: "The goal already exists at each point of the poet's movement; hence we are not impatient to reach an objective, but lovingly linger at each step of the way."

I

Language and Literature

My undertaking is epitomized by Valéry's remark which I shall try to make both exemplary and explicit: "Literature is, and cannot be anything but, a kind of extension and application of certain properties of language."

What allows us to assert such a relationship? The very fact that the literary work is a "verbal work of art" has long provoked investigators to speak of language's "leading role" in literature; an entire discipline—stylistics—has been created on the borderline between literary studies and linguistics; many theses have been written on the "language" of this or that writer. Language is defined here as the material substance of the poet or of the work.

This too-obvious relationship is far from exhausting the many connections between language and literature. Perhaps Valéry was not concerned with language as material, but rather with language as model. Language performs this function in many cases outside literature. Man has constituted himself out of language, as the philosophers of our century have so often observed, and we are likely to discover its schema in all social activity. Or, in Emile Benveniste's phrase, "the configuration of language determines all semiotic systems." Since art is one of these systems, we can be sure of finding it marked by the abstract forms of language.

Literature enjoys, therefore, a particularly privileged status among semiotic activities. It has language as both its point of departure and its destination; language furnishes literature its abstract configuration as well as its perceptible material—it is both mediator and mediatized. Hence literature turns out to be not only the first field whose study takes language as its point of departure, but also the first field of which a knowledge can shed new light on the properties of language itself.

This special position of literature determines our relation to linguistics. It is obvious that in dealing with language we are not entitled to ignore the knowledge accumulated by that science, or by any other investigations of language. Yet, like every science, linguistics often proceeds by reduction and simplification of its object in order to manipulate it more readily; it sets aside or provisionally ignores certain features of language so that it can establish the homogeneity of others and permit their logic to show through. A procedure doubtless justified in the internal development of this science, but one which those who extrapolate its results must thereby regard with a certain suspicion: the features left out of consideration may be precisely those which have the greatest importance in another "semiotic system." The unity of the human sciences abides less in the methods elaborated by linguistics that are beginning to be employed in other fields than in the very object common to them all—language itself. Our image of language today, an image derived from certain studies of linguists must be enriched by what we have learned from these other sciences.

From this point of view, it becomes obvious that all knowledge of literature will follow a path parallel to that of the knowledge of language—more than that, these two paths will tend to coincide. An enormous field lies open to such investigation; only a relatively limited part of it has been explored hitherto in the brilliant pioneer studies of Roman Jakobson and his followers. Such studies have dealt with poetry, and they try to demonstrate the existence of a structure formed by the distribution of certain linguistic elements within a poem. I propose to indicate here, apropos of literary prose, several points where the relationship between language and literature seems particularly noticeable. Of course, because of the present state of our knowledge in this field, I shall limit myself to remarks of a general nature, without the slightest claim to "exhausting the subject."

Indeed, such a relationship has already been explored, with similar hopes. The Russian Formalists, pioneers in more than one field, had already sought to exploit this analogy. They located it, more specifically, between the devices of style and the procedures of narrative organization; one of Victor Shklovsky's first articles was in fact called "The Link between the Devices of Composition and General Stylistic Devices." This author noted that "staircase construction occurred in the same series as repetitions of sounds, tautology, tautological parallelism, repetitions." The three blows Roland strikes upon the rock were for Shklovsky of the same nature as the lexical ternary repetitions in folk poetry.

I do not wish to undertake a historical study here, and I shall confine myself to reviewing briefly several other results of the Formalist investigations, giving them the form which will be useful here. In his studies of narrative typology, Shklovsky had come to distinguish two major types of combination among stories: on the one hand, an open form in which new peripeties can always be added to the end, for instance the adventures of some such hero as Rocambole; and on the other, a closed form which begins and ends with the same motif, while inside it we are told other stories, for instance the story of Oedipus: at the beginning a prediction, at the end its fulfillment, between the two the attempts to evade it. Shklovsky did not realize, however, that these two forms represent the rigorous projection of two fundamental syntactic figures, used in the combination of two propositions between them, coordination and subordination. We may note that contemporary linguistics gives this second operation a name borrowed from the old poetics: embedding (*enchâssement*).

In the passage quoted above, it was *parallelism* that was investigated; this procedure is only one of those observed by Shklovsky. In his analysis of *War and Peace,* he points out, for instance, the *antithesis* formed by pairs of characters: "1. Napoleon—Kutuzov; 2. Pierre Bezukov—André Bolkonsky and at the same time Nicholas Rostov who serves as an axis of reference to one and the other." Shklovsky also notes *gradation:* several members of a family share the same character traits, but to varying degrees. Thus in *Anna Karenina,* "Stiva is located on a lower step in relation to his sister."

But parallelism, antithesis, gradation and repetition are just so many rhetorical figures. We may then formulate as follows the underlying thesis of Shklovsky's remarks: there exist certain narrative figures which are projections of rhetorical figures. Starting from this supposition, we might verify what forms are taken by other, less familiar figures of rhetoric on the level of narrative.

Consider, for example *association,* a figure relating to the use of an inadequate person of the verb. Here is a linguistic example—this sentence which a teacher might say to his pupils: "What do we have for today?" Michel Butor has given an interesting demonstration of the uses of this figure in literature apropos of Descartes; he has also employed it himself in his novel *A Change of Heart (La Modification).*

Here is another figure which might be taken for a definition of the detective novel, if we had not borrowed it from Fontanier's study of rhetoric, written early in the nineteenth century. The figure is *sustentation,* and "consists in keeping the reader or listener in suspense for a long time, and then surprising him by something he was far from expecting." The figure can thus be transformed into a literary genre.

Mikhail Bakhtin, the great Soviet literary critic, has studied Dostoyevsky's particular use of another figure, *occupation,* which Fontanier defines as follows: "It consists in forestalling or rejecting in advance an objection which might be raised." Any utterance of Dostoyevsky's characters implicitly encompasses that of their interlocutor, whether imaginary or real. Monologue is always a dissimulated dialogue, which determines the profound ambiguity of Dostoyevsky's characters.

Finally, I shall review several figures based on one of language's essential properties: the absence of a one-to-one relation between the sounds and the meaning. This absence gives rise to two well-known linguistic phenomena, synonymy and polysemy. Synonymy, the basis of some kinds of wordplay, takes the form of a literary device we call "recognition." The fact that the same character can have two appearances—or, one might say, the existence of two forms for the same content—recalls the phenomenon which results from the comparison of two synonyms.

Polysemy gives rise to several rhetorical figures of which I shall discuss only one: *syllepsis*. A notorious example occurs in this line by Racine:

> *Brûlé de plus de feux que je n'en allumai.*

> Burnt by more fires than any I lighted.

Where does the figure come from? From the fact that the word *feux* (fires), which occurs in each proposition, is taken, in each, in a different sense. The *feux* of the first proposition are imaginary, they burn the character's soul, whereas those of the second correspond to very real flames.

This figure has had a great extension in narrative; we may observe it in the example of one of Boccaccio's novellas. Here we are told that a monk had paid a visit to his mistress, wife of a prosperous townsman. Suddenly the husband returns: what is to be done? The monk and the wife, who had shut themselves up in the baby's room, pretend to be taking care of the child who they say is sick. The reassured husband thanks them warmly. Here the movement of the narrative follows a form similar to syllepsis. The same fact, the monk and the wife in the bedroom, receives one interpretation in the part of the narrative which precedes it and another in the part which follows. According to the first part, the event is a lovers' meeting; according to the second, the care of a sick child. This figure occurs quite frequently in Boccaccio—in such stories as those of the nightingale, the cask, and so forth.

Till now our comparison—following the practice of the Formalists—has juxtaposed certain manifestations of language with certain literary ones. In other words, we have observed only forms. I should now like to sketch another possible approach which would explore the categories underlying these two universes, that of language and that of literature. For this we must depart from the level of forms and turn to that of structures. Thereby, we shall leave literature in order to treat that discourse on literature which is criticism.

The problems of signification could be treated if not successfully, at least promisingly once we come closer to defining the notion of meaning. Linguistics has long neglected this phenomenon, hence it is not in linguistics that we shall find our categories, but among the logicians. We can take as our point of departure Frege's tripartite division: a sign has a reference, a meaning, and an associated image (*Bedeutung, Sinn, Vorstellung*). Only the meaning can be apprehended with the help of rigorous linguistic methods, for only the meaning depends on language alone and is controlled by the power of usage, of linguistic habits. What is the meaning? According to Benveniste, it is the capacity of a linguistic unit to integrate a higher-level unit. A word's meaning is delimited by the combinations in which it can fulfill its linguistic function. A word's meaning is the sum of its possible relations with other words.

To isolate meaning in the sum of significations is a procedure which might greatly aid the work of description, in literary studies. In literary discourse, as in everyday speech, meaning can be isolated from a set of other significations which we might call *interpretations*. In literature the problem of meaning is more complex: whereas in speech, the integration of units does not exceed the level of the sentence, in literature the sentences are once again integrated into utterances and the utterances, in their turn, are integrated into units of larger dimensions, until we reach the work as a whole. The meaning of a monologue or of a description can be grasped and verified by its relations with the other elements of the work: the characterization of a hero, the preparation of a reversal or suspension in the plot. Conversely the *interpretations* of each unit are countless, for they depend on the system in which that unit will be included in order to be understood. According to the type of discourse into which we project the element of the work, we will be dealing with a sociological, psychoanalytical, or philosophical criticism. But this will always be an interpretation of literature in another type of discourse, whereas the investigation of meaning does not lead us outside literary discourse itself. It is here perhaps that we may trace the borderline between those two related and nonetheless distinct activities, poetics and criticism.

Now let us turn to another pair of basic categories. They have been formulated by Benveniste in his studies of verb tenses. He has shown the existence, within language, of two distinct levels of the speech-act: that of discourse and that of the story. These levels refer to the integration of the subject of the speech-act within what is spoken. In the case of the story, Benveniste tells us, "we are dealing with the presentation of phenomena which occurred at a certain moment of time without any intervention on the part of the speaker in the story." Discourse, on the other hand, is defined as "any speech-act supposing a speaker and a listener, and in the speaker an intention to influence the listener in some way." Each language possesses a certain number of elements which serve to inform us exclusively about the subject and the other elements of the speech-act and which effect the conversion of language into discourse; the others serve exclusively to "present the phenomena which have occurred."

We must, then, make an initial distribution within the literary texture according to the level of speech-act manifest there. Let us take these sentences by Proust: "He lavished upon me a kindness as superior to Saint-Loup's as the latter's to the affability of a tradesman. Compared to that of a great artist, the friendliness of *grand seigneur,* however charming, seems like playacting, a pretense." In this text, only the first proposition (up to "kindness") concerns the level of narrative. The comparison which follows as well as the general reflection contained in the second sentence belong to the level of discourse, which is marked by specific linguistic indices (for instance, the change in tense). But the first proposition, too, is linked to discourse, for the subject of the speech-act is indicated in it by the personal pronoun. Hence there is an intersection of means in order to indicate the relation to discourse: they may be either external (direct or indirect style) or internal (when speech does not refer to an exterior reality). The proportion of the two speech-act levels determines the degree of opacity of the literary language:

a discourse has a superior autonomy for it assumes its entire signification starting from itself, without the intermediary of an imaginary reference. The fact that Elstir has lavished his kindness refers to an external representation, that of the two characters and of an action. But the comparison and the reflection which follows are representations in themselves, they refer only to the subject of the speech-act, and they thereby assert the presence of language itself.

The interpenetration of these two categories is, we realize, considerable, and in itself raises many problems which have not yet been touched. The situation is further complicated if we realize that this is not the sole form such categories assume in literature. The possibility of considering any speech as, above all, a communication concerning reality or as a subjective speech-act leads us to another important observation. We can see in it not only the characteristics of two types of speech, but also two complementary aspects of all speech, literary or not. In any utterance, we can temporarily separate these two aspects—which are on the one hand an action on the part of a speaker, a linguistic manipulation; and on the other, the evocation of a certain reality—and this reality has in the case of literature no other existence than that conferred by the utterance itself.

Here again, the Russian Formalists had noted the opposition, though without being able to show its linguistic bases. In any narrative, they distinguished the *fable* (the story), that is, the series of events represented as they would have occurred in life, from the *subject* (the plot), the special arrangement given to these events by the author. Temporal inversions were the example they preferred: it is obvious that the posterior communication of an event which had actually occurred before another event betrays the author's intervention, in other words the intervention of the subject of the speech-act. We now realize that this opposition does not correspond to a dichotomy between the book and represented life, but to two ever-present aspects of an utterance, to its double nature as utterance and speech-act. These two aspects give life to two realities, each as linguistic as the other: the world of the characters and the world of the narrator-reader couple.

The distinction between discourse and narrative affords us a better understanding of another problem of literary theory, that of "point of view." Here we are concerned with the transformations which the notion of "person" undergoes in literary narrative. This problem raised by Henry James has been treated a number of times subsequently—in France, notably by Jean Pouillon, Claude-Edmonde Magny, and Georges Blin. Those studies which failed to take into account the linguistic nature of the phenomenon have not managed to make its nature entirely explicit, though they have described its most important aspects.

Literary narrative, which is a mediatized, not an immediate language and which moreover is subject to the constraints of fiction, knows only one "personal" category, the third person: that is, impersonality. The one who says *I* in the novel is not the *I* of discourse, that is, the subject of the speech-act. He is only a character, and the status of his words (direct style) gives them a maximum objectivity, instead of bringing them closer to the subject of the actual speech-act. But there exists another *I,* an *I* generally invisible, which refers to the narrator, that "poetic personality" we apprehend through the discourse. Hence there is a dialectic of personality and impersonality, between the *I* of the narrator (implicit) and the *he* of the character (which can be an explicit *I*), between discourse and story. Here is the whole problem of "point of view": in the degree of transparency of the impersonal *he* of the story in relation to the *I* of discourse.

It is easy to see, from this perspective, what classification of "point of view" we can adopt; it corresponds closely to the one Jean Pouillon proposes in his book *Temps et Roman:*

——either the *I* of the narrator appears constantly through the *he* of the hero, as in the case of classical narrative, with an omniscient narrator; here discourse supplants story;

——or the *I* of the narrator is entirely effaced by the *he* of the hero; this is the famous "objective narration," a type used chiefly by American authors between the two world wars, in which the narrator knows nothing about his character, but merely sees his movements and gestures, hears his words; here story supplants discourse;

——or else the *I* of the narrator is on a basis of equality with the *he* of the hero, both are informed in the same way as to the development of the action; this type of narrative, which first appeared in the eighteenth century, dominates contemporary literary production; the narrator attaches himself to one of the characters and observes everything through his eyes; in this type, the fusion of *I* and *he* into a narrating *I* makes the presence of the real *I*, that of the narrator, still more difficult to grasp.

This is only a first rough outline; every narrative combines several "points of view"; moreover, there exist many intermediary forms. The character may deceive himself in telling the story, just as he may confess all he knows about it; he may analyze it down to the last detail or be content with the appearance of things; we may be given a dissection of his consciousness ("stream of consciousness") or an articulated speech; all these varieties belong to the point of view which puts the narrator and the character on a basis of equality. Analyses based on linguistic categories will be able to grasp these nuances more surely.

I have tried to sketch the most obvious manifestations of a linguistic category in literary narrative. Other categories await their turn: we must some day discover what time, person, aspect, and voice have become in literature, for they will certainly be present in it if literature is, as Valéry believed, only an "extension and application of certain properties of language."

1966

2

Poetics and Criticism

A comparison of Gérard Genette's *Figures* with Jean Cohen's *Structure du langage poétique* will be instructive; the two books share so many features that the perfect opposition formed by their other aspects is not arbitrary but charged with a meaning we must disclose.

This opposition concerns different aspects of the two books. First of all, theme: *Structure du langage poétique* is a study of properties common to all literary works; *Figures* is devoted to the description of individual poetic systems—that of Etienne Binet, that of Proust, that of *Astrée*. Cohen's book seeks to establish the foundations of poetics in general; Genette's, to reconstruct those of particular poetics. One deals with poetry, the other with works of poetry.

The opposition holds good even with regard to formal properties. Cohen's writing is synthetic and his book seeks to be transparent. Genette's texts, on the other hand, are analytic, descriptive, and, so to speak, opaque: they do not refer to a meaning independent of them, the form chosen is the only form possible. It is no accident that Cohen's coherent exposition is counterbalanced by a collection of articles whose unity is difficult to grasp. Even the singular of Cohen's title, *Structure,* stands in significant opposition to Genette's plural, *Figures.*

Yet there would be no reason for noting such oppositions if the two books did not also testify to a unity quite as significant.

We might say that this unity lies in the immanent approach t
literature common to both authors. The immanent explicatio
of phenomena is a slogan which has become banal enoug
today, but with regard to reflection upon literature, I believ
these are the first two serious attempts (in France) to deal witl
literature in and of itself. This principle would suffice for us t
make a comparison between their method and a contemporar
current of thought. Moreover, there is another peculiarity whicl
reinforces this first impression: the specific goal of both books i
to describe literary *structures*. Is the structural analysis of liter
ature a fait accompli at last? If so, how can it be embodied ii
two books which are so different?

To answer these questions, let us start with one of Genette'
articles, specifically entitled "Structuralism and Literary Criti
cism." To the problem raised by this title, Genette gives fou
successive answers: every critic, whatever his intentions, is
"structuralist" because he makes use of elements of existin,
structures (literary works) in order to create new structures (th,
critical work itself); aspects of the work which treat both liter
ary analysis and linguistics must be studied with the help o
methods elaborated by the latter science; the structuralist i
helpless in the presence of the individual work, especially if th,
critic endows it with meaning, as is always the case once thi
work is sufficiently close to us; literary history, on the othe
hand, can and must become structural, by studying genres anc
their development. To sum up, we might say that in Genette'
conception, the field of literature should be separated into tw,
parts, each lending itself to a different type of analysis: th,
study of the individual work cannot be undertaken by structura
methods, but these methods remain pertinent for the other par
of the field.

Perhaps the vocabulary of a territorial division is not the mos
appropriate one to characterize this essential difference. I
might be more useful to speak of a degree of generality. Struc
tural analysis, we must not forget, was created within a science
it was intended to describe the phonological system of a lan
guage, not a sound—the kinship system in a society, not a
parent. It is a scientific method, and in applying it we are "doing

science." Now what can science do when confronted with the individual object—with a work? At most, science can attempt to describe it; but description itself is not science and becomes so only when it is integrated within a general theory. Hence the description of the work can relate to science (and thus permit the application of structural methods) only if it allows us to discover the properties of the entire system of literary expression or else of its synchronic and diachronic varieties.

We recognize here the directions prescribed by Genette for "structural criticism": the description of the properties of literary discourse and literary history. The individual work remains alien to the goal of the structuralists less because of the investment of meaning which occurs during the reading than because of the force of its very status as an individual object. If the "structuralist critic" has for so long existed only in the optative mode, it is because this label contains a contradiction in terms: it is science which can be structural, not criticism.

Nor does structural literary history exist, for the time being. Jean Cohen's book, however, does give us an image of what might be that investigation of the properties of literary discourse to which, it seems to me, the name *poetics* can best be given. Cohen, starting with his "Introduction," takes a very firm stand: on the one hand, he wants to establish scientific (verifiable and refutable) hypotheses, undaunted by the sacrilege of speaking of a "science of poetry"; on the other hand, he regards poetry, above all, as a particular form of language, hence he limits his work to the study of the "poetic forms of language and of language alone." His goal is as follows: to discover and describe the forms of language proper to poetry, in opposition to prose; for "the difference between prose and poetry is of a linguistic, that is, formal, nature." Here poetics finally takes the place suitable for it, alongside linguistics. We are obviously a long way from the critic whose goal is to characterize specifically *one* work: what interests Cohen is a "constant which remains throughout individual variations" and which exists "in the language of all poets."

But if "structuralist criticism" is a contradiction in terms, then what about Genette's "structuralism"? A close reading will show us that literary structures are indeed the object of his study, but not in the same sense of the word as for Cohen, who studies "the structure of poetic language." Cohen's *structure* is an abstract relation manifest in the individual work in very diverse forms. It is related to law, to rules, and is found at a different level of generality from that of the forms by which it is realized. This is hardly the case for Genette's *structures*. This word must here be taken in a purely spatial sense, as we might speak, for instance, of "graphic structures" in a painting. Structure is the particular arrangement of two forms in relation to each other. In one of his texts, *"L'or tombe sous le fer,"* Genette has even indulged in literally drawing the structure formed by the "elements," the metals and stones in the universe of baroque poetry. We are not concerned here with a principle logically anterior to forms, but with the particular space which separates and connects two or more forms.

This brings us to the very center of Genette's critical vision. It might be said that the sole object of his investigations is to fill, compartment after compartment, every corner of a wide abstract space; he is fascinated by this immense panorama where concealed symmetries wait motionless for an attentive glance to discern them. To reveal structures is only one means of access to this image which becomes richer moment by moment, but whose overall design still remains just as uncertain.

It is evident that no point of doctrine postulates the obligatory existence of such structures in the literary work. Without saying so explicitly, Genette lets it be understood that the writer enjoys a certain freedom as to whether he must submit the universe of his book to structural laws. Though Genette's personal preferences are in fact for authors who organize this universe according to a pre-established design, nothing tells us that others might not have written in ignorance of this mode of thought. The authors Genette chooses are "technicians"—the baroque poets, Robbe-Grillet, and others; in contrast, as we see, to that psychological criticism which delights in "spontaneous" and "inspired" authors.

Nor are we surprised that half of Genette's collection is devoted to the work of critics: he himself has explained that criticism is a particularly rich display of structures. It is this aspect of criticism which attracts him, criticism as object, not as method; it would be futile to seek in this book of criticism, devoted largely to criticism, so much as ten lines on the method of the author himself! Even apropos of critics, Genette is content with an explanation, and does not follow it with the construction of a transcendent critical system: it is not Genette-on-Valéry, Genette-on-Borges we are reading, Valéry and Borges are here to speak for themselves, each one to present us with as text-as-synthesis of all his texts. Thereby Genette performs a real tour de force: we read pages which, at one and the same time, belong to him—and are part of someone else's work.

What then is this fugitive method of Genette's? In any case, he does not adopt that principle of structuralism which holds that the method be in the image of its object (if it is not the object which comes to be in the image of the method) and, dealing with "structures," become structural itself. Genette's procedure remains a commentary which merely espouses the forms of the object in order to make them its own, which leaves the work only in order to reproduce it elsewhere: the relationship between the author's and the critic's texts is one of contagion, not of analogy.

Now let us return to our initial antithesis. The space outlined by these two procedures, contrary and juxtaposed, is the space which separates poetics from criticism: for Genette's analysis deserves the name of literary criticism, in the fullest sense of the term. The two books happen to incarnate, in an exemplary fashion, the two main attitudes reading provokes: criticism and science, criticism and poetics. Let us now try to specify the possibilities and the limits of each.

First, poetics: what it studies is not poetry or literature but "poeticity" or "literariness." The individual work is not an ultimate goal for poetics; if it pauses over one work rather than another, it is because such a work reveals more distinctly the properties of literary discourse. Poetics will have to study not the already existing literary forms but, starting from them, a sum of possible forms: what literature *can* be rather than what it *is*. Poetics is at once less and more demanding than criticism: it does not claim to name the meaning of a work, but it seeks to be much more rigorous than critical meditation.

Partisans of the notion of "analyzing the work for what it is, not for what it expresses" will therefore not be satisfied by poetics. There are always complaints, indeed, about the interpretations of a psychological or sociological criticism: it analyzes the work not as an end in itself but as a means of access to something else, as the effect of a cause. But this is because psychoanalysis and sociology claim to be sciences; thereby, the criticism inspired by them cannot be restricted to the work itself. As soon as literary studies are constituted into a science, as in the case of poetics today, the work itself is transcended again—is considered, once more, as an effect, but now as the effect of its own form. The only difference then—but an important one—is that instead of transposing the work to another type of discourse, we study the underlying properties of literary discourse itself.

This impossibility of being restricted to the particular escapes Cohen's attention in his explicit declarations. Thus he reproaches critics for being more interested in the poet than in the poem, and says apropos of his own work that "literary analysis of the poem as such can be nothing but the exploration of those mechanisms of transfiguration of language by the play of figures." Obviously, in his concern to describe these "mechanisms of transfiguration" he no longer analyzes the "poem as such" at all, for this is impossible. He studies, in fact, a general mechanism, and no poem is discussed in the entire book except as an example.

This confusion is not a serious one, for it is confined to a few isolated declarations; the book as a whole adopts the perspective of poetics, which does not study the poem as such but as a manifestation of poeticity. However, another reduction risks damaging the results obtained, and indeed shows what kind of dangers poetics must fear, the limit it must not venture beyond. This is the excessive generality Cohen attains by taking one of the principles of structuralism literally: to study not phenomena but their difference. The one task of poetics, he tells us, is to

study how poetry differs from prose. The only feature of the figure to be retained is the one whereby poetic expression differs
from "natural" expression. But in order to define poetry, it is not
enough to say how it differs from prose, for the two have a common portion which is literature. Of "poetic language," Cohen re-
tains only the adjective, forgetting that there is also a substantive. The figure is not only an expression different from
another, but also an expression *tout court*. To forget this, to
isolate the two parts, is to consider the figure—or poetry—from
the point of view of something else, and not in itself. Here once
again Cohen infringes upon that principle of immanence which
he elsewhere proclaims, but this time with more serious consequences, for he has in fact a tendency to take poetry for what
differs in it from prose and not for an integral phenomenon.

The extreme which poetics must avoid is an excessive generality, an excessive reduction of the poetic object; the grid it
utilizes risks letting the poetic phenomenon slip through. One
can guess, from the description we have given of Genette's
method, where the limit is which he, in his turn, should avoid
overstepping. His criticism dissolves into the work-as-object to
such a degree that it risks vanishing into it altogether. Long and
frequent quotation is not an accident in Genette's texts, it is one
of the most characteristic features of his method: the poet can
express his thought as well as he, just as he can speak for the
poet. One step more and this criticism will cease being an explication and become only a reprise, a rehearsal. The best description—and it is indeed with description that we are dealing in
Genette's texts—is the one which is not description *all the way*,
the one which makes explicit by reproducing.

The two attitudes would therefore benefit by approaching
each other more closely. One of the finest texts in *Figures*,
"Silences de Flaubert," allows us to glimpse, though from a distance, the possibilities thereby offered. In this text, Genette
seeks to grasp "what is most specific in Flaubert's writing";
simplifying a great deal, we might say that he is concerned with
the special function Flaubert assigns to description, with the extremely important role description plays in his novels. Once
again we confront certain notions of poetics, notions which

seem indeed to illuminate matters; but this is only a foretaste which leaves us hoping for more. For Genette speaks of description as if it were self-explanatory; but indeed what is description? Why does it stand in opposition to narration, whereas both seem to belong to the discourse of the narrator as opposed to the discourse of the characters? What opposes description to narrative—is it simply the substitution of a pause for movement? Are these the only notions on this level of generality or are there others as well? We can no longer trust the definitions of classical poetics; in any case, we have forgotten them; but we must produce new ones. How does it happen that description is present among the rhetorical figures? Is there a change in the mode of expression alone, or also in the narrator's position with regard to the characters (transition from the viewpoint "with" to the viewpoint "behind") in this dazzling phrase from *Madame Bovary* which appears in the middle of a "frenzy of locomotion": "Old men in black coats stroll in the sunshine down a terrace quite green with ivy"? These are some of the questions to which poetics should be able to provide if not an answer, at least the means of finding one.

Hence there is no wall between poetics and criticism, as is demonstrated not only by the project we have just outlined but also by the fact that this pure critic and this pure poetician have found common ground and dealt with one and the same problem: the figures of rhetoric. The choice of this meeting place is already significant (for, among others, the real influence of Valéry on contemporary critical thought): it suggests indeed a rehabilitation of rhetoric. These two writers do not themselves accept, it is true, all the assertions of the classical rhetoricians; but it is henceforth obvious that we cannot dismiss in a few words the problem of rhetorical figures—a problem that is real, important, and complex.

Our two authors develop two different theories of the rhetorical figure, which we shall examine briefly here. To do so, let us consider a single essential point, the definition of the figure. According to Genette, for there to be a figure, there must also be two means of saying the same thing; the figure exists only by opposition to a literal expression. "The existence and character of the figure are absolutely determined by the existence and character of virtual signs to which I compare the real signs by proposing their semantic equivalence." The figure is the space which exists between the two expressions.

According to Cohen, the figure is also defined in relation to something outside itself. But this is not another expression, it is a rule which belongs to the code of language. At the same time he restricts the varieties of relation between the figure and the rule: the relation in question is a transgression, the figure depends on a violation of the rule ("each of the figures being specified as an infraction of one of the rules which compose this code"). The body of Cohen's book represents the development and the verification of this hypothesis, as exemplified by several representative figures. It must be said at once that this development and this verification are, aside from some insignificant exceptions, irreproachable, and that they effectively prove that the figures considered represent infractions of some linguistic rule.

But the problem of the figure is not yet solved thereby. The common denominator of the four or five figures Cohen examines must be found in all the others for it to be a necessary condition of the phenomenon "figure." Otherwise, two possibilities are to be envisaged (just as in Genette's definition): either we declare that what does not possess this denominator is not a figure. But then this definition is purely tautological: we induce the definition from phenomena selected by a criterion furnished by the definition itself. Or else we declare the definition unsatisfactory and seek another common denominator for figures selected according to an independent criterion.

Let us take a figure as common as the antithesis: "Heaven is in her eyes, hell in her heart": What is the literal expression which articulates the space of language here? What is the linguistic rule which has been infringed?

The confusion has different causes in each of the two conceptions. Genette almost formulates his when he deals with description. It is indeed a figure, but why? Because, he tells us, following Fontanier, "Théramène . . . says in four lines what he might have said in two words, and therefore description replaces (that is, might be replaced by) a simple designation: there is the figure." But if the description were absent, there would no longer be the same *meaning;* all that would remain the same is the object evoked, the *referent.* Fontanier and Genette slip from the opposition between two forms of one meaning to the opposition between two meanings relating to one referent. But it is no longer a linguistic space which they enclose: it is a psychological space: to describe or not to describe. Description, like antithesis, gradation, and many other figures, does not refer to a literal expression. The space of language is not within it.

Cohen's reasoning is not erroneous but incomplete. It is true that the figures he examines are infractions; but many others are not so. Alliteration, Cohen says, is a figure because it is in opposition to the phono-semantic parallelism which rules in language: in its case, similar sounds do not correspond to similar meanings. Correct; but then how can *derivation,* or even simple *repetition,* in which the association of similar sounds corresponds to an association of similar meanings, be a figure? If we prove that it is, it is because we possess a "dialectical" method which, we know, wins every time. Every figure is not an anomaly, and we must seek out a criterion other than transgression.

Yet the right definition was already present in Du Marsais' rhetoric (whose failure Genette observes a little too readily): "The ways of speaking," Du Marsais wrote, "which express not just thoughts but thoughts uttered in a particular manner which gives them a character of their own, such ways of speaking, I say, are called figures." A figure is what gives discourse "a character of its own," what renders it perceptible; figurative discourse is an opaque discourse, discourse without figures is transparent. To call the ship "ship" is merely to utilize language as a mediator of signification, thereby killing both object and word. To call the ship "sail" is to fix our attention on the word, giving language a value of its own and the world a chance of surviving.

But for this it is not necessary that there exist another expression in order to say the same thing, nor a linguistic rule that has been infringed. It suffices that there be a form, a particular disposition of language (Du Marsais said as much: "a particular manner") for us to be able to perceive this language itself. A figure is what can be described, what is institutionalized as such. *Gradation* is a figure because we notice the succession of three names for the same species: a look gives life to the figure as it kills Euridice. If there were no figures, we should perhaps still be unaware of the existence of language: let us not forget that the Sophists, who were the first to speak of them, were the creators of a discourse on language, rhetoric.

Figures of speech are the subject of only one chapter in Genette's book, but they are the center of Cohen's attention and his abusive interpretation is a larger threat to the construction of the whole. Figures-as-infractions are the very basis of his theory: they limit the normal functioning of language, letting only the poetic message pass through. But the figures are only a presence of language itself, there is no necessary destruction of ordinary language. Then how does this "other" message manage to get through?

We believe that this "other" message does not get through because it has never existed, at least not in the form Cohen attributes to it. And since it is not his line of argument that we dispute, we must descend, in order to expose the causes of a new confusion, to the logico-linguistic premises from which his reasoning derives.

The signified aspect of the linguistic sign is separated, for Cohen, into two parts: form and substance. This pair of terms, borrowed from Hjelmslev, is used with a certain uncertainty, and it would be to our advantage to establish its meaning from the start. "Form is style," form is what is lost in translation, the expressive and stylistic particularities in the strictest sense of the word. Substance is the "thing existing in itself and independent of any verbal or non-verbal expression." On this basis, Cohen's poetic theory is developed as follows: substance (objects) cannot be poetic in itself; hence poetry derives exclusively from form. For poetry to be achieved, we must prevent the normal functioning of language which habitually transmits substances, not forms: this is the role of figures. Once the denotative message is jammed, we can perceive the form which resolves itself into pure affectivity. At this moment, "it is no longer a question of the message itself, as a system of signs, but of the subjective effect produced on the receiver"; the effect of poetry is in the emotions and its study belongs to a psychology, not to semantics. And Cohen quotes this significant sentence of Carnap's which "expresses very nicely our own conception": "The purpose of a poem . . . is . . . to express certain emotions of the poet and to excite analogous emotions in us."

Let us begin with the premises. What is striking about this theory of signification—and this is paradoxical—is that words do not have meaning: they have only a referent (substance) and a stylistic and emotional value (form). Now logic and linguistics have long asserted that aside from these two elements there exists a third, the most important element, which we call *meaning* or *intention*. "The satellite of the earth" and "that golden sickle," Cohen tells us, are in opposition exclusively by their form: the first expression contains no figure and is affectively neutral, the second is figurative and emotional. "The moon is poetic as 'queen of the night' or as 'that golden sickle'; it remains prosaic as 'the satellite of the earth.' " Now it is not only the stylistic value which differs in these two expressions, it is also the meaning; what they have in common is a referent, not a signification; but this latter is interior to language. The essential difference is not in the emotional reaction which they provoke in the receiver (and do they do so?), but in the meaning they have.

"Lamartine's *Le Lac,* Hugo's *Tristesse d'Olympio,* Musset's *Le Souvenir* all say the same thing, but each one says it in a new way," Cohen asserts. Or again: the poem's esthetic value resides not in what it says but in the manner in which it says it. Now there are no two ways of saying the same thing; only the referent can remain the same; the two "ways" create two different significations.

There is, then, no proof that poetry resides in what Cohen calls "form": if he manages to prove that it is not in the referent, he has told us nothing with regard to the meaning. There are, on the other hand, many arguments against the reduction of the poem to a complex of emotions. Jakobson, more than forty years ago, put us on our guard: "Poetry can use the means of emotional language, but always with intentions which are its own. This resemblance between the two linguistic systems, as well as the use made by poetic language of the means proper to emotional language, often provokes the identification of the two. Such an identification is erroneous, since it does not take account of the fundamental functional difference between the two linguistic systems." To reduce poetry to an analogous "sentiment" in the poet and his reader, as Rudolf Carnap seeks to do, is to return to psychological conceptions long since superseded. Poetry is not a matter of sentiments, but of signification.

The gulf opened by Cohen between two opposing types of signification of which only one is esthetically valid manages to reestablish, in all its former grandeur, the old "form" and "content" couple. The danger of this conception (which Valéry himself did not entirely avoid) is not in the primacy given to content at the expense of form—to say the opposite would be quite as false—but in the very existence of this dichotomy. If structuralism has taken one step forward since Formalism, it is precisely in having ceased to isolate an exclusively valid form and to ignore whatever the content may be. The literary work does not have a form and a content but a structure of significations whose relations must be apprehended.

Here too Cohen's reductive conception collides with the facts: many a poetics cannot be explained as an infraction of the principles of language. But "the classical esthetic is an anti-poetic esthetic," Cohen assures us. No; poetics is a category broader than the category he offers us, and the esthetic of the classics readily finds its own place within it.

The critical remarks we have just formulated must not lead us to mistake the importance of Cohen's endeavor. Many of his analyses remain an incontestable acquisition, and if the premises and conclusions lend themselves to discussion, this may be no more than an additional merit: for it was high time to begin discussing the problems of poetics.

1966

3

The Typology of Detective Fiction

> Detective fiction cannot be subdivided into kinds.
> It merely offers historically different forms.
>
> —Boileau and Narcejac, *Le Roman policier*, 1964

If I use this observation as the epigraph to an article dealing precisely with "kinds" of "detective fiction," it is not to emphasize my disagreement with the authors in question, but because their attitude is very widespread; hence it is the first thing we must confront. Detective fiction has nothing to do with this question: for nearly two centuries, there has been a powerful reaction in literary studies against the very notion of genre. We write either about literature in general or about a single work, and it is a tacit convention that to classify several works in a genre is to devalue them. There is a good historical explanation for this attitude: literary reflection of the classical period, which concerned genres more than works, also manifested a penalizing tendency—a work was judged poor if it did not sufficiently obey the rules of its genre. Hence such criticism sought not only to describe genres but also to prescribe them; the grid of genre preceded literary creation instead of following it.

The reaction was radical: the romantics and their present-day descendants have refused not only to conform to the rules of the genres (which was indeed their privilege) but also to recognize the very existence of such a notion. Hence the theory of genres has remained singularly undeveloped until very recently. Yet now there is a tendency to seek an intermediary between the too-general notion of literature and those individual objects which are works. The delay doubtless comes from the fact that typology implies and is implied by the description of these individual works; yet this task of description is still far from having received satisfactory solutions. So long as we cannot describe the structure of works, we must be content to compare certain measurable elements, such as meter. Despite the immediate interest in an investigation of genres (as Albert Thibaudet remarked, such an investigation concerns the problem of universals), we cannot undertake it without first elaborating structural description: only the criticism of the classical period could permit itself to deduce genres from abstract logical schemas.

An additional difficulty besets the study of genres, one which has to do with the specific character of every esthetic norm. The major work creates, in a sense, a new genre and at the same time transgresses the previously valid rules of the genre. The genre of *The Charterhouse of Parma,* that is, the norm to which this novel refers, is not the French novel of the early nineteenth century; it is the genre "Stendhalian novel" which is created by precisely this work and a few others. One might say that every great book establishes the existence of two genres, the reality of two norms: that of the genre it transgresses, which dominated the preceding literature, and that of the genre it creates.

Yet there is a happy realm where this dialectical contradiction between the work and its genre does not exist: that of popular literature. As a rule, the literary masterpiece does not enter any genre save perhaps its own; but the masterpiece of popular literature is precisely the book which best fits its genre. Detective fiction has its norms; to "develop" them is also to disappoint them: to "improve upon" detective fiction is to write "literature," not detective fiction. The whodunit par excellence is not the one which transgresses the rules of the genre, but the one which conforms to them: *No Orchids for Miss Blandish* is an incarnation of its genre, not a transcendence. If we had properly described the genres of popular literature, there would no longer be an occasion to speak of its masterpieces. They are one and the same thing; the best novel will be the one about which there is nothing to say. This is a generally unnoticed phenomenon, whose consequences affect every esthetic category. We are today in the presence of a discrepancy between two essential manifestations; no longer is there one single esthetic norm in our society, but two; the same measurements do not apply to "high" art and "popular" art.

The articulation of genres within detective fiction therefore promises to be relatively easy. But we must begin with the description of "kinds," which also means with their delimitation. We shall take as our point of departure the classic detective fiction which reached its peak between the two world wars and is often called the whodunit. Several attempts have already been made to specify the rules of this genre (we shall return below to S. S. Van Dine's twenty rules); but the best general characterization I know is the one Butor gives in his own novel *Passing Time* (*L'Emploi du temps*). George Burton, the author of many murder mysteries, explains to the narrator that "all detective fiction is based on two murders of which the first, committed by the murderer, is merely the occasion for the second, in which he is the victim of the pure and unpunishable murderer, the detective," and that "the narrative . . . superimposes two temporal series: the days of the investigation which begin with the crime, and the days of the drama which lead up to it."

At the base of the whodunit we find a duality, and it is this duality which will guide our description. This novel contains not one but two stories: the story of the crime and the story of the investigation. In their purest form, these two stories have no point in common. Here are the first lines of a "pure" whodunit:

a small green index-card on which is typed:
    Odel, Margaret.
184 W. Seventy-first Street. Murder: Strangled about
11 P.M. Apartment robbed. Jewels stolen. Body found by
Amy Gibson, maid.   [S. S. Van Dine, *The "Canary" Murder Case*]

The first story, that of the crime, ends before the second begins. But what happens in the second? Not much. The characters of this second story, the story of the investigation, do not act, they learn. Nothing can happen to them: a rule of the genre postulates the detective's immunity. We cannot imagine Hercule Poirot or Philo Vance threatened by some danger, attacked, wounded, even killed. The hundred and fifty pages which separate the discovery of the crime from the revelation of the killer are devoted to a slow apprenticeship: we examine clue after clue, lead after lead. The whodunit thus tends toward a purely geometric architecture: Agatha Christie's *Murder on the Orient Express,* for example, offers twelve suspects; the book consists of twelve chapters, and again twelve interrogations, a prologue, and an epilogue (that is, the discovery of the crime and the discovery of the killer).

This second story, the story of the investigation, thereby enjoys a particular status. It is no accident that it is often told by a friend of the detective, who explicitly acknowledges that he is writing a book; the second story consists, in fact, in explaining how this very book came to be written. The first story ignores the book completely, that is, it never confesses its literary nature (no author of detective fiction can permit himself to indicate directly the imaginary character of the story, as it happens in "literature"). On the other hand, the second story is not only supposed to take the reality of the book into account, but it is precisely the story of that very book.

We might further characterize these two stories by saying that the first—the story of the crime—tells "what really happened," whereas the second—the story of the investigation—explains "how the reader (or the narrator) has come to know about it." But these definitions concern not only the two stories in detective fiction, but also two aspects of every literary work which the Russian Formalists isolated forty years ago. They distinguished, in fact, the *fable* (story) from the *subject* (plot) of a narrative: the story is what has happened in life, the plot is the way the author presents it to us. The first notion corresponds to the reality evoked, to events similar to those which take place in our lives; the second, to the book itself, to the narrative, to the literary devices the author employs. In the story, there is no inversion in time, actions follow their natural order; in the plot, the author can present results before their causes, the end before the beginning. These two notions do not characterize two parts of the story or two different works, but two aspects of one and the same work; they are two points of view about the same thing. How does it happen then that detective fiction manages to make both of them present, to put them side by side?

To explain this paradox, we must first recall the special status of the two stories. The first, that of the crime, is in fact the story of an absence: its most accurate characteristic is that it cannot be immediately present in the book. In other words, the narrator cannot transmit directly the conversations of the characters who are implicated, nor describe their actions: to do so, he must necessarily employ the intermediary of another (or the same) character who will report, in the second story, the words heard or the actions observed. The status of the second story is, as we have seen, just as excessive; it is a story which has no importance in itself, which serves only as a mediator between the reader and the story of the crime. Theoreticians of detective fiction have always agreed that style, in this type of literature, must be perfectly transparent, imperceptible; the only requirement it obeys is to be simple, clear, direct. It has even been attempted—significantly—to suppress this second story altogether. One publisher put out real dossiers, consisting of police reports, interrogations, photographs, fingerprints, even locks of hair; these "authentic" documents were to lead the reader to the discovery of the criminal (in case of failure, a sealed envelope, pasted on the last page, gave the answer to the puzzle: for example, the judge's verdict).

We are concerned then in the whodunit with two stories of which one is absent but real, the other present but insignificant. This presence and this absence explain the existence of the two in the continuity of the narrative. The first involves so many conventions and literary devices (which are in fact the "plot" aspects of the narrative) that the author cannot leave them unexplained. These devices are, we may note, of essentially two types, temporal inversions and individual "points of view": the tenor of each piece of information is determined by the person who transmits it, no observation exists without an observer; the author cannot, by definition, be omniscient as he was in the classical novel. The second story then appears as a place where all these devices are justified and "naturalized": to give them a "natural" quality, the author must explain that he is writing a book! And to keep this second story from becoming opaque, from casting a useless shadow on the first, the style is to be kept neutral and plain, to the point where it is rendered imperceptible.

Now let us examine another genre within detective fiction, the genre created in the United States just before and particularly after World War II, and which is published in France under the rubric *"série noire"* (the thriller); this kind of detective fiction fuses the two stories or, in other words, suppresses the first and vitalizes the second. We are no longer told about a crime anterior to the moment of the narrative; the narrative coincides with the action. No thriller is presented in the form of memoirs: there is no point reached where the narrator comprehends all past events, we do not even know if he will reach the end of the story alive. Prospection takes the place of retrospection.

There is no story to be guessed; and there is no mystery, in the sense that it was present in the whodunit. But the reader's interest is not thereby diminished; we realize here that two entirely different forms of interest exist. The first can be called *curiosity;* it proceeds from effect to cause: starting from a certain effect (a corpse and certain clues) we must find its cause (the culprit and his motive). The second form is *suspense,* and here the movement is from cause to effect: we are first shown the causes, the initial *données* (gangsters preparing a heist), and our interest is sustained by the expectation of what will happen, that is, certain effects (corpses, crimes, fights). This type of interest was inconceivable in the whodunit, for its chief characters (the detective and his friend the narrator) were, by definition, immunized: nothing could happen to them. The situation is reversed in the thriller: everything is possible, and the detective risks his health, if not his life.

I have presented the opposition between the whodunit and the thriller as an opposition between two stories and a single one; but this is a logical, not a historical classification. The thriller did not need to perform this specific transformation in order to appear on the scene. Unfortunately for logic, genres are not constituted in conformity with structural descriptions; a new genre is created around an element which was not obligatory in the old one: the two encode different elements. For this reason the poetics of classicism was wasting its time seeking a logical classification of genres. The contemporary thriller has been constituted not around a method of presentation but around the milieu represented, around specific characters and behavior; in other words, its constitutive character is in its themes. This is how it was described, in 1945, by Marcel Duhamel, its promoter in France: in it we find "violence—in all its forms, and especially the most shameful—beatings, killings. . . . Immorality is as much at home here as noble feelings. . . . There is also love—preferably vile—violent passion, implacable hatred." Indeed it is around these few constants that the thriller is constituted: violence, generally sordid crime, the amorality of the characters. Necessarily, too, the "second story," the one taking place in the present, occupies a central place. But the suppression of the first story is not an obligatory feature: the early authors of the thriller, Dashiell Hammett and Raymond Chandler, preserve the element of mystery; the important thing is that it now has a secondary function, subordinate and no longer central as in the whodunit.

This restriction in the milieu described also distinguishes the thriller from the adventure story, though this limit is not very distinct. We can see that the properties listed up to now—danger, pursuit, combat—are also to be found in an adventure story; yet the thriller keeps its autonomy. We must distinguish several reasons for this: the relative effacement of the adventure story and its replacement by the spy novel; then the thriller's tendency toward the marvelous and the exotic, which brings it closer on the one hand to the travel narrative, and on the other to contemporary science fiction; last, a tendency to description which remains entirely alien to the detective novel. The difference in the milieu and behavior described must be added to these other distinctions, and precisely this difference has permitted the thriller to be constituted as a genre.

One particularly dogmatic author of detective fiction, S. S. Van Dine, laid down, in 1928, twenty rules to which any self-respecting author of detective fiction must conform. These rules have been frequently reproduced since then (see for instance the book, already quoted from, by Boileau and Narcejac) and frequently contested. Since we are not concerned with prescribing procedures for the writer but with describing the genres of detective fiction, we may profitably consider these rules a moment. In their original form, they are quite prolix and may be readily summarized by the eight following points:

1. The novel must have at most one detective and one criminal, and at least one victim (a corpse).
2. The culprit must not be a professional criminal, must not be the detective, must kill for personal reasons.
3. Love has no place in detective fiction.
4. The culprit must have a certain importance:
    (a) in life: not be a butler or a chambermaid.
    (b) in the book: must be one of the main characters.
5. Everything must be explained rationally; the fantastic is not admitted.
6. There is no place for descriptions nor for psychological analyses.
7. With regard to information about the story, the following homology must be observed: "author : reader = criminal : detective."
8. Banal situations and solutions must be avoided (Van Dine lists ten).

If we compare this list with the description of the thriller, we will discover an interesting phenomenon. A portion of Van Dine's rules apparently refers to all detective fiction, another portion to the whodunit. This distribution coincides, curiously, with the field of application of the rules: those which concern the themes, the life represented (the "first story"), are limited to the whodunit (rules 1–4a); those which refer to discourse, to the book (to the "second story"), are equally valid for the thriller (rules 4b–7; rule 8 is of a much broader generality). Indeed in the thriller there is often more than one detective (Chester Himes's *For Love of Imabelle*) and more than one criminal (James Hadley Chase's *The Fast Buck*). The criminal is almost obliged to be a professional and does not kill for personal reasons ("the hired killer"); further, he is often a policeman. Love—"preferably vile"—also has its place here. On the other hand, fantastic explanations, descriptions, and psychological analyses remain banished; the criminal must still be one of the main characters. As for rule 7, it has lost is pertinence with the disappearance of the double story. This proves that the development has chiefly affected the thematic part, and not the structure of the discourse itself (Van Dine does not note the necessity of mystery and consequently of the double story, doubtless considering this self-evident).

Certain apparently insignificant features can be codified in either type of detective fiction: a genre unites particularities located on different levels of generality. Hence the thriller, to which any accent on literary devices is alien, does not reserve its surprises for the last lines of the chapter; whereas the whodunit, which legalizes the literary convention by making it explicit in its "second story," will often terminate the chapter by a particular revelation ("You are the murderer," Poirot says to the narrator of *The Murder of Roger Ackroyd*). Further, certain stylistic features in the thriller belong to it specifically. Descriptions are made without rhetoric, coldly, even if dreadful things are being described; one might say "cynically" ("Joe was bleeding like a pig. Incredible that an old man could bleed so much," Horace McCoy, *Kiss Tomorrow Goodbye*). The comparisons suggest a certain brutality (description of hands: "I felt that if ever his hands got around my throat, they would make the blood gush out of my ears," Chase, *You Never Know with Women*). It is enough to read such a passage to be sure one has a thriller in hand.

It is not surprising that between two such different forms there has developed a third, which combines their properties: the suspense novel. It keeps the mystery of the whodunit and also the two stories, that of the past and that of the present; but it refuses to reduce the second to a simple detection of the truth. As in the thriller, it is this second story which here occupies the central place. The reader is interested not only by what has happened but also by what will happen next; he wonders as much about the future as about the past. The two types of interest are thus united here—there is the curiosity to learn how past events are to be explained; and there is also the suspense: what will happen to the main characters? These characters enjoyed an immunity, it will be recalled, in the whodunit; here they constantly risk their lives. Mystery has a function different from the one it had in the whodunit: it is actually a point of departure, the main interest deriving from the second story, the one taking place in the present.

Historically, this form of detective fiction appeared at two moments: it served as transition between the whodunit and the thriller and it existed at the same time as the latter. To these two periods correspond two subtypes of the suspense novel. The first, which might be called "the story of the vulnerable detective" is mainly illustrated by the novels of Hammett and Chandler. Its chief feature is that the detective loses his immunity, gets beaten up, badly hurt, constantly risks his life, in short, he is integrated into the universe of the other characters, instead of being an independent observer as the reader is (we recall Van Dine's detective-as-reader analogy). These novels are habitually classified as thrillers because of the milieu they describe, but we see that their composition brings them closer to suspense novels.

The second type of suspense novel has in fact sought to get rid of the conventional milieu of professional crime and to return to the personal crime on the whodunit, though conforming to the new structure. From it has resulted a novel we might call "the story of the suspect-as-detective." In this case, a crime is committed in the first pages and all the evidence in the hands of the police points to a certain person (who is the main character). In order to prove his innocence, this person must himself find the real culprit, even if he risks his life in doing so. We might say that, in this case, this character is at the same time the detective, the culprit (in the eyes of the police), and the victim (potential victim of the real murderers). Many novels by William Irish, Patrick Quentin, and Charles Williams are constructed on this model.

It is quite difficult to say whether the forms we have just described correspond to the stages of an evolution or else can exist simultaneously. The fact that we can encounter several types by the same author, such as Arthur Conan Doyle or Maurice Leblanc, preceding the great flowering of detective fiction, would make us tend to the second solution, particularly since these three forms coexist today. But it is remarkable that the evolution of detective fiction in its broad outlines has followed precisely the succession of these forms. We might say that at a certain point detective fiction experiences as an unjustified burden the constraints of this or that genre and gets rid of them in order to constitute a new code. The rule of the genre is perceived as a constraint once it becomes pure form and is no longer justified by the structure of the whole. Hence in novels by Hammett and Chandler, mystery had become a pure pretext, and the thriller which succeeded the whodunit got rid of it, in order to elaborate a new form of interest, suspense, and to concentrate on the description of a milieu. The suspense novel, which appeared after the great years of the thriller, experienced this milieu as a useless attribute, and retained only the suspense itself. But it has been necessary at the same time to reinforce the plot and to re-establish the former mystery. Novels which have tried to do without both mystery and the milieu proper to the thriller—for example, Francis Iles's *Premeditations* and Patricia Highsmith's *The Talented Mr Ripley*—are too few to be considered a separate genre.

Here we reach a final question: what is to be done with the novels which do not fit our classification? It is no accident, it seems to me, that the reader habitually considers novels such as those I have just mentioned marginal to the genre, an intermediary form between detective fiction and the novel itself. Yet if this form (or some other) becomes the germ of a new genre of detective fiction, this will not in itself constitute an argument against the classification proposed; as I have already said, the new genre is not necessarily constituted by the negation of the main feature of the old, but from a different complex of properties, not by necessity logically harmonious with the first form.

1966

4

Primitive Narrative

Now and then critics invoke a narrative that is simple, healthy, and natural—a primitive narrative untainted by the vices of modern versions. Present-day novelists are said to have strayed from the good old ways and no longer follow the rules, for reasons not yet entirely agreed upon: innate perversity on their part, or a futile pursuit of originality, or a blind submission to fashion?

One wonders about the real narratives which have permitted such an induction. In any case, it is instructive from this perspective to reread the *Odyssey*, that first narrative which should, a priori, correspond best to the image of primitive narrative. Few contemporary works reveal such an accumulation of "perversities," so many methods and devices which make this work anything and everything but a simple narrative.

The image of primitive narrative is not a fictive one, prefabricated for the needs of an argument. It is as implicit in certain judgments on contemporary literature as in certain scholarly remarks on works of the past. Adopting a position based on an esthetic proper to primitive narrative, commentators on early narrative declare one or another of its parts alien to the body of the work; and worse still, they believe themselves to be referring to no particular esthetic. Yet it is precisely in the case of the *Odyssey*, where we have no historical certainty, that this very esthetic determines scholarly decisions as to "insertions" and "interpolations."

It would be tiresome to list all the laws of this esthetic. But we can review the main ones:

The law of verisimilitude: All of a character's words and actions must agree with a psychological verisimilitude—as if at all periods the same combination of qualities had been judged to possess the same verisimilitude. For example we are told: "Such and such a passage has been regarded as an interpolation since Antiquity, because these words seem to contradict the portrait of Nausicaa drawn elsewhere by the poet."

The law of stylistic unity: The low and the sublime cannot mix. Hence we are told that a certain "unseemly" passage must naturally be regarded as an interpolation.

The law of the priority of the serious: Any comic version of a narrative is subsequent in time to its serious version; a corollary is the temporal priority of the good to the bad—the version nowadays considered best is the earliest. "This entrance of Telemachus into Menelaus' household is an imitation of Odysseus' entrance into that of Alcinous, which would indicate that the *Wanderings of Telemachus* were composed after the *Alcinous Narratives.*"

The law of noncontradiction (cornerstone of all scholarly criticism): If a referential incompatibility ensues from the juxtaposition of two passages, at least one of the two is inauthentic. The nurse is called Euryclea in the first part of the *Odyssey,* Eurynome in the last; hence the two parts have different authors. According to the same logic, the two parts of *A Raw Youth* could not both be written by Dostoyevsky. Odysseus is said to be younger than Nestor, yet he meets Iphitus, who died during Nestor's childhood: how could this passage fail to be an interpolation? In the same way, we should exclude as inauthentic a good many pages from Proust's novel in which young Marcel seems to have several different ages at the same moment of the story. Or again: "In these lines we observe the clumsy seam of a long interpolation; for how can Odysseus speak of going to sleep when it had been agreed that he would set out again on the same day?" The different acts of *Macbeth,* too, must have different authors, for we are told in the first that Lady Macbeth had children, and in the last that she never had any.

Passages which do not obey the principle of noncontradiction are said to be inauthentic, but is not this principle itself inauthentic?

The law of nonrepetition (incredible as it seems that anyone could imagine such an esthetic law): In an authentic text, there are no repetitions. "The passage which begins here repeats for the third time the scenes in which Antinous and Eurymachus have previously thrown stools at Odysseus. . . . This passage may rightly be regarded as suspect." According to this principle, we may regard a good half of the *Odyssey* as "suspect" or even as "a shocking repetition." But it is difficult to imagine a description of the epic genre that does not account for repetitions, which appear to have so fundamental a role in the form.

The antidigressive law: Any digression from the main action is added later, by a different author. "Between lines 222 and 286 a long narrative has been inserted concerning the unexpected arrival of a certain Theoclymenus, whose genealogy is given in detail. This digression, as well as the subsequent passages which relate to Theoclymenus, is of no use in forwarding the main action." Or better still: "This long passage, lines 394–466, cannot fail to be regarded by today's reader as a digression not only useless but inappropriate, for it suspends the narrative at a crucial moment. It can be excised from the context without difficulty." Consider what would remain of a *Tristram Shandy* were we to "excise" all the digressions which "so annoyingly interrupt the narrative"!

The innocence of scholarly criticism is, of course, a false innocence; consciously or not, such criticism applies to all narrative criteria elaborated on the basis of specific narratives (I do not know which ones). But there is also a more general conclusion to be drawn: there is no "primitive narrative." No narrative is natural; a choice and a construction will always preside over its appearance; narrative is a discourse, not a series of events. There exists no "proper" narrative as opposed to "figurative" ones (just as there is no "proper" meaning); all narratives are figurative. There is only the myth of the proper narrative, and indeed it refers to a doubly figurative narrative: the obligatory figure is seconded by another, which Du Marsais called the "corrective": a figure which is there to conceal the presence of the other figures.

Before the Song

Now let us examine some of the properties of narrative in the *Odyssey*. And first of all, let us attempt to characterize the types of discourse used by the narrative and to be met with in the society described by the poem.

The *Odyssey* employs two major types of speech, whose properties are so different that we may question whether they even belong to the same phenomenon: speech-as-action and speech-as-narrative.

Speech-as-action is always concerned to perform an act which is not simply the utterance of these words. This act is generally accompanied, for the speaker, by *risk*. One must not be afraid in order to speak ("fear made them all turn pale, and only Eurymachus could answer him"). Piety corresponds to silence, speech is linked to rebellion ("Man must always guard against impiety, but enjoy *in silence* the gifts the gods send").

Ajax, who assumes the risk of speech, perishes, punished by the gods: "And Ajax would have escaped his doom, though Athena hated him, had he not gone mad and uttered impious words; for he said that despite the gods he had escaped the great gulf of the sea, and Poseidon heard his loud boast and at once catching up the trident in his ponderous hands, he drove it against the Gyrean rock and sent a splinter crashing into the water, and this was where Ajax had been sitting when he raved in his blasphemy. It carried him down to the depths of the endless sea."

Odysseus' vengeance, in which cunning alternates with boldness, is expressed by a series of silences and words, some necessitated by his reason, others by his heart. "Without uttering a word," Athena warns him upon his arrival in Ithaca, "you must endure many evils and suffer everything, even violence." In order not to run a risk, Odysseus must keep silent, but if he follows the impulses of his heart, he speaks: "Cowherd, and you, swineherd, may I speak one word to you? . . . Would it be better to keep silence? . . . I yield to my heart, and I speak." There may be pious words which do not involve risk, but in principle to speak is to be audacious, to dare. Hence the answer to Odysseus' words (which are not lacking in respect for his interlocutor) is as follows: "Wretch! You shall be punished for that! What a way to speak! You stand boasting before all these heroes—indeed you are fearless!" The very fact that someone dares to speak justifies the observation "you are fearless."

Telemachus' passage from adolescence to manhood is marked almost exclusively by the fact that he begins to speak: "All stood amazed, biting their lips, that Telemachus dared speak to them so boldly." To speak is to assume a responsibility, which is why it is also to incur a danger. The chief of the tribe is entitled to speak, the others speak at their own risk.

If speech-as-action is chiefly regarded as a risk, speech-as-narrative is an *art*—on the speaker's part—as well as a pleasure for both listener and speaker. Here what is said is accompanied not by mortal danger, but by joy and delight: "In this hall, give yourself up to the pleasure of speech as to the joys of feasting!" "Now are the long nights, which give leisure for sleep and for the pleasure of story-telling!"

Just as the tribal chief was the incarnation of speech-as-action, here another member of society becomes its uncontested champion: the bard. The bard is generally admired because he knows how to speak well; he deserves the highest honors: "He is such that his voice makes him equal to the Immortals"; it is happiness to hear him. An auditor never remarks on the content of the song but only on the bard's art and his voice. On the other hand, it is unthinkable that Telemachus, when he ascends the agora to speak, should be received by remarks on the *quality* of what he says; his speech is transparent and invokes reactions exclusively to its reference: "What a wrongheaded speaker! . . . Telemachus, come away, leave off such plans and such wicked words!"

We may note here that this opposition between speech which is said to be accurate and speech which is described as beautiful has vanished from our society; today we ask the poet, in princi-

ple, to speak the truth, we argue about the signification of his
words, not about their beauty.

Speech-as-narrative finds its sublimation in the song of the
Sirens, which at the same time transcends the basic dichotomy.
The Sirens have the most beautiful voices in the world, and
their song is the most beautiful—without being very different
from the bard's: "have you seen his hearers turn to the bard,
inspired by the gods for the joy of mortal men? As long as he
sings, they wish only to hear him, and forever!" Already, one
cannot leave the bard so long as he sings; the Sirens are like a
bard who never stops singing. The song of the Sirens, then, is a
higher degree of poetry, of the poet's art. Here we must note
especially Odysseus' description of it. What is this irresistible
song about, which unfailingly makes those who hear it die, so
great is its allure? It is a song about itself. The Sirens say only
one thing: that they are singing! "Come to us, come, much-
vaunted Odysseus, honor of Achaia! . . . Stop your ship: come
listen to our voices! Never has a black vessel rounded this cape
without listening to the sweet airs which come from our
lips. . . ." The loveliest speech is the one which speaks itself.

At the same time, it is a speech which is equal to the most violent act of all: to inflict death (upon oneself). The man who
hears the song of the Sirens cannot survive: singing signifies
living if hearing equals dying. "But a later version of the
legend," say the commentators on the *Odyssey,* "has it that the
Sirens, in their chagrin that Odysseus sailed past, threw themselves from their rock into the sea." If hearing equals living,
singing signifies dying. The speaker suffers death if the hearer
escapes it. The Sirens make those who hear them lose their life
because otherwise they must lose their own.

The song of the Sirens is, at the same time, that poetry which
must disappear for there to be life, and that reality which must
die for literature to be born. The song of the Sirens must cease
for a song about the Sirens to appear. If Odysseus had not escaped the Sirens, if he had perished on their rock, we would not
have known their song; all those who heard it had died of it and
could not pass it on. By depriving the Sirens of life, Odysseus

has given them, through the intermediary of Homer, immortality.

Feigned Speech

If we try to discover what internal properties distinguish the two types of speech, two independent oppositions appear. First, in the case of speech-as-action, we react to the referential aspect of what is said (as we have seen in the case of Telemachus); if the speech is a narrative, the only aspect which the interlocutors retain seems to be its literal aspect. Speech-as-action is perceived as information, speech-as-narrative as a discourse. Second, and this seems contradictory, speech-as-narrative derives from the constative mode of discourse, whereas speech-as-action is always performative. It is in the case of speech-as-action that the whole process of speaking assumes a primordial importance and becomes the essential factor of the message; speech-as-narrative deals with something else and evokes the presence of an action other than that of the speech itself. Contrary to our custom, transparency accompanies the performative, opacity the constative.

The song of the Sirens is not the only one which blurs this already complex configuration. Added to it is another verbal register, very widespread in the *Odyssey*, which we might call "feigned speech": the lies uttered by the characters.

Lying belongs to a more general category, that of any inadequate speech. We may thus designate discourse in which a discrepancy appears between reference and referent, between designatum and denotatum. Along with lies, we find here errors, hallucinations, irony. Once we become aware of this type of discourse, we realize the fragility of that conception according to which the signification of a discourse is constituted by its referent.

Our difficulties begin when we ask to which type of speech in the *Odyssey* feigned speech belongs. On the one hand, it can belong only to the constative; only constative speech can be true or false, the performative escapes this category. On the other hand, speaking in order to lie does not equal speaking in order to constate, but in order to act: every lie is necessarily performative. Feigned speech is both narrative and action.

Constative and performative continually interpenetrate, but this interpenetration does not do away with the opposition itself. Within speech-as-narrative, we now see two distinct poles, though there is a possible communication between them. At one pole, there is the bard's song; we never speak of truth and lies with regard to it; what holds the listeners is exclusively the literal aspect of what is said. At the other pole, we read the many brief narratives the characters utter throughout the poem, without thereby becoming bards. This category of discourse marks a stage in the movement toward speech-as-action: here speech remains constative, but it also assumes another dimension which is that of action; every narrative is uttered in order to serve a precise purpose, which is not the pleasure of the listeners alone. The constative is here embedded in the performative. Whence the profound kinship of narrative to feigned speech. We always graze against the lie, as long as we are in narrative. Telling truths is already almost lying.

We encounter such speech throughout the *Odyssey*. (But on only one level: the characters lie to one another, the narrator never lies to us. The surprises experienced by the characters are not surprises for us. The narrator's dialogue with the reader is not isomorphic with that of the characters among themselves.) The appearance of feigned speech is indicated by a special clue: the speaker necessarily invokes truth.

Telemachus asks: "But see here, answer me *without pretense,* point by point; what is your name, your people, your city, and your race?" Athena answers: "Yes, I shall answer your questions *without pretense.* My name is Mentor: I have the honor of being the son of Anchialus the wise, and I am in command of our splendid oarsmen of Taphos," and so forth.

Telemachus himself lies to the swineherd and to his mother, in order to conceal Odysseus' arrival in Ithaca; and he accompanies his words by such formulas as "I like to *speak frankly,*" and "Here, at length, mother, is the *truth.*"

Odysseus says: "All I ask, Eumaeus, is to tell the wise Penelope, daughter of Icarus, *all the truth.*" Then a little later comes

Odysseus' narrative before Penelope, all lies. Similarly, Odysseus meeting his father, Laertes, says: "Yes, I shall answer you *without pretense.*" And new lies follow.

Invocation of the truth is a sign of lying. This law seems so powerful that Eumaeus the swineherd deduces a corollary from it: truth for him bears the marks of a lie. Odysseus tells him about his life; this narrative is entirely invented (and of course preceded by the formula: "I shall answer you without pretense"), except for one detail: the fact that Odysseus is still alive. Eumaeus believes everything, but adds: "There is only one point, you see, which seems to me invented. No, I cannot believe such tales about Odysseus! In your state, why these monstrous lies? I am very well informed about my master's return! The hatred of all the gods has overwhelmed him. . . ." The only part of the narrative Eumaeus treats as false is the only part which is true.

The Narratives of Odysseus

We see that lies appear most frequently in the narratives of Odysseus. These narratives are numerous and cover a good part of the *Odyssey*. The *Odyssey* then is not a simple narrative, but a narrative of narratives, it consists of the relation of the narratives the characters address to each other. Once again, nothing here of a natural, a "primitive" narrative; the latter should, apparently, dissimulate its nature as narrative, whereas the *Odyssey* constantly exhibits it. Even the narrative uttered in the narrator's name does not escape this rule, for within the *Odyssey* there is a blind bard who sings, precisely, the adventures of Odysseus. We confront a discourse which makes no attempt to dissimulate the speech-act but rather to make it explicit. At the same time, this explicitness rapidly reveals its limits. To deal with the speech-acts within what is uttered is to produce a new utterance which, as speech-act, still remains to be described. The narrative which deals with its own creation can never break off, except arbitrarily, for there still remains a narrative-to-be-spoken; it still remains to be told how this narrative we are reading or writing could have appeared. Literature is infinite, in this sense that it always speaks its own creation. The effort of narrative to speak itself by an auto-reflection can only be a failure each new declaration adds a new layer to that thickness which hides the speech-act. This infinite spiral ends only if the dis course acquires a perfect opacity: then discourse speaks itself without needing to speak *of* itself.

In his narratives, Odysseus experiences no such remorse The stories he tells form, it would appear, a series of variations for he always tells the same thing: his life. But the tenor of the story changes according to the interlocutor, who is always dif ferent: Alcinous (our narrative of reference), Athena, Eumaeus Telemachus, Antinous, Penelope, Laertes. The multitude of these narratives not only makes Odysseus a living incarnation of feigned speech, but also permits us to discover certain con stants. Every one of Odysseus' narratives is determined by its end, by its point of arrival: it serves to justify the present situa tion. These narratives always concern something which has al ready been done, they link a past to a present: they must end by an "I . . . here . . . now." If the narratives diverge, it is be cause the situations in which they have been uttered are dif ferent. Odysseus appears well dressed before Athena and Laer tes: the narrative must explain his wealth. Conversely, in other cases he is covered with rags, and the story told must justify this condition. The content of what is spoken is entirely dictated by the speech-act: the singularity of this type of discourse would be even more evident if we were to think of more recent narra tives, where it is not the point of arrival but the point of depar ture which is the sole fixed element. Here, a step forward is a step into the unknown, the direction to be followed is called into question with each new movement. In the *Odyssey,* it is the point of arrival which determines the road to be taken, whereas Tristram Shandy's narrative does not link a present to a past, or even a past to a present, but a present to a future.

There are two Odysseuses in the *Odyssey:* one has the adven tures, the other tells them. It is difficult to say which of the two is the main character. Athena herself is in some doubt: "Poor eternal storyteller! All your hunger is for ruses. . . . You return to your country and still you think only of robbers' tales and the lies dear to your heart since childhood." If Odysseus takes so

ng to return home, it is because home is not his deepest de-
ire: his desire is that of the narrator (who is telling Odysseus'
es, Odysseus or Homer?). But the narrator desires to tell.
)dysseus resists returning to Ithaca so that the story can con-
nue. The theme of the *Odyssey* is not Odysseus' return to
thaca; this return is, on the contrary, the death of the *Odyssey*,
s end. The theme of the *Odyssey* is the narrative forming the
dyssey, it is the *Odyssey* itself. This is why, returning home,
)dysseus does not think about it, does not rejoice over it; he
hinks only of "robbers' tales and lies"—he thinks the *Odyssey*.

A Prophetic Future

Odysseus's lying narratives are a form of repetition: different
iscourses dissimulate an identical reference. Another form of
epetition is constituted by a special use of the future tense in
he *Odyssey*, which we might call the prophetic future. Here
gain we are concerned with an identity of the reference; but
longside this resemblance to lies, there is also a symmetrical
pposition. We are concerned with identical utterances whose
peech-acts differ: in the case of lies, the speech-acts were iden-
ical, the difference occurring among the utterances.

The prophetic future tense in the *Odyssey* comes closer to our
abitual image of repetition. This narrative modality appears in
ifferent kinds of predictions, and it is always seconded by a
escription of the predicted action once it has occurred. Most of
he events in the *Odyssey* are thus recounted two or more times
Odysseus' return is predicted many times). But these two nar-
atives of the same events do not occur on the same level; they
tand in opposition within that discourse which is the *Odyssey*,
ust as a discourse stands in opposition to a reality. Along with
ll the other tenses of the verb, the future seems to enter into an
pposition whose terms are the absence and presence of a re-
erent. Only the future tense exists exclusively within the dis-
ourse; the present and the past refer to an act which is not the
iscourse itself.

We can discern several subdivisions within the prophetic fu-
ure. First from the viewpoint of the state or attitude of the au-
hor of the speech-act. Sometimes it is the gods who speak in

the future; this future is then not a supposition, but a certitude
what they predict will occur. Thus Circe, or Calypso, or Athena
predicts to Odysseus what will happen to him. Alongside this
divine future, there is the divinatory future of men—men trying
to read the signs sent by the gods. When an eagle flies over
head, Helen stands up and says: "Here is the prophecy which
god sends into my heart, and which will come true. . . . Odys
seus will return home and take his revenge." Many other
human interpretations of the divine signs are to be found
throughout the *Odyssey*. Finally, men sometimes project their
own future; thus Odysseus, at the beginning of Book 19, fore
sees in every detail the scene which soon afterward takes place
Certain imperatives offer a similar case.

The predictions of the gods, the prophecies of soothsayers
the projects of men: all come true, all turn out to be accurate
The prophetic future cannot be false. Yet in one case this im
possible combination occurs: Odysseus, meeting Telemachus or
Penelope in Ithaca, predicts that Odysseus will return to his
country and see his family. The prophetic future can be false
only if what it predicts is true—already true.

Another range of subdivisions is to be found in the relations of
the future tense with the instance of discourse. The future
which will come about in the course of the pages that follow is
only one of these types: let us call it the prospective future
Alongside it exists the retrospective future, in which we are told
an event while also being told or reminded that it had been fore
told. Thus the Cyclops, learning that the name of his execu
tioner is Odysseus, cries: "Ah, Misery! The oracles of our old
soothsayer have come true! He foretold what would happen to
me, and that I would be blinded by the hands of Odysseus."
Thus Alcinous, seeing his ships sink in his own harbor, cries
"Ah, Misery! The oracles from the days of my father spoke
true," and so forth. Every nondiscursive event is merely the in
carnation of a discourse, reality is only a realization.

This certitude as to the fulfillment of foretold events pro
foundly affects the notion of plot. The *Odyssey* contains no sur
prises; everything is recounted in advance, and everything
which is recounted occurs. This puts the poem, once again, in

radical opposition to our subsequent narratives in which plot plays a much more important role, in which we do not know what will happen. In the *Odyssey*, not only do we know what will happen but we are told what will happen with indifference. Hence, apropos of Antinous: "It was he who would first taste the arrows sent by the hand of the eminent Odysseus." This sentence, which appears in the narrator's discourse, would be unthinkable in a more recent novel. If we still call "plot" the thread of events followed within the story, it is only to facilitate matters: what does "our" plot of causality have in common with that plot of predestination which belongs to the *Odyssey*?

1967

5

Narrative-Men

"What is character but the determination of incident? What is incident but the illustration of character? What is either a picture or a novel that is *not* of character? What else do we seek in it and find in it?"

These questions occur in a famous essay by Henry James, *The Art of Fiction* (1884). Two general ideas emerge from them; the first concerns the unbreakable link between the different elements of narrative: action and character. There is no character except in action, no action independent of character. But surreptitiously, a second idea appears in the last lines: if the two are indissolubly linked, one is more important than the other nonetheless—character, that is, characterization, that is, psychology. Every narrative is "an illustration of character."

We rarely have occasion to observe so pure a case of egocentricity presenting itself as universality. Though James's theoretical ideal may have been a narrative in which everything is subservient to the psychology of the characters, it is difficult to ignore a whole tendency in literature, in which the actions are not there to "illustrate" character but in which, on the contrary, the characters are subservient to the action; where, moreover, the word "character" signifies something altogether different from psychological coherence or the description of idiosyncrasy. This tendency, of which the *Odyssey,* the *Decameron,* the *Arabian Nights,* and *The Saragossa Manuscript* are among the most famous examples, can be considered as a limit-case of literary *a-psychologism*.

Let us try to observe this situation more closely, taking the last two works as our examples.

We are usually satisfied, in speaking of such works as the *Arabian Nights*, with saying that they lack internal analysis of the characters, that there is no description of psychological states. But this way of describing a-psychologism is tautological. To characterize this phenomenon more accurately, we should start from a certain image of narrative movement when narrative obeys a causal structure. We might then represent each moment of the narrative in the form of a simple proposition, which enters into a relation of consecution (noted by +) or a relation of consequence (noted by →) with the propositions preceding and following it.

The first opposition between the narrative James extols and that of the *Arabian Nights* can be illustrated as follows: if there is a proposition "X sees Y," the important thing for James is X; for Scheherazade, Y. Psychological narrative regards each action as a means of access to the personality in question, as an expression if not a symptom. Action is not considered in itself, it is *transitive* with regard to its subject. A-psychological narrative, on the contrary, is characterized by intransitive actions: action is important in itself and not as an indication of this or that character trait. The *Arabian Nights* derive, we might say, from a *predicative* literature: the emphasis will always fall on the predicate and not on the subject of the proposition. The best-known example of this effacement of the grammatical subject is the story of Sinbad the Sailor. Even Odysseus emerges more clearly characterized from his adventures than Sinbad. We know that Odysseus is cunning, prudent, and so forth. Nothing of the kind can be said about Sinbad, whose narrative (though told in the first person) is impersonal; we should note it not as "X sees Y" but as "Y is seen." Only the coldest travel narrative can compete with Sinbad's tales in impersonality—though we have Sterne's *Sentimental Journey* to remind us that not all travel narratives are cold.

The suppression of psychology occurs here within the narra
tive proposition; it continues even more successfully in the field
of relations among propositions. A certain character trait pro
vokes an action; but there are two different ways of doing this.
We might speak of an *immediate* causality as opposed to a *me
diated* causality. The first would be of the type "X is brave→X
challenges the monster." In the second, the appearance of the
first proposition would have no immediate consequence, but in
the course of the narrative X would appear as someone who
acted bravely. This is a diffused, discontinuous causality, which
is expressed not by a single action but by secondary aspects of a
series of actions, often remote from one another.

But the *Arabian Nights* does not acknowledge this second
causality. No sooner are we told that the sultana's sisters are
jealous than they substitute a dog, a cat, and a piece of wood for
her children. Kassim is greedy; therefore he goes looking for
money. All character traits are immediately causal; as soon as
they appear, they provoke an action. Moreover the distance between the psychological trait and the action it provokes is minimal; rather than an opposition between quality and action, we
are concerned with an opposition between two aspects of the action, durative and punctual or iterative and noniterative. Sinbad
likes to travel (character trait)→Sinbad takes a trip (action): the
distance between the two tends toward a total reduction.

Another way of observing the reduction of this distance is to
inquire if the same attributive proposition can have, in the
course of the narrative, several different consequences. In a
nineteenth-century novel, the proposition "X is jealous of Y" can
lead to "X withdraws from society," "X commits suicide," "X
courts Y," "X hurts Y." In the *Arabian Nights*, there is only one
possibility: "X is jealous of Y→X hurts Y." The stability of the
relationship between the two propositions deprives the first of
any autonomy, of any intransitive meaning. The implication
tends to become an identity. If the consequences are more numerous, the first proposition will have a greater value of its own.

Here we touch on a curious property of psychological causality. A character trait is not simply the cause of an action, nor
simply its effect: it is both at once, just as action is. X kills his

wife because he is cruel; but he is cruel because he kills his
wife. Causal analysis of narrative does not refer back to a first
and immutable origin, which would be the meaning and law of
subsequent images. In other words, in its pure state, we must
be able to grasp this causality outside of linear time. The cause
is not a primordial *before,* it is only one element of the "cause-
and-effect" couple, in which neither is thereby superior to the
other.

Hence it would be more accurate to say that psychological
causality duplicates the causality of events (of actions) rather
than that it takes its place. Actions provoke one another, and as
a by-product a psychological cause-and-effect coupling appears,
but on a different level. Here we can raise the question of psychological coherence; such psychological by-products may or
may not form a system. The *Arabian Nights* again affords us an
extreme example, in the tale of Ali Baba. The wife of Kassim,
Ali Baba's brother, is anxious about her husband's disappearance. "She wept all night long." The next day, Ali Baba brings
home the pieces of his brother's body and says, by way of consolation: "Sister-in-law, your suffering is all the greater because
you had so little reason to expect it. Though the harm is past
remedy, if something is yet capable of consoling you, I offer to
unite what little God has granted me to whatever you possess,
by marrying you." The sister-in-law's reaction: "She did not refuse the match, but rather regarded it as a reasonable cause of
consolation. Drying her tears, which she had begun to shed in
abundance, stifling the shrill cries customary to women who
have lost their husbands, she gave Ali Baba sufficient evidence
that she would accept his offer." In this fashion Kassim's wife
moves from despair to joy. Similar examples are countless.

Obviously, by contesting the existence of a psychological coherence in such a case we enter the realm of common sense.
There is doubtless another psychology in which these two con-
secutive actions form a unity. But the *Arabian Nights* belong to
the realm of common sense (of folklore), and the abundance of
examples suffices to convince us that we are not concerned
here with another psychology, nor even with an antipsychology,
but with an a-psychology.

Character is not always, as James claims, the determination of incident, nor does every narrative consist of "the illustration of character." Then what *is* character? The *Arabian Nights* gives us a very clear answer, which is repeated and confirmed by *The Saragossa Manuscript:* a character is a potential story that is the story of his life. Every new character signifies a new plot. We are in the realm of narrative-men.

This phenomenon profoundly affects the structure of narrative.

Digression and Embedding

The appearance of a new character invariably involves the interruption of the preceding story, so that a new story, the one which explains the "now I am here" of the new character, may be told to us. A second story is enclosed within the first; this device is called *embedding.*

This is obviously not the only excuse for embedding. The *Arabian Nights* already affords us a number of others: for example, in "The Fisherman and the Genie," the embedded stories serve as arguments. The fisherman justifies his pitilessness toward the genie by the story of Duban; within the latter story, the king defends his position by the story of the jealous man and the parrot; the vizier defends his by the story of the prince and the ghoul. If the characters remain the same in the embedded story and in the embedding one, this kind of motivation becomes pointless. In the "Story of the Two Jealous Sisters," the narrative of the kidnapping of the sultan's children from the palace and of their recognition by the sultan encloses the narrative of the acquisition of the magic objects; temporal succession is the only motivation. But the presence of narrative-men is certainly the most striking form of embedding.

The formal structure of embedding coincides (nor is such a coincidence an accident) with that of a syntactic form, a particular case of subordination, which in fact modern linguistics calls *embedding.* To reveal this structure, let us take a German example, since German syntax permits much more spectacular examples of embedding than English or French:

Derjenige, der den Mann, der den Pfahl, der auf der Brücke, der auf dem Weg, der nach Worms führt, liegt, steht, umgeworfen hat, anzeigt, bekommt eine Belohnung.

(Whoever identifies the one who upset the post which was placed on the bridge which is on the road which goes to Worms will get a reward.)

In the German sentence, the appearance of a noun immediately provokes a subordinate clause which, so to speak, tells its story; but since this second clause also contains a noun, it requires in its turn a subordinate clause, and so on, until an arbitrary interruption, at which point each of the interrupted clauses is completed one after the other. The narrative of embedding has precisely the same structure, the role of the noun being played by the character: each new character involves a new story.

The *Arabian Nights* contain examples of embedding quite as dizzying. The record seems to be held by the narrative which offers us the story of the bloody chest. Here

    Scheherazade tells that
      Jaafer tells that
        the tailor tells that
          the barber tells that
            his brother (and he has six brothers) tells that . . .

The last story is a story to the fifth degree; but it is true that the two first degrees are entirely forgotten and no longer have any role to play. Which is not the case in one of the stories of *The Saragossa Manuscript,* where

    Alfonso tells that
      Avadoro tells that
        Don Lope tells that
          Busqueros tells that
            Frasquetta tells that . . .

and where all the degrees, except for the first, are closely linked and incomprehensible if isolated from one another.

Even if the embedded story is not directly linked to the embedding story (by identity of characters), characters can pass from one story to the other. Thus the barber intervenes in the tailor's story (he saves the hunchback's life). As for Frasquetta she crosses all the intermediary degrees to appear in Avadoro's story (she is the mistress of the Knight of Toledo); so does Busqueros. Such shifts from one degree to the next have a comic effect in *The Saragossa Manuscript*.

Embedding reaches its apogee with the process of self-embedding, that is, when the embedding story happens to be, at some fifth or sixth degree, embedded by itself. This "laying bare of the device" is present in the *Arabian Nights,* as Borges has pointed out: "No [interpolation] is more disturbing than that of the six hundred and second night, most magical of all. On this night, the king hears from the queen's mouth her own story. He hears the initial story, which includes all the others, which—monstrously—includes itself. . . . If the queen continues, the king will sit still and listen forever to the truncated version of the *Arabian Nights,* henceforth infinite and circular. . . ." Nothing will ever again escape the narrative world, spreading over the whole of experience.

The importance of embedding is indicated by the dimensions of the embedded stories. Can we even call them digressions when they are longer than the story from which they digress? Can we regard as an addition or as a gratuitous embedding all the tales of the *Arabian Nights* because they are embedded in Scheherazade's tale? The same is true of *The Saragossa Manuscript:* whereas the basic story seemed to be Alfonso's, actually it is the loquacious Avadoro's tales which spread over more than three-quarters of the book.

But what is the internal significance of embedding, why are all these means assembled to give it so much emphasis? The structure of narrative provides the answer: embedding is an articulation of the most essential property of all narrative. For the embedding narrative is the *narrative of a narrative.* By telling the story of another narrative, the first narrative achieves its fundamental theme and at the same time is reflected in this image of itself. The embedded narrative is the image of that great abstract narrative of which all the others are merely infinitesimal parts as well as the image of the embedding narrative which directly precedes it. To be the narrative of a narrative is the fate of all narrative which realizes itself through embedding.

The *Arabian Nights* reveal and symbolize this property of narrative with a particular clarity. It is often said that folklore is characterized by the repetition of the same story; and indeed it is not rare, in one of the *Nights,* for the same adventure to be related twice if not more often. But this repetition has a specific function which is unknown: it serves not only to reiterate the same adventure but also to introduce the narrative which a character makes of it. Most of the time it is this narrative which counts for the subsequent development of the plot. It is not the adventures Queen Badur survives which win her King Armanos' pardon, but the narrative of them she recounts. If Turmente cannot further his plot, it is because he is not permitted to tell his story to the caliph. Prince Firuz wins the heart of the Princess of Bengal not by having his adventure but by telling it to her. The act of narrating is never, in the *Arabian Nights,* a transparent act; on the contrary, it is the mainspring of the action.

Loquacity and Curiosity—Life and Death

The speech-act receives, in the *Arabian Nights,* an interpretation which leaves no further doubt as to its importance. If all the characters incessantly tell stories, it is because this action has received a supreme consecration: narrating equals living. The most obvious example is that of Scheherazade herself, who lives exclusively to the degree that she can continue to tell stories; but this situation is ceaselessly repeated within the tale. The dervish has incurred a genie's wrath, but by telling him the story of the envious man, he wins pardon. The slave has committed a crime; to save his life, his master, as the caliph tells him, has but one recourse: "If you tell me a story more amazing than this one, I shall pardon your slave. If not, I shall have him put to death." Four persons are accused of the murder of a hunchback; one of them, the inspector of kitchens, tells the king: "O fortunate King, will you give us the gift of life if I tell you the adventure which befell me yesterday, before I met the hunchback who was put into my room by stealth? It is surely more amazing than this man's story." "If it is as you say," replies the king, "I shall grant all four of you your lives."

Narrative equals life; absence of narrative, death. If Scheherazade finds no more tales to tell, she will be beheaded. This is what happens to the physician Duban when he is threatened by death: he asks the king permission to tell the story of the crocodile; permission is not granted, and Duban perishes. But he is revenged by the same means, and the image of this vengeance is one of the finest in all the *Arabian Nights:* he offers the pitiless king a book to read while the decapitation is taking place. The executioner does his work; Duban's severed head speaks:

O king, you may look through the book."
The king opened the book. He found its pages stuck together. Putting his finger in his mouth, he wet it with saliva and turned the first page. Then he turned the second, and those that followed. He continued in this fashion, for the pages parted only with difficulty, until he came to the seventh leaf. He looked at the page and saw nothing written there.
"Physician," he said, "I see nothing written on this leaf."
"Keep turning the pages," replied the head.
He opened more leaves, and still found nothing. Scarcely a moment had elapsed, when the drug entered his body; the book was impregnated with poison. Then he took a step, staggered, and fell to the ground.

The blank page is poisoned. The book which tells no story kills. The absence of narrative signifies death.

Consider, after such a tragic illustration, this pleasanter version of the power of nonnarrative. A dervish tells every passerby how to gain possession of a certain talking bird, but all have failed and been turned into black stones. Princess Parizade is the first to capture the bird, and she releases the other less fortunate candidates. "All sought to find the dervish as they passed by, to thank him for his welcome and his counsel, which they had found sincere if not salutary; but he had died and none could discover whether it had been of old age or because he was no longer necessary to teach the way to the conquest of the three things over which Princess Parizade had just triumphed." The man is merely a narrative; once the narrative is no longer necessary, he can die. It is the narrator who kills him, for he no longer has a function.

Finally, the imperfect narrative also equals, in such circumstances, death. Hence the inspector of kitchens who claimed that his story was better than the hunchback's ends it by addressing the king: "Such is the amazing tale I wanted to tell you yesterday and which I recount today in all its details. Is it not more astounding than the hunchback's adventure?" "No, it is not, and your boast bears no relation to the truth," answered the King of China, "I must have all four of you hanged."

Absence of narrative is not the only counterpart of narrative-as-life; to want to hear a narrative is also to run mortal risks. If loquacity saves from death, curiosity leads to it. This law underlies the plot of one of the richest tales, "The Porter and the Ladies." Three young ladies of Baghdad receive several unknown men in their house; they stipulate only one condition in return for the pleasures they promise to bestow: "about anything you are going to see, ask no explanation." But what the men see is so strange that they ask the three ladies to tell their story. No sooner has this desire been expressed than the ladies call in their slaves: "Each slave chose his man, rushed upon him, and cast him to the ground, striking him with the flat of his sword." The men must be killed because their request for a narrative, their curiosity, is liable to the death penalty. How do they escape? Thanks to the curiosity of their executioners. For one of the ladies says: "I shall give each of them permission to continue on his way, on condition that he tell his story, recounting the series of adventures which led to his visiting us here. If they refuse, you will cut off their heads." The listener's curiosity, when it does not mean his own death, restores life to the condemned men, who in return can escape only on condition that they tell a story. Finally, a third reversal: the caliph, who was present in disguise among the guests of the three ladies, invites them the next day to his palace; he forgives them everything, but on one condition: they must tell. . . . The characters of this book are obsessed by stories; the cry of the *Arabian Nights* is not "Your money or your life!" but "Your story or your life!"

This curiosity is the source of both countless narratives and incessant dangers. The dervish can live happily in the company of the ten young men, all blind in the right eye, on one condition: "ask no indiscreet question about our infirmity or our condition." But the question is asked, and peace is at an end. To discover the answer, the dervish ventures into a magnificent palace; there he lives like a king, surrounded by forty lovely ladies. One day they depart, telling him, if he would remain in such happiness, not to enter a certain room. They warn him: "We fear you will not be able to protect yourself against that indiscreet curiosity which will be the cause of your downfall." Naturally, faced with the choice between happiness and curiosity, the dervish chooses curiosity. Just as Sinbad, for all his misfortunes, sets out again after each voyage: he wants life to tell him stories, one narrative after the other.

The palpable result of such curiosity is the *Arabian Nights*. If its characters had preferred happiness, the book would not exist.

Narrative: Supplier and Supplied

For the characters to be able to live, they must narrate. Thus the first narrative subdivides and multiplies into a thousand and one nights of narratives. Now let us attempt to take the opposite point of view, no longer that of the embedding narrative but that of the embedded narrative, and inquire: why does the embedded narrative need to be included within another narrative? How can we account for the fact that it is not self-sufficient but requires an extension, a context in which it becomes simply a part of another narrative?

If we consider the narrative in this way, not as enclosing other narratives but as being enclosed by them, a curious property is revealed. Each narrative seems to have something excessive, a supplement which remains outside the closed form produced by the development of the plot. At the same time, and for this very reason, this something-more, proper to the narrative, is also something-less. The supplement is also a lack; in order to supply this lack created by the supplement, another narrative is necessary. Hence the narrative of the ungrateful king who puts

Duban to death after the latter has saved his life has something more than this narrative itself; besides, it is for this reason, with a view to this supplement, that the fisherman tells the story, a supplement which can be summed up in a formula: never pity the ungrateful. The supplement must be integrated into another story; hence it becomes the simple argument which the fisherman employs when he becomes involved in an adventure similar to Duban's, with the genie. But the story of the fisherman and the genie also has a supplement which requires another story; and there is no reason for this process to stop anywhere. The attempt to supply is therefore vain—there will always be a supplement awaiting a narrative-to-come.

This supplement takes several forms in the *Arabian Nights*. One of the most familiar is that of the argument, as in the preceding example; the narrative becomes a means of convincing the interlocutor. Further, at higher levels of embedding, the supplement is transformed into a simple verbal formula, a sentence or proverb meant to be used by the characters as much as by the readers. Finally a wider integration of the reader is also possible (though it is not characteristic of the *Arabian Nights*). Behavior provoked by reading is also a supplement, and a law is established: The more this supplement is consumed within the narrative, the less reaction this narrative provokes on the part of its reader. We may weep when reading *Manon Lescaut*, but not when reading the *Arabian Nights*.

Here is an example of a one-sentence proverb or moral. Two friends argue about the origin of wealth: Is it enough to have some money to begin with? There follows a story illustrating one of the positions being defended, then comes a story which illustrates the other; and at the end, a conclusion is reached: "Money is not always a sure means of amassing more and becoming rich."

As in the case of psychological cause and effect, we must here conceive of this logical relation outside of linear time. The narrative precedes or follows the maxim, or both at once. Similarly, in the *Decameron*, certain novellas are created to illustrate a metaphor (for example, "scraping the bottom of the barrel") and at the same time they create that metaphor. It is pointless to ask today whether the metaphor engendered the narrative, or the narrative engendered the metaphor. Borges has even suggested an inverted explanation of the existence of the entire *Arabian Nights:* "This invention [the stories Scheherazade tells] . . . is apparently posterior to the title and was imagined in order to justify it." The question of origins need not be raised; we are beyond the origin and unable to conceive of it. The supplied narrative is no more original than the supplying narrative, nor vice versa. Each narrative refers us to another, in a series of reflections which can end only by becoming perpetual—for example, by self-embedding.

Such is the incessant proliferation of narratives in this marvelous story-machine, the *Arabian Nights.* Every narrative must make its own narration explicit; but to do so a new narrative must appear in which this narration is no more than a part of the story. Hence the narrating story always becomes a narrated story as well, in which the new story is reflected and finds its own image. Furthermore, every narrative must create new ones—within itself, in order that its characters can go on living, and outside itself, so that the supplement it inevitably produces may be consumed there. The many translators of the *Arabian Nights* all seem to have yielded to the power of this narrative machine. None has been content with a simple translation merely faithful to the original; each translator has added and suppressed stories (which is also a way of creating new narratives, narrative always being a selection); a secondary speech-act, translation represents in itself a new tale which no longer awaits its narrator. Borges has told a part of this tale in his "Translators of the *Arabian Nights.*"

There are, then, so many reasons for narrative never to stop that we cannot help wondering: What happened before the first narrative? And what will happen after the last? The *Arabian Nights* have not failed to provide an answer, ironic though it may be, for those who want to know the "before" and the "after." The first story, Scheherazade's, begins with these words, meaningful on every level (but one should not open the book to look for them—it should be possible to guess what they are, so appropriate are they to their place): "It is told . . ." No need to search out the origin of narrative in time—it is time which originates in narrative. And if before the first narrative there is an "it *has been* told," after the last there will be an "it *will be* told." For the story to stop, we must be told that the marveling caliph orders it to be inscribed in letters of gold in the annals of the realm; or again that "this story . . . spread and was told everywhere down to the last detail."

1967

6

An Introduction to Verisimilitude

One day in Sicily, in the fifth century B.C., a dispute between two men ended in violence, with damages. The next day they appeared before the authorities empowered to decide which of the two was guilty. But how to reach such a decision? The dispute did not occur before the eyes of the judges, who were unable to observe and ascertain the truth. When the senses are powerless, only one means remains—to hear the narratives of the litigants themselves, whose position is thereby altered, for their problem is no longer to establish a truth (which is impossible) but to approach it, to produce an impression of it. And this impression will be stronger in direct proportion to the skill of the narrative. To win the trial, it is more important to speak well than to have behaved well. Plato writes bitterly: "In law courts, indeed, there is no concern whatsoever to tell the truth, but rather to persuade, and persuasion depends on verisimilitude." But for this very reason, discourse, narrative, ceases to be, in the speakers' consciousness, a docile reflection of events and acquires an independent value. Thus words are not simply the transparent names of things, they form an autonomous entity governed by its own laws and susceptible of being judged for itself. The importance of words exceeds that of the things they were supposed to reflect.

That day witnessed the simultaneous birth of the consciousness of language, of a science which formulates the laws of language (rhetoric), and of a concept (verisimilitude) which would fill the gap between these laws and what is claimed to be language's constitutive property: its reference to reality. The discovery of language soon produced its first results: rhetorical theory, the sophists' philosophy of language. But later a contrary effort was made to forget language, to behave as if words were, once again, merely the obedient names of things; and today we are just beginning to glimpse the end of this antiverbal period in humanity's history. For twenty-five centuries men have tried to convince one another that reality is a sufficient reason of speech; for twenty-five centuries, men have had to keep reconquering the right to perceive language. Literature, though it symbolizes the autonomy of discourse, has not sufficed to vanquish the notion that words reflect things. The fundamental feature of our whole civilization remains this conception of language-as-shadow whose forms may change but which are nonetheless the direct consequences of the objects they reflect. Studying verisimilitude is equivalent to showing that discourses are not governed by a correspondence with their referent but by their own laws, and to denouncing the phraseology which, within these discourses, would make us believe the contrary. We must disengage language from its illusory transparence, learn to perceive it, and at the same time study its techniques of disappearing—like Wells's invisible man swallowing his chemical formula—before our eyes.

The concept of verisimilitude is no longer fashionable. We no longer find it in "serious" scientific literature; on the other hand, it continues to thrive in second-rate commentaries, in school editions of the classics, in pedagogical practice. Here is an example of such use, taken from a commentary on *Le Mariage de Figaro*:

Movement makes us overlook the lack of verisimilitude.
The Count, at the end of the second act, has sent Bazile and Gripe-Soleil to the village for two specific reasons: to summon the judges and to get hold of the peasant who had written the anonymous note. . . . It is scarcely likely that the Count, now quite aware of Chérubin's presence in the Countess's bedroom that morning, would ask no explana-

tion of Bazile's lie, nor attempt to confront him with Figaro, whose attitude has come to seem increasingly equivocal. We know, and our
knowledge will be confirmed in the fifth act, that the Count's antici-
pation of a rendezvous with Suzanne is insufficient to disturb him to
such a point when the Countess is involved.

Beaumarchais was aware of this failure of verisimilitude (there is a
note to this effect in his manuscripts), but he assumed, and with reason, that in the theater it would be overlooked.

Or again:

Beaumarchais himself admitted to his friend Gudin de la Brenellerie
"that there was not much verisimilitude in the mistaken identities of
the nighttime scenes." But he added: "The public willingly accepts
such illusions when they produce an amusing imbroglio."

The term "verisimilitude" is used here in its most naive
sense—"consistent with reality." Certain actions, certain attitudes are said to lack verisimilitude when they seem unable to
occur in reality. Corax, verisimilitude's first theoretician, had already gone further; for him verisimilitude was a relation not
with reality (as is truth) but with what most people believe to be
reality—in other words, with public opinion. Hence discourse
must be consistent with another (anonymous, impersonal) discourse, not with its referent. But if we reread the commentary I
have just quoted, we see that Beaumarchais was alluding to
something else entirely; he explains the state of the text by a
reference not to common opinion but to the particular rules of
his own genre ("in the theater it would be overlooked" . . . "the
public willingly accepts such illusions," and so forth). In the
first sentences of the commentary we are concerned not with
common opinion but simply with a literary genre which is not
that of Beaumarchais.

Hence several meanings of the term *verisimilitude* appear,
and we must take care to distinguish them, for the word's polysemy is precious and we shall not reject it. We shall discard
only the first naive meaning, according to which a relation with
reality is expressed. The second meaning is that of Plato and
Aristotle: verisimilitude is the relation of the specific text to
another, generalized text which is called "common opinion."
Among the French classics, we already find a third meaning—

comedy has its own verisimilitude, different from tragedy's; there are as many verisimilitudes as there are genres, and the two notions tend to melt into each other (the appearance of this meaning of the word is an important step in the discovery of language; here we move from the level of the *said* to the level of *saying*). Finally, in our own day, another meaning has become predominant: we speak of a work's verisimilitude insofar as the work tries to convince us it conforms to reality and not to its own laws. In other words, verisimilitude is the mask which is assumed by the laws of the text and which we are meant to take for a relation with reality.

Consider another example of these different meanings (and different levels) of verisimilitude; we take it from one of the books most refractory to realistic phraseology, *Jacques le fataliste*. Throughout the narrative, Diderot is aware of the many possibilities confronting him: the narrative is not determined in advance, any direction is (in the absolute sense) as good as any other. The censorship which forces the author to choose only one is what we call *verisimilitude:*

They . . . saw a host of men armed with pikes and pitchforks bearing down upon them as fast as their legs could carry them. You will suppose these were people from the inn, their servants, and the brigands we have mentioned. . . . You will suppose this little army is about to fall upon Jacques and his master, that a bloody action will ensue, with blows exchanged, shots fired, and if it were left to me alone, such indeed would be the case, but then farewell to the truth of the story, farewell to the tale of Jacques and his loves. . . . It is evident I am not writing a novel, since I overlook just what no novelist would fail to utilize. He who takes what I write for truth may err less than he who takes it for fiction.

In this brief passage, Diderot alludes to the chief properties of verisimilitude. The narrative's freedom is limited by the internal requirements of the book itself ("the truth of the story," "the tale of Jacques and his loves"), in other words by its participation in a genre. If the work belonged to another genre, the requirements would have been different ("I am not writing a novel," "what no novelist would fail to utilize"). At the same time, even as he openly asserts that the narrative obeys its own economy, its own function, Diderot feels the need to add: what I write is the truth; if I choose this development rather than some other, it is because the events I am relating actually occurred in this way. He must disguise freedom as necessity, the relation to writing as a relation to reality by a sentence made all the more ambiguous (but also more convincing) by the preceding declaration. These are the two essential levels of verisimilitude: verisimilitude as discursive law—absolute and inevitable—and verisimilitude as mask, as a system of rhetorical methods tending to present these laws as so many submissions to the referent.

ii

Alberta French wants to save her husband, accused of having murdered his mistress, from the electric chair. She must find the real killer, and has only one clue: a matchbook monogrammed with an M which the murderer has left at the scene of the crime. Alberta gets hold of the victim's address-book and manages to meet successively everyone in it whose name begins with M. The third is the man to whom the matchbook belongs, but Alberta, convinced of his innocence, goes hunting for a fourth M. Thus *Black Angel,* one of William Irish's finest novels, is built on a logical flaw. By discovering the matchbook's owner, Alberta has lost her clue. It is no more likely that the murderer should be the fourth person whose name begins with M than anyone else whose name is in the address-book. From the point of view of the plot, this fourth episode has no raison d'être.

How could Irish have overlooked such a logical inconsistency? Why not put the episode about the owner of the matchbook after the other three, so that this revelation will not deprive what follows of its plausibility? The answer is easy—the author needs suspense; down to the last moment, he must not let us know the criminal's name. Now according to a general narrative law, temporal succession corresponds to a gradation of intensity, so that the final episode is to be the most impressive one, and the last suspect the guilty man. It is to evade this law, to frustrate an overly simple revelation, that Irish puts the murderer in the penultimate position within the series of suspects. Hence it

is in order to respect a rule of the genre—in order to obey the
verisimilitude of the murder mystery—that the writer violates
the verisimilitude of the world he is evoking.

This violation is important; it shows, by the contradiction it
sets up, both the multiplicity of verisimilitudes and how the
murder mystery submits to the rules of its convention. This submission is not self-evident—quite the contrary: the murder mystery tries to appear quite detached from it, and to do so, an
ingenious means has been devised. If every discourse enters
into a relation of verisimilitude with its own laws, the murder
mystery takes verisimilitude for its very theme; verisimilitude is
not only its law but also its object. An inverted object, so to
speak—for the law of the murder mystery consists in establishing an *antiverisimilitude*. Moreover, there is nothing
new about this logic of inverted verisimilitude; it is as old as any
reflection upon verisimilitude, for we find the following example
in the inventors of this notion, Corax and Tisias: "That a strong
man should have beaten a weak one has *physical* verisimilitude,
for he had every material means of doing so; yet such a situation lacks *psychological* verisimilitude, for it is impossible that
the accused should not have anticipated our suspicion."

We find the same "regularity" in any whodunit; a crime has
been committed, the criminal must be found. Given several
isolated clues, a whole is to be reconstructed. But the law of
reconstruction is never the law of ordinary verisimilitude; on the
contrary, precisely the obvious suspects turn out to be innocent,
and the innocent are "suspect." The guilty man in a murder
mystery is the man who does not seem guilty. In his summing
up, the detective will invoke a logic which links the hitherto
scattered clues; but such logic derives from a scientific notion of
possibility, not from one of verisimilitude. The revelation must
obey these two imperatives: possibility and absence of verisimilitude.

The revelation, that is, the truth, is incompatible with verisimilitude, as we know from a whole series of detective plots
based on the tension between them. In Fritz Lang's film
Beyond a Reasonable Doubt, this antithesis is taken to ex-
tremes. Tom Garett wants to prove that the death penalty is ex-

cessive, that innocent men are often sent to the chair. With the help of his future father-in-law, he selects a crime which is currently baffling the police and pretends to have committed it: he skillfully plants the clues which lead to his own arrest. Up to this point, all the characters in the film believe Garett to be guilty; but the spectator knows he is innocent—the truth has no verisimilitude, verisimilitude has no truth. Then a double reversal occurs: the police discover documents proving Garett's innocence, but at the same time *we* learn that his attitude has been merely a clever way of concealing his crime—it is in fact Garett who has committed the murder. Again the divorce between truth and verisimilitude is total: if we know Garett to be guilty, the characters are obliged to believe he is innocent. Only at the end do truth and verisimilitude coincide, but this signifies the death of the character as well as the death of the narrative, which can continue only if there is a gap between truth and verisimilitude.

Verisimilitude is the theme of the murder mystery; its law is the antagonism between truth and verisimilitude. But by establishing this law, we are once again confronted by verisimilitude. By relying on antiverisimilitude, the murder mystery has come under the sway of another verisimilitude, that of its own genre. No matter how much it contests ordinary verisimilitudes, it will always remain subject to *some* verisimilitude. And this fact represents a serious threat to the life of the murder mystery, for the discovery of this law involves the death of the riddle. We have no need to follow the detective's ingenious logic to discover the killer—we need merely refer to the much simpler law of the author of murder mysteries. The culprit will not be one of the suspects; he will not be brought to light at any point in the narrative; he will always be linked in a certain way with the events of the crime, but some reason—apparently quite important, actually secondary—keeps us from regarding him as a potential culprit. Hence it is not difficult to discover the killer in a murder mystery: we need merely follow *the verisimilitude of the text* and not the truth of the world evoked.

There is something tragic in the fate of the murder-mystery writer; his goal is to contest verisimilitudes, yet the better he succeeds, the more powerfully he establishes a *new* verisimilitude, one linking his text to the genre to which it belongs. Hence the murder mystery affords our purest image of the impossibility of escaping verisimilitude: the more we condemn verisimilitude, the more we are enslaved by it.

The murder-mystery writer is not alone in suffering this fate; all of us do, and all the time. From the very first we find ourselves in a situation less favorable than his: he can contest the laws of verisimilitude, and even make antiverisimilitude his law. Though we may discover the laws and conventions of the life around us, it is not within our power to change them—we shall always be obliged to obey them, though such obedience is twice as difficult after this discovery. It comes as a bitter surprise when we realize that our life is governed by the same laws we discovered in our morning paper and that we cannot change them. To know that justice obeys the laws of verisimilitude, not of truth, will keep no one from being sentenced.

But independent of this serious and immutable character of the laws of verisimilitude, with which we are concerned here, verisimilitude lies in wait for us at every turn, and we cannot escape it—any more than the murder-mystery writer can. The constitutive law of our discourse binds us to it. If I speak, my utterance will obey a certain law and participate in a verisimilitude I cannot make explicit and reject without thereby utilizing another utterance whose law will be *implicit*. Being an act and not only an utterance, my discourse will always participate in *some* verisimilitude; a speech-act cannot, by definition, be made altogether explicit: if I speak of it, I am no longer speaking of it but of its utterance, which is an act in its turn and one which I cannot utter.

The law the Hindus seem to have formulated apropos of self-knowledge has a direct bearing on the subject of discourse: "Among the many philosophical systems of India listed by Paul Deussen, the seventh denies that the self can be an immediate object of knowledge, 'for if our soul were knowable, it would require a second soul to know the first one and a third to know the second.' " The laws of our own discourse are at once verisimilar (by the very fact of being laws) and unknowable, for it is only another discourse which can describe them. By contesting verisimilitude, the murder-mystery writer settles into a verisimilitude on another level, but one no less powerful.

Thus this text itself, which discusses verisimilitude, possesses a verisimilitude of its own: it obeys an ethical, literary, ideological verisimilitude which leads us today to concern ourselves with verisimilitude. Only the destruction of discourse can destroy its verisimilitude, though the verisimilitude of silence is not so difficult to imagine either. . . . Yet these last sentences participate in a different, a higher verisimilitude, and in that they resemble truth: for what is truth but a distanced and postponed verisimilitude?

1967

7

Speech according to Constant

The *word* seems to be endowed with a magical power in *Adolphe*. "A word from me would have calmed her: why could I not utter that word?" "She allowed me to understand that no more than a word would restore her to me utterly." "A word caused this host of worshipers to vanish."

This potency of the word merely translates, in a condensed form, the role granted to speech in Constant's world. For him man is above all a man speaking, and the world a discursive world. Throughout *Adolphe*, the characters do nothing but utter words, write letters, or immure themselves in ambiguous silences. Every quality, every attitude is translated by a certain way of speaking. Solitude is a verbal behavior; desire for independence, another; love, a third. The erosion of Adolphe's love for Ellénore is merely a series of different linguistic attitudes: the "irreparable words" of the fourth chapter, the secret and dissimulation in the fifth, the revelation made before a third person in the eighth, Adolphe's promise in front of the baron and the letter he writes him in the ninth. All the way to death: the last act Ellénore attempts to perform is to speak. "She wanted to speak, but there was no more voice; as if resigned, she let her head fall on the arm that supported her; her breathing became slower; a few moments later, she was no more." Death is nothing but the impossibility of speaking.

This relation of language to death is not gratuitous. Speech is violent, "words, cruel." Ellénore describes words sometimes as a sharp instrument which lacerates the body ("lest that voice I have so loved, that voice which echoed deep in my heart, pierce and lacerate my being"), sometimes as strange nocturnal beasts which pursue and devour her to the death ("Those stinging words echo around me: I hear them at night, they follow me, they devour me, they despoil whatever you do. Must I die then, Adolphe?"). And indeed it is words which will cause the book's most serious action: Ellénore's death. A letter from Adolphe to Baron de T*** kills Ellénore. Nothing is more violent than language.

To understand the full meaning of speech, we must first consider its relation to what it signifies, a relation which may assume several forms. First of all there is the most classical relation, which we might call symbolic. Here, verbal behavior merely translates a certain inner disposition, without having a relation of necessity; it is an arbitrary and conventional relation between two series which exist independently of one another. For example Adolphe will say: "Sometimes I attempted to control my boredom and took refuge in a profound taciturnity." Here there is a sentiment to communicate—the control of boredom—and a manner of doing so—taciturnity; the second symbolizes the first.

Verbal attitudes have several meanings, which also proves the unmotivated character of the relation between signifier and signified. Consider silence: depending on the context, it signifies a great variety of sentiments. For instance, "contempt is silent"; "when she saw me, the words died on her lips; she remained quite speechless" (here it is astonishment which is translated by silence); "one of her friends, struck by her silence and her dejection, asked her whether she was ill" (hence silence = illness). Or again: "Count de P***, taciturn and preoccupied"; but we read "taciturn = preoccupied." "Then, offended by my silence"; that is, silence signifies an offense. The case is the same for the act of speaking or of writing.

It would be interesting, on the basis of similar phrases, to make a study of the linguistic forms which allow us, as readers, to interpret this language of verbal behavior without difficulty.

The most widely used form would be coordination; syntactic parallelism enables us to discover a semantic resemblance. Thus: "I grew lively again, I began speaking," "silence and bad temper," "taciturn and preoccupied," "I tried to impose my will . . . , I took refuge in silence," and so forth. Here we also find attributive sentences; the verb *to be* or a substitute establishes the relation of signification between the two parts of the sentence. For example, "my words were considered as proof of a hate-filled soul"; "scorn is silent"; "the silence became embarrassing." Sometimes a relation of causality will be established from one to the other: "I was supported by no impulse which came from the heart. I *therefore* expressed myself awkwardly"; "the excuses I offered were weak *because* they were not the genuine ones." Or again: "Offended *by* my silence . . ."

The symbolic relation, in which the nature of the sign is indifferent to the nature of the object designated, does not cover every incidence of speech. Let us take for example the dinner scene during which Adolphe manages to amuse Ellénore. Adolphe's brilliant conversation symbolizes the qualities of his soul, and at the same time, it constitutes a part of that soul. One of Adolphe's qualities will be precisely his art of conversation. One can no longer speak of a verbal attitude which symbolizes an inner property, since it belongs to that property. Or again: in order to reach the conclusion that "Ellénore had never been loved in such a fashion," Adolphe merely quotes us one of his letters. In other words, the tenderness and the density of this letter designate, symbolize Adolphe's love; but at the same time they constitute part of it. Love is, if not exclusively, at least partially, this tenderness, this density of emotion; they do not symbolize it in an arbitrary and conventional manner. Thus we are here dealing with another relation between the sign and the object designated, the relation of the index, as opposed to that of the symbol, or—one may also say—of synecdoche as opposed to allegory.

Sometimes verbal behavior designates nothing but itself. Indicial power is so great that it leads to a self-reference; whereby the relation of signification is reduced to zero. Thus in this scene, so important for the development of feeling in *Adolphe*, of dissimulation, of secrecy (chapter 5): Here there is a silence which in fact *signifies* silence, the absence of words, secrecy, dissimulation. "We therefore kept silent about the sole thought that constantly occupied our minds. . . . Once a secret exists between two hearts that love one another, once one of them has brought itself to be able to conceal a single idea from the other, the spell is broken, happiness is destroyed. . . . Dissimulation casts into love a foreign element which denatures it and stigmatizes it in its own eyes." What kills love is precisely dissimulation, silence; this silence therefore designates only itself.

Very often an apparent symbolic signification will have as its sole purpose to dissimulate the indicial signification which is to be found in the very act of speaking or of keeping silent. Thus Adolphe, speaking about himself, says: "I allowed myself to give way to a few agreeable remarks. . . . It was the need to speak which determined me to do so, and not confidence." Confidence would have been the symbolic signified, but it is not confidence that matters—confidence is not even present; what these words designate is the need to speak, speech itself. Or again: "We spoke of love, but we spoke of love for fear of speaking to each other of something else." The apparent symbolic content of these words is love, but their hidden indicial content is the very fact that they are uttered, instead of other words.

This indicial relation explains Constant's tendency to identify the human being with the conversation he can conduct (a tendency which will become an absolute law in Proust). It is manifest in *Amélie et Germaine,* his first journal, much more clearly than in *Adolphe;* here Amélie is represented only as a series of words. "There is a perpetual chattering, almost always sneering or sewn together with remarks without consistency and to which it is impossible that she should attach any meaning." "She was quite gay this evening, and in her gaiety she made some rather amusing remarks, but still, they were the remarks of a child of ten." This importance extends to the point of involuntary comedy: "I should marry her without illusions, prepared for a conversation frequently ordinary." One marries the conversation rather than the woman! And last of all this sentence which, by its very precision, might figure as it stands in Proust:

"One can never make oneself understood without speaking in the first person and as clearly as possible, and her lack of finesse is such that at the first impersonal remark, she no longer knows what one is trying to tell her." Not to understand impersonal remarks is a serious personal defect.

This identification of the character with the speech he utters explains the importance someone's voice or handwriting can assume. Hence Adolphe says, "I was glad to postpone the moment when I would hear her voice again"; here one does not speak about the meaning of the words but about the voice which utters them. Similarly for Ellénore, who, upon hearing Adolphe, exclaims: "That is the voice which has hurt me so." The voice becomes almost a material object, it moves from the auditive to the tactile order. Or in *Cécile:* "the disturbance I felt at the sight of her handwriting . . ."

What Does It Mean to Speak?

One might say that Constant proposes a theory of the sign, that the existence of "contiguous" signs, which are part of the object designated, contests a naive image of the sign, which sees the signifiers at an unvarying distance from the signifieds (what analytic philosophy calls the descriptive fallacy). But if the theory of speech according to Constant were limited to that, it would have only a historical interest today, and we should simply add its author to the predecessors of semiotics. But this theory goes much farther—so far that our traditional image of the sign turns out to be entirely changed. What Constant opposes is the notion that words designate things in an adequate fashion, that the signs can be faithful to their designata. To suppose that words can faithfully account for things is to admit that (1) "things" are there, (2) words are transparent, harmless, without consequence for what they designate, (3) words and things enter into a static relation. But none of these implicit propositions is true, according to Constant. Objects do not exist before being named, or in any case they do not remain the same before and after the act of denomination. And the relation of words and things is a dynamic, not a static relation.

One cannot verbalize with impunity; to name things is to

change them. Adolphe makes this experiment over and over again. "No sooner had I written a few lines than my mood changed," he complains. To think a thing, on the one hand, and to speak or write or hear or read it, on the other, are two very different acts. Yet, one might say, thoughts too are verbal—one does not think without words. True enough; but the word "speech" designates something more than the simple series of words. The difference is a double one—first of all, there is that act of utterance or of writing which is not at all gratuitous (we remember the "voice which has hurt me so," in Ellénore's words); then, and this is crucial, speech is constituted of words addressed to someone else, whereas thought, even verbal thought, is addressed only to oneself. The notion of speech implies the notion of others, of an interlocutory second-person; thereby speech is profoundly linked to the other person who plays a decisive role in Constant's world.

Let us take an example: Adolphe's meetings with Baron de T***. Adolphe knows everything the baron tells him, but he had never heard it spoken, and it is the fact that such words have been pronounced which becomes significant. "These fatal words, 'between every kind of success and yourself, there exists an insurmountable obstacle, and that obstacle is Ellénore,' echoed in the air around me." It is not the idea's novelty which strikes Adolphe, it is the sentence that, by its very existence, changes the relation between Ellénore and Adolphe which it was supposed to describe. Similarly, Adolphe has told himself a thousand times (but without *saying* it) that he must leave Ellénore; one day, he says it to the baron. The situation is thereby entirely transformed: "I had prayed heaven to raise some sudden obstacle between Ellénore and myself which I could not surmount. That obstacle had been raised." Adolphe's having designated, verbalized his decision, changes its very nature, which leads Constant to formulate this maxim: "There are things one goes a long time without saying, but once they are said, one never stops repeating them."

Adolphe's feelings exist only through speech, which also means that they exist only through others. The presence of others in speech gives speech its creative quality; just as the im-

tation of others determines the character's feelings: Adolphe
will discover Ellénore because one of his friends has taken a
mistress; and at the height of his dreams of another woman, an
ideal companion, he will describe her only in terms of his father's imaginary desire: "I imagined my father's joy," "if heaven
had granted me a wife . . . whom my father would not blush to
accept as his daughter." Marriage does not consist of the subject's choice of a wife for himself, but of a daughter for someone
else, for the father.

To designate feelings, to verbalize thoughts, is to change
them. Let us consider more closely the nature and direction of
these changes. This direction is double, according to the qualities of the very words one utters, and it affects above all their
truth value. The first rule of modification can be formulated
thus: if a speech claims to be true, it becomes false. To seek to
describe an existing mood is to give a false description of it, for
after the description it will no longer be what it was before. This
is what Adolphe suffers constantly: "As I went on speaking
without looking at Ellénore, I felt my ideas become vaguer and
my resolve weaken." Once one names the resolve, it no longer
exists. Or again: "I left the room upon completing these words;
but who will explain to me by what mobility the sentiment
which led me to speak them vanished even before I had finished uttering them?" We know the answer now: the sentiment
has vanished precisely because the words designating it have
been uttered. Or once more: "I was oppressed by the words I
had just uttered, and I scarcely believed the promise I had
given." One ceases to believe the promise as soon as it is uttered.

This law, according to which a speech becomes false if it tries
to be true, has its corollary (which we might have deduced by
symmetry) as follows: if a speech claims to be false, it becomes
true. Or, to adopt Constant's own formula: "The sentiments we
feign, we end by feeling." All of Adolphe's feeling for Ellénore is
born of certain words, at first deliberately formulated as false:
"Aroused as I was by my own manner, I experienced, as I finished writing, a little of the passion which I had sought to
express with all possible strength." And, with the help of a fa-

vorable circumstance: "Love, which an hour before I applauded myself for feigning, I suddenly believed I was feeling with a frenzy." False words become true, one cannot speak or write with impunity. A similar scene is described in *The Red Notebook:* "By dint of saying it, I almost managed to believe it." And if words create the reality they had previously evoked fictively, silence makes this same reality vanish: "The disappointments I concealed, I partially forgot."

These two rules, simple as they may be, cover the entirety of verbal production. From them ensues a paradox concerning sincerity or veracity, which Constant has nicely formulated: "Almost no one is ever altogether sincere nor altogether in bad faith." This assertion refers as much to the absence of unity in the personality as to the properties of speech itself which, when mendacious, becomes true, and when sincere, becomes false. There is no pure lie, and no pure truth.

Signs and what they designate no longer present themselves as two independent series, each capable of representing the other; they form a whole, and any territorial delimitation distorts their image. We cannot name or communicate a feeling without altering it; there does not exist a purely constative speech. Or, more generally, we must not speak of the essence of an act or of a feeling, while trying to disregard our experience of it. Constant offers us a dynamic conception of the psyche; there exists no stable context, fixed once and for all, in which would appear, one after the other, certain new elements. The appearance of each element modifies the nature of the others, and they define themselves only by their mutual relations. Not that feelings do not exist outside of the words which designate them, but they are not what they are except by their relation to these words. Any effort to know psychic functioning in a static context is doomed to failure.

We have seen that false speech became true, that it had that power to create the referent which it first evoked "jokingly." We may generalize this rule and say that words do not come after a psychic reality which they verbalize, but that they are its very origin: In the beginning was the word. . . . Words create things instead of being a pale reflection of them. Or as Constant says in *Cécile,* apropos of a special case: "As often happens in life, the precautions he took to keep this sentiment from developing were precisely what caused it to develop."

All transactions of love, for example, obey this law; Constant's characters acknowledge it and act in consequence. When Elénore wants to protect herself from her love for Adolphe, she first attempts to ward off the words which designate it: "She consented to receive me only infrequently . . . with the promise that I never speak a word of love to her." Ellénore is suspicious, for she knows that to accept language is to accept love itself; the words will lose no time in creating the thing. Which is what happens, very soon afterward: "She allowed me to tell her of my love; by degrees she grew familiar with such language; soon she admitted to me that she loved me." To accept language, to accept love: the distance between the two is only that of a proposition. The same is true of Germaine, in *Amélie et Germaine:* "Germaine needs the language of love, that language which is every day more impossible for me to speak to her." Germaine does not ask for love, but for the language of love, which, we now know, is not less but more. Constant knows this too; it is not love which has become impossible but specifically the use of this language. Adolphe will act in the same way when he tries to break off his relations with Ellénore: "I congratulated myself when I could substitute the words affection, friendship, devotion for the word love. . . ."

Another remarkable scene in *Adolphe* describes the appearance of pity in this way. Ellénore says to Adolphe: "You think you feel love and you feel only pity." And he comments, "Why did she utter these fatal words? Why did she reveal to me a secret of which I wanted to remain ignorant? . . . The mechanism was destroyed; I was determined upon my sacrifice, but I was no longer happy to be making it." Thus pity takes the place of love by the power of a sentence; pity, whose very existence had hitherto been problematical, becomes Adolphe's ruling passion.

All words, and not only the magician's, have an incantatory character. In his tale "Les Fées," Charles Perrault describes the marvelous gift a fairy bestows upon two sisters. To the first:

" 'The gift I give you,' the fairy continued, 'is that upon each word you speak, a flower or a precious stone will fall from your lips.' " And to the second: " 'The gift I give you is that with each word you speak, a snake or a toad will fall from your lips.' " And the prediction immediately comes true: " 'Indeed, good mother,' the haughty sister replied, and two vipers and two toads at once fell from her mouth." But all of us, Constant would say, have received this same gift, and the words which come out of our mouths are infallibly transformed into palpable reality. An unsuspected responsibility is laid upon us: we cannot speak for the sake of speaking, words are always more than words, and there is a great danger in not taking into account the consequences of what we say. Constant himself formulates as follows the "main idea" of *Adolphe:* to signal the danger "in the simple habit of borrowing the language of love." By speaking thus, "we commit ourselves to a path whose end we cannot foresee."

Thus words are more important—and more difficult—than the actions they designate. Adolphe cannot defend Ellénore's honor by his words, whereas he does not hesitate to fight a duel for her, and he remarks: "I should have greatly preferred to fight them than to have answered them." And Constant will say about himself: "What has always betrayed me is my words. They have always spoiled the merit of my actions." Words weigh more heavily than things. Thus Ellénore will reflect: "You are kind; your actions are noble and devoted; but what actions might efface your words?"

This priority of speech over action (or perhaps, of speech among actions) is so obvious that society has made it its law. Constant thus characterizes in *Cécile* "French public opinion . . . which forgives all vices but is inexorable about the proprieties" and will repeat the same observation in the preface to the third edition of *Adolphe:* "Public opinion in France is willing enough to welcome vice when scandal is not attached to it." Words are more important than things; even more, words create things.

Personal and Impersonal Speech—Present and Absent Things

Not all speech has the same power of bringing what it names into the world. A scene in the eighth chapter affords us a good illustration of this. Ellénore arranges for Adolphe to meet one of her friends, who is to serve as an intermediary between the alienated lovers. Adolphe, in a burst of sincerity, reveals his true feelings for Ellénore in the friend's presence: "I had never told anyone, until that moment, that I no longer loved Ellénore"; and as we already know, between thinking a thing—however frequently—and saying it, there is an infinite distance. But the fact here becomes particularly significant, for this speech is addressed to a *third person:* "This truth, hitherto imprisoned in my heart, and only occasionally revealed to Ellénore in outbursts of anger and desperation, assumed more power and truth in my own eyes simply because someone else had now become its recipient." The same words addressed to Ellénore did not have the same meaning, could not play the same role, for Ellénore was a "thou" and not a "he." The opposition of the two is that of a *personal* speech, which knows only "I" and "thou," to an *impersonal* speech, which is that of "he" and especially, as we shall see, of "one." The difference between the two is clearly perceived by Adolphe: "It is a great step, and an irreparable one, when one suddenly reveals to the eyes of a third person the hidden ways of an intimate relation." Impersonal speech transforms emotion into reality: but is reality anything except what is uttered by that impersonal speech, by the speech of nonpersons?

We may now account for the importance Adolphe grants (as does Constant in his journals) to public opinion: public opinion is precisely this impersonal speech, whose (acting) subject remains anonymous and empowered to create facts. In trying to determine his own value, Adolphe does not question himself but attempts to call to mind impersonal judgments: "I recalled . . . the praise bestowed upon my first efforts." "Any praise, any approval of my mind or of my learning seemed to me an unendurable reproach." We may note, on the one hand, the incontestable character (for Adolphe) of these judgments and, on the

other, the fact that it is meaningless to search for their author.
Here is what Constant calls, for himself, "a situation analogous
to hell": "the perpetual chatter, that amazement of the most
enlightened men in France about the strange association into
which I had entered . . ." (*Amélie et Germaine*). There is no
question of contesting the fairness of public opinion (just as
Adolphe cannot do so when he must decide whether or not to
reject society's condemnation of Ellénore); such things are not
dispute l. On the contrary, every character will try to adapt himself to it as best he can. Hence the narrator of *The Red Notebook,* who is courting a young woman, will attempt to gain not
her favors, but those of public opinion: "My goal was that others
should speak about me." Out of these "others," out of this
"one," emerges the surest, the most real speech, one more real
than reality—since it is worth more than the fact it designates.

Writing partakes of the characteristics of impersonal speech.
Constant frequently questions himself, especially in his *Journal,*
as to the bearing and signification of writing, and he notes, each
time, certain affinities between writing and public speech. Here
is a frequently quoted passage from the *Journal:* "In beginning
this journal, I resolved to write whatever I might feel. I have
abided by this resolve as best I could, and yet such is the influence of speaking to the gallery that sometimes I have not entirely observed it." To write is "to speak to the gallery": by the
simple fact that he writes (and does not speak), Constant sees
his discourse approach that impersonal speech which might be
addressed to a public. He will remark upon this presence of the
public in writing many times more: "Let us be of good faith and
not write for each other as we do for the public" (*Amélie et Germaine*). His consciousness of a reader who is no one in particular, who is the nonperson, is—so to speak—constant: "You will
see that . . ." "If one were to read what I have sometimes written of this matter . . ." (*Journal*). By the very fact that one
writes, the words no longer are addressed to the "I" (as in
"thought"), nor to a specific "thou" (which was the case in
speech; personal letters are thus the writing closest to speech),
but to "others," to a "one." And the consequences are there: to
write is to institute reality, just as in the case of impersonal

speech. Hence Constant writes: "I consign my impression at least here so that it may not be altered." Or, once he has described the death of Julie Talma in his *Journal,* he finds himself obliged to abandon the journal in order to cease feeling the presence of death.

We see here, among others, what risks are run by those who consider Constant's journals as pure testimony, as reflecting Constant's life without participating in that life. To identify him with the character of the journals is illegitimate precisely because Constant is writing this journal (and the Constant we project in Adolphe's features is never anything but a *written* Constant: the one of the journal, the one of the letters). He himself constantly puts us on our guard. The journal is not a transparent description, a pure reflection of "life"; writing can never be that. "I must indicate here that I treat my journal as my life," he will write. Or again: "This journal has become for me a sensation for which I have a kind of need." The journal supplants life, it is more opaque, more material than life. This accounts for those odd notations where the time of life is replaced by the space of writing: "I certainly hope at the bottom of the next page to be away from here," or "at the end of the twenty-fifth page after this one, I might well be amazed by all that I am now experiencing."

The impersonality of writing may explain the ease with which the characters in *Adolphe* write, compared to their difficulty in speaking. Hence Adolphe's father: "His letters were affectionate, but no sooner were we in one another's presence than there was something constrained in him." Hence Adolphe himself: "Convinced by these repeated experiences that I should never have the courage to speak to Ellénore, I determined to write her." And one might say that, more generally, Adolphe finds it difficult to explain himself to Ellénore (in speech) but that he manages to do so readily to the reader (in writing).

To return once more to the rules we articulated above: speech, if true, is false; if false, is true. If we want to combine these two rules into one, we must say: words do not signify the presence of things but their absence. Thus formulated, this law is pertinent for the totality of the referents, and not merely for one of its parts. Verbalization changes the nature of psychic activities and indicates its absence; it does not change the nature of material objects but establishes their absence rather than their presence.

All the cases hitherto analyzed conform to this law. Here is another particularly eloquent one which we find in *Cécile:* "The care she took to assure me that, once married, she had never repented of this union, convinced me she had repented of it forthwith." Or, again, this sentence in *Adolphe:* "O spell of love—he who experiences you cannot describe you!" The description of love designates its absence, just as the affirmation of the absence of regret designates its presence (the absence of absence). Words do not designate things but the contrary of things.

We must understand these paradoxical affirmations precisely as such. We cannot replace words by their contraries in order to palliate the threats which endanger communication; it is not a question here of a wrong use of language. The meaning of the paradox would be obliterated if there existed but one law which postulates that the use of words implies the absence of their referent. Words designate the contrary of what they seem to designate; if this appearance, this "semblance," vanished, the whole meaning of the contradictory law of language would collapse at once.

We are constantly reminded, in *Adolphe,* of this primary reality, necessary in order that transgression be possible. Hence Baron de T*** will say to Adolphe: "The facts are positive, they are public [here again public opinion makes a "fact" "positive"]; by preventing me from recalling them, do you suppose you are destroying them?" And Adolphe himself will affirm: "What one does not say exists no less for that." These sentences therefore do not contradict the doctrine of speech which emerges from the preceding; they provide, on the contrary, its necessary condition, that primary relation without which the paradox of speech would not have existed.

Reflection on the nature of speech and thereby of all communication produces, in Constant, a sentiment which we might characterize as "tragic utterance." Communication is nothing out a concealed or postponed misunderstanding; the effort to communicate is a diversion for children. This Constant must have profoundly experienced, if we judge by these remarks drawn from his journal: "One is never known but to oneself, one cannot be judged but by oneself; between the others and oneself there is an invincible barrier." "The others are . . . the others, one can never bring it about that they might be oneself. . . . There is between ourselves and what is not ourselves an insurmountable barrier." "My life in fact is nowhere but in myself, . . . its inwardness is surrounded by some barrier which others cannot cross." This obsessive barrier which Constant cannot help feeling resides in the very nature of speech, and it is, in effect, insurmountable—a sufficient reason for that pessimism which often strikes us when we read Constant's texts. We cannot take comfort in the notion that if communication does not occur, the feelings which were to have become its object remain intact; we know now that they exist only in this communication. We act then, Constant will say, "as if we wanted to take revenge upon our very feelings for the pain we feel in not being able to make them known." Cut off from others, the self no longer exists.

The one comfort we might offer Constant derives from his theory itself: since every true speech becomes false, once it is articulated (because of the change it produces in the object described), hence this very theory is certainly false, insofar as speech, after the articulation of the theory, is no longer the same.

Speech and Desire

A great deal of the text of *Adolphe* concerns speech, as we have seen. There is perhaps only one theme which is represented as abundantly: that of desire. The coexistence of the two within a text is not gratuitous, and it will be instructive to compare the structure of speech, as we have just observed it, with that of desire. In this connection, let us summarize that structure of desire so exhaustively studied in Maurice Blanchot's essay "Adolphe ou le malheur des sentiments vrais," published in *La Part du feu*.

Adolphe's desire will last only as long as it is unsatisfied, for he desires his desire more than its object. Living with Ellénore, he will no longer be happy, dreaming only of the independence he lacks. But once free, he cannot enjoy that independence either: "How heavily it weighed upon me, that freedom I had so longed for! How much my heart craved now that dependence which had so often disgusted me!" The abolition of the distance between desire's subject and object abolishes desire itself.

Whence several consequences: first of all, desire will never be so strong as in the absence of its object—which leads Constant to an absolute valuation of absence, to a devaluation of presence. He will write in his journal: "My imagination, which so readily responds to the disadvantages of any present situation . . ."; "whatever my will, it is only in absence that any resolution can be carried out." He even arrives at this formula, unique in its concision: "I love only in absence. . . ."

The satisfaction of desire signifies its death and therefore disaster, misery. To be loved is to be unhappy. "No one was more beloved, more praised, more petted and caressed than I, and never was a man less happy," Constant will write again. Once one is loved, one can no longer love. How explain that one ceases to desire the object aspired to so ardently a quarter of an hour before, how can the same object provoke, one after the other, two such different attitudes? It is because this object is the same only materially and not symbolically; yet only this latter dimension matters to us here. We must once again abandon any static image of consciousness. The object is not the same whether it is absent or present; it does not exist independent of our relation to it. Or as Constant himself formulates it: "The object which escapes us is necessarily quite different from the one which pursues us."

Nothing favors desire so much as obstacles. Adolphe's love begins only with the first obstacle which opposes it (a cold letter from Ellénore), and thereafter, each obstacle removed will diminish his desire. Further: obstacles not only reinforce but create desire (a favorite theme of myths and folk tales, as we know from so many stories of prohibition). Constant will write apropos of his second wife: "Horribly weary of her when she wanted to be united to me, yet as soon as she told me that according to her father's wishes she wanted to postpone the match, I felt myself once again overwhelmed by a devouring passion."

At the same time, it is not enough to say we desire not the presence of an object but its absence; once again, it is not a question of wrong linguistic usage, of simply replacing words by their contraries. The paradox and tragedy of desire proceed precisely from its double nature. We desire at the same time desire and its object; Adolphe would be miserable not obtaining Ellénore's love, just as he is miserable having done so. The choice is merely between different miseries. Constant will say as much in his commentary on Adolphe's character: "His position and Ellénore's were without recourse, and that is precisely what I wanted. I have shown him tormented because he loved Ellénore only slightly; but he would not have been any less tormented if he had loved her more. He suffered *because of* her, lacking feelings; with more impassioned feelings, he would have suffered *for* her." Or in the same fashion, apropos of Mme de Staël: "She has always had that kind of anxiety about our relationship which kept her from finding it tiresome, because she never believed herself sufficiently sure of it." The choice, then, is between anxiety and weariness, between pain and indifference.

In this world lacerated by the contradictory law which constitutes it, Constant sees only one positive certainty: to spare others pain. If the logic of desire puts us in a relative world, the pain of others is an absolute value, and its negation, its refusal, is the only positive reference. This principle will determine Adolphe's conduct, just as it has determined Constant's (which is what we mean when we speak of their "weakness of character"). Happiness, or rather what replaces it here, the absence of misery, depends once again entirely on others: "The *ne plus ultra* of happiness would be to do each other as little harm as possible."

We can now readily re-establish the profound relation between speech and desire. Both function analogously; words imply the absence of things, just as desire implies the absence of its object, and these absences are imposed despite the "natural" necessity of things and of the object of desire. Both defy the traditional image which represents objects in themselves, independent of their relation to the person for whom they exist. Both reach an impasse: that of communication, that of happiness. Words are to things what desire is to its object.

This does not mean, evidently, that we desire what we say. The equivalence is more profound, it consists in the analogy of the mechanism, of the functioning, and it can be realized as much in identity as in opposition: "All the more violent in that I felt myself to be all the weaker," Adolphe will say of himself; words echoed by Constant's own: "I am harsh because I am weak" (*Journal*). Here words replace things; but things are, precisely, desire.

We could now ask to what degree this theory of speech, sketched by Constant, has something to do with literature; is it not rather a matter of another chapter in the history of psychology (as Jean Hytier suggests in *Les Romans de l'individu:* "The name Constant should figure in psychology textbooks")? Yet there is a material fact which already should put us on our guard: almost all the elements of this theory are to be found in *Adolphe,* and even exclusively in *Adolphe.* The journals or the other writings merely confirm a portion of Constant's ideas. Could it be an accident that his one strictly literary text should be almost entirely devoted to this theme?

We can propose the following explanation for this phenomenon. It is reasonable to suppose that the thematic variety of literature is only apparent, that at the basis of all literature are to be found what might be called the same semantic universals, very few in number, but whose combinations and transformations furnish the whole variety of existing texts. If this were the case, we can be sure that desire would be one of these universals (exchange might be another). Now in dealing with speech, Constant also deals with desire; we have observed the formal equivalence of the two. We can then say that this entire problematics is fundamentally literary; desire would even be one of those constants which permit us to define literature itself.

But why, one may ask, would desire be one of the semantic

universals of literature (merely its importance in human life is not a sufficient reason)? We have just seen that desire functions the way speech does (as does exchange, moreover); but literature, too, is speech, though a different speech. By taking desire as one of its thematic constants, literature indirectly reveals its secret which is its first law: literature remains its own essential object. By speaking of desire it continues to speak . . . itself. Hence we can now advance a hypothesis as to the nature of the semantic universals of literature: they will never be anything but transformations of literature itself.

1967

8

The Grammar of Narrative

The metaphorical usage enjoyed by certain terms—"language," "grammar," "syntax," and so forth—makes us habitually forget that these words might have a precise meaning, even when they do not refer to a natural language. In proposing a discussion of "the grammar of narrative," we must first specify what meaning the word "grammar" will assume.

In the very earliest reflections on language, a hypothesis appears according to which there may be discovered a common structure that transcends the obvious differences among languages. Investigations of this common structure, a kind of universal grammar, have been pursued, with varying degrees of success, for more than twenty centuries. Before our own period, their apogee was doubtless reached by the "modists" of the thirteenth and fourteenth centuries. Here is how one of them, Robert Kilwardby, formulated their credo: "Grammar can constitute a science only if it is one and the same for all men. It is by accident that grammar lays down rules proper to a particular language, such as Latin or Greek; for just as geometry is not concerned with concrete lines or surfaces, so grammar established the correctness of discourse insofar as the latter ignores actual language [current usage would here invert the terms *discourse* and *language*]. The object of grammar is the same for all men."

But if we admit the existence of a universal grammar, we must no longer limit it to languages alone. It will have, evidently, a psychological reality; here we might quote George Boas, whose testimony is all the more valuable in that its author has inspired an antiuniversalist linguistics: "The appearance of the most fundamental grammatical concepts in every language must be regarded as the proof of the unity of certain fundamental psychological processes." This psychological reality makes plausible the existence of the same structure elsewhere than in speech.

Such are the premises which permit us to search for this same universal grammar by studying other symbolic activities besides natural language. Since this grammar still remains a hypothesis, it is obvious that the results of a study of such an activity will be at least as pertinent to its knowledge as the results of a study of, say, French. Unfortunately there exist very few extended explorations of the grammar of symbolic activities; one of the rare examples we might cite is Freud's study of oneiric language. Yet linguists have failed to consider it when they inquire into the nature of a universal grammar.

A theory of narrative will also contribute, then, to the knowledge of this grammar, insofar as narrative is such a symbolic activity. Here a two-way relation is set up: we can borrow categories from the rich conceptual apparatus of linguistic studies, but at the same time we must avoid following the prevailing theories of language too docilely. Perhaps the study of narration will permit us to correct the image of discourse as we find it in the grammars.

I should like to illustrate here, by several examples from the *Decameron* (roman numerals indicate the day, arabic numbers the tale), the problems which arise in the attempt to describe narrative, when this attempt is placed in a similar perspective.

1. Let us consider first the problem of the parts of speech. Any semantic theory of the parts of speech must be based on the distinction between description and denomination. Language performs these two functions equally well, and their interpenetration in the lexicon often makes us forget this distinction. If I say "the child," this word serves to describe an object, to enumerate its characteristics (age, size, and so forth); but at

the same time it permits me to identify a spatio-temporal unit, to give it a name (particularly, here, by means of the article). These two functions are irregularly distributed within language: proper nouns, pronouns (personal, demonstrative, and so forth), and articles are chiefly denominative, whereas common nouns, verbs, adjectives, and adverbs are chiefly descriptive. Yet this is only a matter of predominance, which is why it is useful to conceive of description and denomination as detached, so to speak, from proper nouns and common nouns; these parts of speech are a quasi-accidental form of description and denomination. This explains why common nouns can easily become proper nouns (Hotel "Universe") and conversely ("a Svengali"): each of the two forms serves the two processes, but to different degrees.

To study the structure of a narrative's plot, we must first present this plot in the form of a summary, in which each distinct action of the story has a corresponding proposition. The opposition between denomination and description will appear much more clearly here than in language. The agents (subjects and objects) of the propositions will always be ideal proper nouns (we may usefully recall that the first meaning of "*proper* noun" is not "a name which is someone's property" but "a name in the proper sense," "a name par excellence"). If the agent of a proposition is a common noun (a substantive), we must subject it to an analysis which will distinguish, within the word itself, its denominative and descriptive aspects. To say, as Boccaccio often does, "the king of France" or "the widow" or "the servant" is both to identify a unique person and to describe certain of his properties. Such an expression is equivalent to an entire proposition: its descriptive aspects form the predicate of the proposition, whereas its denominative aspects constitute the subject. "The king of France sets out on a journey" actually contains two propositions—"X is king of France" and "X sets out on a journey"—in which X plays the part of the proper noun, even if this noun is absent from the tale. The agent cannot be endowed with any property, but is rather a blank form which is complete by different predicates. The agent has no more meaning than a pronoun such as "he" in "he who runs" or "he who is brave." The grammatical subject is always devoid of internal properties, for these derive only from a temporary junction with a predicate.

We shall therefore keep description solely within the predicate. In order now to distinguish several classes of predicates, we must consider the construction of narratives more closely. The minimal complete plot consists in the passage from one equilibrium to another. An "ideal" narrative begins with a stable situation which is disturbed by some power or force. There results a state of disequilibrium; by the action of a force directed in the opposite direction, the equilibrium is re-established; the second equilibrium is similar to the first, but the two are never identical.

Consequently there are two types of episodes in a narrative: those which describe a state (of equilibrium or of disequilibrium) and those which describe the passage from one state to the other. The first type will be relatively static and, one might say, iterative; the same kind of actions can be repeated indefinitely. The second, on the other hand, will be dynamic and in principle occurs only once.

This definition of the two types of episodes (and hence of propositions designating them) permits us to relate them to two parts of speech, the adjective and the verb. As has often been remarked, the opposition between verb and adjective is not that of an action having no common denominator with a quality, but that of two aspects, probably iterative and noniterative. Narrative "adjectives" will therefore be those predicates which describe states of equilibrium or disequilibrium, narrative "verbs" those which describe the passage from one to the other.

It may seem surprising that our list of parts of speech does not include substantives. But the substantive can always be reduced to one or more adjectives, as some linguists have already pointed out. For example, H. Paul writes: "The adjective designates a simple property, or one which is represented as simple; the substantive contains a complex of properties." In the *Decameron*, substantives are almost always reduced to an adjective; thus "gentleman" (II,6; II,8; III,9), "king" (X,6; X,7), and "angel" (IV,2) all reflect a single property, which is "to be well born." It should be noted here that the words—in French, or in English—by which we designate some property or action are not pertinent to determining the part of (narrative) speech. A property can just as well be designated by an adjective as by a substantive or even by a whole locution. We are here concerned with adjectives or verbs of the grammar of narrative, and not with those of the grammar of French or English.

Let us take an example which will let us illustrate these parts of (narrative) speech. Peronella receives her lover when her husband, a poor mason, is away from home. But one day the husband returns early. Peronella hides her lover in a cask and tells her husband that someone wants to buy it—that this someone is in fact examining the cask right now. The husband believes her and is delighted by the prospect of the sale. He climbs inside the cask in order to scrape it out, and while he does so the lover makes love to Peronella, who has thrust her head and arms into the opening of the cask to keep her husband from seeing what is going on (VII,2).

Peronella, the lover, and the husband are the agents of this story. All three are narrative proper nouns, though the last two are not named; we can designate them by X, Y, and Z. The words lover and husband further indicate a certain state (it is the legality of the relation with Peronella which is here in question); they therefore function as adjectives. These adjectives describe the initial equilibrium: Peronella is the mason's wife, hence she is not entitled to make love with other men.

Then comes the transgression of this law: Peronella receives her lover. Here we are obviously dealing with a "verb" which we might designate as to violate, to transgress (a law). It produces a state of disequilibrium, for the family law is no longer respected.

From this moment on, two possibilities exist by which equilibrium can be re-established. The first would be to punish the unfaithful wife, but this action would serve to re-establish the initial equilibrium. Now, the novella (or at least Boccaccio's novellas) never describes such a repetition of the initial order. The verb "to punish" is therefore present within the tale (it is the danger which hangs over Peronella) but it is not realized—it remains in a virtual state. The second possibility consists in finding a means of avoiding punishment; this is what Peronella will do. She succeeds by disguising the situation of disequilibrium (the transgression of the law) into a situation of equilibrium (the purchase of a cask does not violate the family law). Hence there is a third verb here: "to disguise." The final result is again a state, hence an adjective; a new law is established, though it is not an explicit one, according to which the wife can follow her natural inclinations.

Thus analysis of narrative permits us to isolate formal units which present striking analogies with the parts of speech: proper noun, verb, adjective. Since no account is taken here of the verbal substance which supports these units, it becomes possible to give descriptions of them which may be clearer than those we could produce in the study of a language.

2. We habitually distinguish in a grammar the *primary* categories, which permit us to define the parts of speech, from the *secondary* categories, which are the properties of these parts: for instance, voice, aspects, mood, tense, and so forth. Here let us take the example of one of these secondary categories, mood, in order to observe its transformations within the grammar of narrative.

The mood of a narrative proposition makes explicit the relation which the character concerned sustains with it; hence this character takes the role of the subject of the utterance. First we shall distinguish two classes: the indicative on the one hand, and all the other moods on the other. These two groups stand in opposition, as real to unreal. Propositions uttered in the indicative are perceived as designating actions which have really taken place; if the mood is different, it is because the action has not been performed but exists in potentiality, virtually (Peronella's virtual punishment has provided us an example of this).

The former grammars accounted for the existence of modal propositions by the fact that language serves not only to describe and therefore to refer to reality, but also to express our will. Whence too the close relation, in some languages, between the moods and the future tense, which habitually signifies only an intention. We shall not follow these grammars all the way:

we may establish a first dichotomy between the moods proper to the *Decameron,* of which there are four, by discovering whether or not they are linked to a human will. This dichotomy gives us two groups: moods of *will* and moods of *hypothesis.*

There are two moods of will: the obligative and the optative. The *obligative* is the mood of a proposition which must occur; it is a coded, nonindividual will which constitutes the law of a society. For this reason, the obligative has a special status; the laws are always implied, never named (it is unnecessary), and risk passing unnoticed by the reader. In the *Decameron,* punishment must be written in the obligative mood—it is a direct consequence of the laws of the society, and it is present even if it does not take place.

The *optative* corresponds to the actions desired by the character. In a certain sense, any proposition can be preceded by the same proposition in the operative mood, insofar as each action in the *Decameron*—though to different degrees—results from someone's desire to see this action realized. *Renunciation* is a special case of the optative: it is an optative initially affirmed, subsequently denied. Thus Gianni renounces his initial desire to transform his wife into a mare when he learns the details of the transformation (IX,10). Similarly, Ansaldo renounces his desire to possess Dianora when he learns of her husband's generosity (X,5). One novella also demonstrates a second-degree optative: in III,9, Giletta not only wants to sleep with her husband, but even wants her husband to love her, to become the subject of an optative proposition: she desires another's desire.

The other two moods, conditional and predictive, not only offer a common semantic characteristic (hypothesis) but are distinguished by a special syntactic structure: they refer to a succession of two propositions and not to an isolated proposition. More precisely, they concern the relation between these two propositions, which is always implied but with which the subject of the utterance may sustain varying relations.

The *conditional* is defined as the mood which puts two attributive propositions into an implied relation, so that the subject of the second proposition and whoever makes the condition are one and the same character (the conditional has sometimes been designated as a *test*). Hence in IX,1, Francesca makes it a condition of granting her love that Rinuccio and Alessandro must each perform a heroic deed; if the proof of their courage is forthcoming, she will yield to their claims. Similarly in X,5, Dianora demands of Ansaldo "a garden which will bloom in January even as in the month of May"; if he succeeds, he can possess her. One novella takes the test itself as a central theme. Pyrrhus demands that Lidia, as a proof of her love, perform three actions: kill her husband's favorite falcon before his eyes, tear out a tuft of her husband's beard, and finally, extract one of his best teeth. Once Lidia has passed the test, he will agree to sleep with her (VII, 9).

Last, the *predictive* has the same structure as the conditional, but the subject who predicts need not be the subject of the second proposition (the consequence); whereby the predictive approaches what Benjamin Whorf has identified as the *transrelative mood*. No restriction burdens the subject of the first proposition. Hence that subject can be the same as the subject of the prediction (in I,3: if I cause Melchisedech discomfort, Saladin decides, he will give me money; in X,10: if I am cruel to Griselda, Gautier muses, she will try to do me harm). The two propositions can have the same subject (IV,8: if Girolamo leaves the city, his mother speculates, he will no longer love Salvestra; VII,7: if my husband is jealous, Beatrice supposes, he will get up and leave). These predictions are sometimes highly elaborated. Thus in this last novella, in order to sleep with Ludovico, Beatrice tells her husband that Ludovico has been flirting with her; similarly, in III,3, in order to provoke a knight's love, a lady complains to the knight's friend that he does nothing but flirt with her. The predictions in these two novellas (which both turn out to be accurate) are not a matter of course: here words create things instead of reflecting them.

This phenomenon allows us to see that the predictive is a special manifestation of the logic of verisimilitude. We suppose that one action will lead to another, because such causality corresponds to a common probability. Yet we must take care not to confuse this verisimilitude of the *characters* with the verisimilitude of the *reader*. Such a confusion would lead us to seek the probability of each individual action; whereas the verisimilitude of the characters has a precise formal reality, the predictive.

If we try to articulate more clearly the relations presented by the four moods, we will have, as well as the opposition, presence-of-will/absence-of-will, another dichotomy which will oppose the optative and the conditional to the obligative and the predictive. The first pair is characterized by an identity of the author of the verbal act with the subject of the utterance: here one puts oneself in question. The second pair, on the other hand, reflects actions external to the speaking subject: they are social and not individual laws.

3. If we seek to go beyond the level of propositions, more complex problems appear. For hitherto we could compare the results of our analysis with those of linguistic studies. But there is hardly any linguistic theory of discourse; hence we shall not make the attempt to refer to it. Here are some general conclusions which can be drawn from the analysis of the *Decameron* about the structure of narrative discourse.

The relations established between propositions can be of three kinds. The simplest is the *temporal* relation in which events follow one another in the text because they follow one another in the imaginary world of the book. The *logical* relation is another type of relation; narratives are habitually based on implications and presuppositions, whereas texts more remote from fiction are characterized by the presence of a movement from the general to the particular, and vice versa. Finally, a third relation is of a *spatial* type, insofar as the two propositions are juxtaposed because of a certain resemblance between them, thereby indicating a space proper to the text. Here we are dealing, evidently, with parallelism and its many subdivisions; this relation seems dominant in poetry. Narrative possesses all three types of relations, but in a constantly varying proportion and according to a hierarchy proper to each individual text.

We may establish a syntactic unit superior to the proposition; let us call it the *sequence*. The sequence will have different characteristics, according to the type of relation between propositions. But in each case, an incomplete repetition of the initial proposition will mark its end. Moreover, the sequence provokes an intuitive reaction on the reader's part, that is, that he is faced with a complete story, an integral anecdote. A novella coincides frequently, though not always, with a sequence; the novella may contain several sequences or only a part of one.

From the perspective of the sequence, we may distinguish several types of propositions. These types correspond to the logical relations of exclusion (either-or), of disjunction (and-or), and of conjunction (and-and). We shall call the first type of propositions *alternative*, for only one among them can appear at one point of the sequence; this appearance, moreover, is obligatory. The second type will be that of *optional* propositions whose place is not specified and whose appearance is not obligatory. Last, a third type will be formed by the *obligatory* propositions; these must always appear at a specific place.

Let us take a novella which will permit us to illustrate these various relations. A Gascony lady is "abused by several lewd fellows" during her sojourn in Cyprus. She wishes to lodge a complaint with the king of the island, but is told that her efforts would be futile, for the king remains indifferent to the insults he himself receives. Nonetheless, she meets the king and makes several bitter remarks to him. The king is touched and abandons his indifferent attitude (I,9).

A comparison between this novella and the other texts which form the *Decameron* will permit us to identify the status of each proposition. There is first of all the obligatory proposition: this is the lady's desire to modify the preceding situation. We encounter this desire in all the novellas of the collection. Further, two propositions contain the causes of this desire (the abuse by the boys and the unhappiness of the lady), and we may label them as optional. Here we are dealing with a psychological motivation for our heroine's modifying action, a motivation which is frequently absent from the *Decameron* (contrary to what occurs in the nineteenth-century tale). In the story of Peronella (VII,2), there is no psychological motivation, but here we also find an optional proposition: this is the fact that the lovers once again make love behind the husband's back. Let there be no mistake: by labeling this proposition optional, we mean that it is not necessary to our perception of the novella's plot as a completed whole. The novella itself certainly needs it, it is in fact the "salt of the story," but we must be able to separate the concept of plot from the concept of tale.

Finally there exist alternative propositions. Let us take for instance the lady's action which modifies the king's character. From the syntactic point of view, it has the same function as Peronella's in concealing her lover in the cask; both aim at establishing a new equilibrium. Yet here this action is a direct verbal attack, whereas Peronella made use of disguise. "To attack" and "to disguise" are therefore two verbs which appear in alternative propositions; in other words, they form a paradigm.

If we try to establish a typology of narratives, we can do so only by relying on the alternative elements: neither the obligatory propositions which must always appear, nor the optional ones which can always appear, will help us here. Further, the typology might be based on purely syntactic criteria. We said earlier that the narrative consisted in a passage from one equilibrium to another. But a narrative can also present only a portion of this trajectory. Hence it can describe only the passage from an equilibrium to a disequilibrium, or conversely.

The study of the novellas of the *Decameron* has led us, for example, to discern in this collection only two types of story. The first, of which the tale about Peronella was an example, could be called "punishment evaded." Here the complete trajectory is followed (equilibrium—disequilibrium—equilibrium); moreover, the disequilibrium is provoked by the transgression of a law, an act which deserves punishment. The second type of story, illustrated by the novella about the Gascony lady and the king of Cyprus, can be designated as a "conversion." Here, only the second part of the narrative is present; we start from a state of disequilibrium (a weak king) to arrive at the final equilibrium. Further, this disequilibrium is caused not by a particular action (a verb) but by the very qualities of the character (an adjective).

These few examples may suffice to give some notion of the grammar of narrative. One could object that, in doing so, we have not managed to "explicate" narrative, to draw general conclusions from it. But the state of studies of narrative implies that our first task is the elaboration of a descriptive apparatus; before being able to explain the facts, we must learn to identify them.

Imperfections may (and should) also be found in the concrete categories proposed here; my purpose was to raise questions rather than to provide answers. It seems to me, nonetheless, that the notion itself of a grammar of narrative cannot be contested. This notion rests on the profound unity of language and narrative, a unity which obliges us to revise our ideas about both. We shall understand narrative better if we know that the character is a noun, the action a verb. But we shall understand noun and verb better by thinking of the role they assume in the narrative. Ultimately, language can be understood only if we learn to think of its essential manifestation—literature. The converse is also true: to combine a noun and a verb is to take the first step toward narrative. In a sense, what the writer does is to read language.

1968

9

The Quest of Narrative

Literature must be treated as literature. This slogan, uttered in this very form for over fifty years, ought to have become a commonplace, thereby losing its polemical force. Yet it has not, and the appeal for a "return to literature" in literary studies is as timely as ever; indeed it seems forever doomed to be no more than a force rather than an established condition.

This is because such an imperative is doubly paradoxical. On the one hand, such sentences as "literature is literature" have a specific name: they are tautologies, sentences in which the junction of subject and predicate produces no meaning insofar as this subject and this predicate are identical. In other words, these are sentences which constitute a "zero degree" of meaning. On the other hand, to write about a text is to produce another text; with the first sentence the commentator produces, he falsifies the tautology, which could subsist only at the price of his silence. We can no longer remain faithful to a text once we begin writing. And even if our new text also "belongs" to literature, it is no longer the same literature which is involved. Willy nilly, we write: literature is *not* literature, this text is *not* this text. . . .

The paradox is a double one, but within this duplicity we find the possibility of transcending it. To speak a tautology is not futile precisely to the degree that the tautology will never be perfect. We can play on the ambiguity of the rule, and the requirement "to consider literature as literature" regains its legitimacy.

This is evident when we consider a specific text and its current exegeses; we realize at once that the demand to treat a literary text as a literary text is neither a tautology nor a contradiction. An extreme example is afforded by the literature of the Middle Ages: it is altogether an exception to find a medieval work examined in a strictly literary perspective. N. S. Trubetzkoy, the founder of structural linguistics, wrote in 1926 apropos of the literary history of the Middle Ages:

Glance at the manuals or the university lectures concerned with this field. They rarely deal with literature as such. They deal with instruction (more exactly, with the absence of instruction), aspects of social life reflected (more exactly, insufficiently reflected) in sermons, chronicles, and "lives," with the emendation of ecclesiastical texts; in a word, they deal with many questions. But they rarely speak of literature. There exist a few stereotyped appreciations, which are applied to very different literary works of the Middle Ages: some of these works are written in a "flowery" style, others in a "naive" or "ingenuous" manner. The authors of these manuals or lectures have a specific attitude with regard to these works—it is always dismissive, disdainful; in the best cases, it is disdainful and condescending, but sometimes it is frankly indignant and disapproving. A literary work of the Middle Ages is judged "interesting" not for what it is, but to the degree that it reflects aspects of social life (that is, it is judged in the perspective of social, not literary history), or again, to the degree that it contains direct or indirect indications about the author's literary knowledge (bearing, preferably, on foreign works).

Except for a few details, this judgment can also be applied to present studies of medieval literature (Leo Spitzer was to repeat it some fifteen years later).

These details have their importance, of course. A scholar like Paul Zumthor has blazed new trails in the understanding of medieval literature. A good number of texts have been studied and commented upon with an exactitude and a seriousness which must not be underestimated. Trubetzkoy's words remain valid, however, for the field as a whole, however significant the exceptions.

The text of which I want to sketch a reading has already been the object of an attentive and detailed study of this kind. I refer to *The Quest of the Holy Grail,* an anonymous work of the thirteenth century, and to Albert Pauphilet's *Etudes sur la Queste del Saint Graal;* Pauphilet's analysis considers strictly literary aspects of the text; it remains for us to take his analysis further.

The Signifying Narrative

"Most of the episodes, once recounted, are interpreted by the author," Pauphilet writes, "in the same way the theologians of the period interpreted the details of Scripture."

This text, then, contains its own gloss. No sooner is an adventure completed than its hero meets some hermit who informs him that what he has experienced is no mere adventure but the sign of something else. For example, at the outset, Galahad sees several wonders but fails to understand them until he has encountered a sage. "Sire," the sage replies, "you have asked me the meaning of your adventure, here it is. The adventure consisted of three dreadful ordeals: the stone which was so heavy to lift, the body of the knight which had to be flung outside, and the voice you heard which made you lose consciousness and memory. Of these three things, here is the meaning. . . ." And the sage will conclude: "Now you know the meaning of the adventure." Galahad declares that it has "much more meaning than he supposed."

No knight eludes such explanations. The sage tells Gawain: "It has a meaning, this custom of confining damsels which the seven brothers had devised." "Ah, Sire," says Gawain, "explain to me this meaning, that I may tell it when I return to the court." And in the case of Lancelot: "Lancelot told him of the three words which the voice had uttered in the chapel, when he was called stone, and shaft, and fig tree. 'For the love of God,' he concluded, 'tell me the meaning of these three things. For never have I heard speech that I had such desire to understand.' " The knight can divine that his adventure has a second meaning, but he cannot find it by himself. Thus, "Bors was much amazed by this adventure and did not know what it meant; but he realized indeed that it had a marvelous meaning."

The possessors of meaning form a special category among the characters: they are "sages," hermits, abbots, and recluses. Just as the knights could not *know,* these latter cannot *act;* none of them participates in a peripety, except in the episodes of interpretation. The two functions are strictly parceled out between the two classes of characters; this distribution is so well known that the heroes refer to it themselves: " 'We have seen so much, sleeping or waking,' Gawain replied, 'that we must seek out some hermit who might explain the meaning of our dreams.' " Should no such assistance be available, heaven itself intervenes, and "a voice is heard" which explains everything.

We are confronted, then, from the outset and in a systematic fashion, with a double narrative, with two types of episodes, of a distinct nature but referring to the same event and alternating regularly. Interpreting earthly events as signs of heavenly purposes was common enough in the literature of the period. But whereas other texts totally separated signifier from signified, omitting the latter because they counted on its notoriety, *The Quest of the Holy Grail* juxtaposes the two type of episodes; the interpretation is included within the texture of the narrative. One half of the text deals with adventures, the other with the text which describes them. Text and meta-text are brought into continuity.

This kind of equation might warn us against too sharp a distinction between signs and their interpretations. The episodes resemble each other (though without ever becoming identical) by having this in common: the signs, like their interpretation, are *narratives.* The narrative of an adventure signifies another narrative; the spatio-temporal coordinates of the episode change but its very nature does not. This, once again, was a common enough phenomenon in the Middle Ages, when it was habitual to translate Old Testament narratives as designating those of the New Testament (typology), and we find examples of this transposition in *The Quest of the Holy Grail.* "The death of Abel, in that time when there were yet only three men on earth, foretold the death of the true Crucified One; Abel signified Victory, and Cain represented Judas. Even as Cain greeted his brother before killing him, Judas was to greet his Lord before betraying him unto death. These two deaths are thus in agreement, if not in degree, at least in significance." Medieval Bible commentators searched for an invariable, common to the different narratives.

In *The Quest of the Holy Grail,* the interpretations refer, with varying degrees of ambiguity, to two series of events. The first belongs to a past remote by some hundreds of years; it relates to Joseph of Arimathea, to his son Josephes, to King Mordrain, and to King Méhaignié; this series is habitually designated by the knights' adventures or by their dreams. In itself this series is merely a new "semblance" in relation to the life of Christ, this time. The relation of the three series is clearly established during the narrative of the three tables, which is recounted to Perceval by his aunt: "You know that since the coming of Jesus Christ, there have been three chief tables in the world. The first was the table of Jesus Christ, at which the apostles ate several times. . . . After this table, there was another in the semblance and the remembrance of the first, which was the Table of the Holy Grail, whereon was seen such a great miracle in this country in the time of Joseph of Arimathea, in the beginnings of Christendom upon earth. . . . After this table, there was yet the Round Table, established according to the council of Merlin and of high renown." Each event of the last series signifies events of the preceding ones. Thus, during Galahad's very first ordeals, occurs the event of the shield; once the adventure is over, heaven's envoy appears on the scene. "Hear me, Galahad. Forty-two years after the passion of Jesus Christ, it came to pass that Joseph of Arimathea . . . left Jerusalem with many of his family. They made their way. . . ." There follows another adventure, more or less similar to the one which Galahad has just had and therefore constituting its meaning. References to the life of Christ are treated the same way, though more discreetly, insofar as the material is more familiar: "By semblance if not by degree, your coming must be likened unto that of Christ," a sage tells Galahad. "And even as the prophets, long before Jesus Christ, had foretold his coming and that he would deliver man from hell, just so the hermits and the saints have foretold your coming for over twenty years."

The resemblance between the signs-to-be-interpreted and their interpretation is not purely formal, as is best shown by the fact that sometimes events which belonged to the first group subsequently appear in the second. This is the case, in particular, regarding a strange dream of Gawain's, in which he sees a herd of spotted bulls. The first sage he encounters explains that this herd means the quest for the Grail, in which Gawain takes part. The bulls in the dream say, "Let us search for a better pasture elsewhere," which refers to the knights of the Round Table who said on the day of Pentecost: "Let us search for the Holy Grail." Now the narrative of the vow made by the knights of the Round Table occurs in the first pages of *The Quest for the Holy Grail,* and not in some legendary past. Hence there is no difference of nature between the narratives-as-signifier and the narratives-as-signified, since they can appear in place of each other. The narrative is always a signifier; it signifies another narrative.

The passage from one narrative to the other is possible because of the existence of a code. This code is not the personal invention of the author of *The Quest for the Holy Grail,* it is common to all the works of the period; it consists in linking one object to another, one representation to another; we can easily envisage the constitution of a veritable lexicon.

Here is an example of this exercise in translation. "When she had won you over by her lying words, she ordered her tent pitched and said to you, 'Perceval, come and rest until the night falls, and shield yourself here from the burning sun.' These words are of a great significance, and she meant much besides what you might understand by them. The tent, which was round in the fashion of the universe, represents the world, which will never be without sin; and because sin always abides there, she did not wish you to lodge elsewhere. By telling you to sit and rest, she meant you to be idle and feed your body upon earthly delicacies. . . . She called you, claiming that the sun would burn you, and it is not surprising that she should fear so. For when the sun, by which we understand Jesus Christ, the true light, warms man with the fire of the Holy Ghost, the cold and rime of the Enemy can no longer do him harm, his heart being fixed upon the great sun."

The translation always proceeds from the more to the less

well known, surprising as this might seem. It is the everyday actions—to sit, to eat—and the ordinary objects—the tent, the sun—which turn out to be incomprehensible signs for the characters and which need to be translated into the language of religious values. The relation between the series-to-be translated and the translation is established by a rule which we might call "identification by predicate." The tent is round, the universe is round; hence the tent can signify the universe. The existence of a common predicate permits the two subjects to become each other's signifier. Or again: the sun is luminous, Jesus Christ is luminous; hence the sun can signify Jesus Christ.

In this rule of identification by predicate we recognize the mechanism of metaphor. This figure, for the same reason as the other rhetorical figures, is to be found at the base of every symbolic system. The figures inventoried by rhetoric are so many particular cases of an abstract rule, which governs the birth of signification in all human activity, from dreams to magic. The existence of a common predicate makes the sign a motivated one; the arbitrariness of the sign, which characterizes everyday speech, seems to be an exceptional case.

Yet the number of predicates (or of properties) that can be attached to a subject is limitless; the possible signifieds of any object, of any action are therefore infinite. Within a single system of interpretation, several meanings are already proposed. The sage who explains to Lancelot the phrase "you are harder than stone," as soon as his first explanation is completed, broaches a new one: "But, if it please you, 'stone' may be understood in yet another fashion." The color black signifies sin in one of Lancelot's adventures, but means the Holy Church and therefore virtue in a dream of Bors's. This is what permits the Enemy, disguised as a priest, to propose false interpretations to the credulous knights. Here he addresses himself to Bors: "The bird which resembled a swan signifies a maiden long lovesick for you and who will soon come to plead for your friendship. . . . The black bird is the great sin which would lead you to turn her away." And then, a few pages later, the other interpretation is given by an authentic priest: "The black bird which has ap-

eared to you is Holy Church, which says, 'I am black but I am
omely, know that my dark color is worth more than the
whiteness of others.' As for the white bird that resembled a
wan, it was the Enemy. Indeed the swan is white without and
lack within," and so forth.

How is one to make one's way through this arbitrary labyrinth
of significations so much more dangerous than the arbitrariness
of ordinary language? The representative of good and the repre-
entative of evil make use of the same general rule of "iden-
ification by predicate." It is not by means of this rule that we
could have discovered the falseness of the first interpretation,
but because, and this is essential, the number of signifieds is
educed and their nature is known in advance. The white bird
could not signify an innocent maiden because dreams never
speak of such a thing. It can signify, in the last resort, only two
hings: God and the Devil. The psychoanalytic interpretation of
dreams proceeds in the same way; the overdetermined arbi-
rariness afforded by every "interpretation by predicate" is cir-
cumscribed and regularized by the fact that we know what we
will find: "ideas of oneself and of immediate blood relatives,
phenomena of birth, love, and death" (Ernest Jones). The signifieds are given in advance, in both cases. The interpretation of
dreams, as we find it in *The Quest of the Holy Grail,* obeys the
same laws as Jones's, and involves as much *a priori* thinking; it
is only the nature of what is *a priori* which is changed. Here is
a final example (the analysis of a dream of Bors's): "One of the
flowers leaned toward the other in order to despoil its whiteness,
even as the knight tried to ravish the maiden. But the sage separated them, which signifies that Our Lord, who did not desire
their ruin, sent you in order to separate them and to save the
whiteness of both."

It will not suffice that signifiers and signifieds, the narratives-
to-be-interpreted and the interpretations, be of the same nature.
The Quest of the Holy Grail goes further; it tells us that the signified *is* a signifier, the intelligible *is* sensible. An adventure is
at the same time a real adventure and the symbol of another adventure; in this the medieval narrative is distinguished from the
allegories to which we are accustomed and in which the literal

meaning has become purely transparent, without any logic of its own. Let us consider Bors's adventures. This knight one evening comes to a "strong, high tower"; he remains there for the night. While he is sitting at table with "the lady of the place," a servant enters to announce that the lady's older sister contests her property, that unless she sends a knight to meet the older sister's representative in single combat the next day, she will be stripped of her lands. Bors offers his services to defend the cause of his hostess. The next day, he proceeds to the field of battle and a fierce combat takes place. "The two knights took their distance from each other, then flung themselves into a gallop and each struck the other so grievously that their shields were pierced and their hauberks were broken. . . . At top and bottom they rend their shields, they tear their hauberks at hip and arm; they wound each other grievously, shedding blood beneath the bright, sharp blades. Bors meets with more resistance from the knight than he had thought." This is indeed a real combat, where a man can be wounded, where he must engage all his (physical) powers in order to succeed.

Bors wins the battle; the cause of the younger sister is saved, and our knight leaves in search of other adventures. Meanwhile he happens upon a sage who explains to him that the lady was not a lady at all, nor the adversary knight a knight. "By this lady, we understand Holy Church, who keeps Christendom within the true faith, and who is the patrimony of Jesus Christ. The other lady, who had been disinherited and made war upon her, is the Old Law, the enemy who ever wars against Holy Church and her own." Hence this combat was not a terrestrial and material combat, but a symbolic one; it was two ideas that were doing battle, not two knights. The opposition between material and spiritual is continually proposed and withdrawn.

Such a conception of the sign contradicts our habits. For us, the combat must occur either in the material world or else in the world of ideas; it is earthly or celestial, but not both at once. If it is two ideas which are in combat, Bors's blood cannot be shed, only his mind is concerned. To maintain the contrary is to infringe upon one of the fundamental laws of our logic, which is the law of the excluded middle. X and its contrary cannot be true at the same time, says the logic of ordinary discourse. *The Quest of the Holy Grail* says exactly the contrary. Every event has a literal meaning *and* an allegorical meaning.

This conception of signification is fundamental for *The Quest of the Holy Grail*, and because of it we have difficulty understanding what the Grail is, an entity at once material and spiritual. The impossible intersection of contraries is constantly asserted, however: "They who hitherto were nothing but spirit though they had a body," we are told of Adam and Eve, and of Galahad, "he began to tremble, for his mortal flesh was perceiving spiritual things." The dynamism of the narrative rests on this fusion of the two in one.

Starting from this image of signification, we may gain a first approximation of the nature of the quest and the meaning of the Grail: the quest of the Grail is the quest of a code. To find the Grail is to learn how to decipher the divine language, which means, as we have seen, to appropriate the a priori aspects of the system. Moreover, just as in psychoanalysis, this does not involve an abstract apprenticeship (anyone knows the principles of religion, as today, those of analytic treatment), but a highly personalized practice. Galahad, Perceval, and Bors succeed, more or less readily, in interpreting the signs of God; Lancelot the sinner, for all his good will, does not. On the threshold of the palace, where he might contemplate the divine apparition, he sees two lions on guard. Lancelot translates: danger, and unsheathes his sword. But that is the profane and not the divine code. "At once he saw coming from on high a fiery hand which struck him grievously on the arm and knocked away his sword. A voice spoke to him, saying, 'Ah, man of little faith and pitiful belief, why trust your arm rather than your Creator? Wretch, do you suppose that He who has taken you into His service is not more powerful than your weapons?' " Thus the episode should have been translated as: test of faith. For this very reason, once inside the palace, Lancelot will see only a fraction of the mystery of the Grail. To be ignorant of the code is to see oneself forever denied the Grail.

Structure of Narrative

Pauphilet writes: "This tale is an assemblage of transpositions, each of which, taken separately, exactly renders the nuances of thought. We must trace them back to their moral signification in order to discover their connection. The author composes, so to speak, on the abstract level, and then translates."

The organization of the narrative is therefore produced on the level of the interpretation and not on that of the events-to-be-interpreted. The combinations of these events are sometimes singular, incoherent, but this does not mean that the narrative lacks organization; simply this organization is situated on the level of ideas, not on that of events. We had spoken in this regard of the opposition between phenomenal causality and ideological causality. And Pauphilet astutely compares this narrative to the philosophical tale of the eighteenth century.

The substitution of one logic for another involves certain problems. In this movement, *The Quest of the Holy Grail* reveals a fundamental dichotomy, by means of which various mechanisms are elaborated. It thus becomes possible to make explicit, starting from the analysis of this particular text, certain general categories of narrative.

Let us take the ordeal or test, one of the most frequent events in *The Quest of the Holy Grail*. The ordeal is already present in the earliest folklore tales; it consists in the uniting of two events in the logical form of a conditional phrase: "If X does this or that thing, then this or that will happen (to him)." In principle, the event of the antecedent presents a certain difficulty, whereas that of the consequent is favorable to the hero. *The Quest of the Holy Grail* presents, of course, such ordeals, with their variations: positive ordeals, or exploits (Galahad draws the sword out of the stone), and negative ordeals, or temptations (Perceval succeeds in withstanding the charms of the Devil disguised as a lovely maiden); successful ordeals (those of Galahad, chiefly), and failed ordeals (those of Lancelot), which inaugurate respectively two symmetrical series—ordeal-success-reward or ordeal-failure-penitence.

But there is another category which makes it easier to situate the various ordeals. If we compare the ordeals that Perceval or Bors undergoes on the one hand, with those of Galahad on the other, we discover an essential difference. When Perceval goes on a quest, we do not know in advance whether or not he will be victorious; sometimes he fails and sometimes he succeeds. The ordeal modifies the preceding situation: before the ordeal, Perceval (or Bors) was not worthy to continue the search for the Grail; after it, if he succeeds, he is worthy. The same is not so with regard to Galahad. From the beginning of the text, Galahad is designated as the Good Knight, the invincible, the one who will complete the quest of the Grail, the image and reincarnation of Jesus Christ. It is unthinkable that Galahad fail; the conditional form of setting out is no longer respected. Galahad is not elect because he succeeds in the ordeals, but succeeds in the ordeals because he is elect.

This profoundly modifies the nature of the ordeal; it becomes necessary in fact to distinguish two types of ordeals and to say that those of Perceval or Bors are narrative ordeals, whereas those of Galahad are ritual ordeals. Indeed, Galahad's actions resemble rites much more than they do ordinary adventures. To sit upon the Siege Perilous without harm, to draw the sword from the stone, to bear the shield without danger, and so forth, are not true ordeals. The Siege was initially destined for "its master," but when Galahad approaches it, the inscription changes into "Here is Galahad's siege." Is it an exploit, then, on Galahad's part to sit there? Similarly in the case of the sword: King Arthur declares that "the most famous knights of my house have failed today to draw this sword from the stone." To which Galahad judiciously replies: "Sire, there is no wonder in that, because the adventure, being mine, could not be for them." And in the case of the shield which brings disaster to all save one, the celestial knight had already explained: "Take this shield and bear it . . . to the good knight who is called Galahad. . . . Tell him that the Master orders him to bear it. . . ." There is, again, no exploit here, Galahad merely obeys orders from on high, merely follows the rite prescribed for him.

When we have discovered the opposition between narrative and ritual in *The Quest of the Holy Grail,* we discover that the two terms of this opposition are projected on the continuity of the tale, so that the tale is divided schematically into two parts. The first part resembles the folklore narrative, that is, it is narrative in the classical sense of the word. The second is ritual, for starting from a certain moment nothing surprising happens any more, the heroes are turned into the servants of a great rite, the rite of the Grail (Pauphilet refers in this regard to Ordeals and Rewards). This moment is located at the meeting of Galahad with Perceval, Bors, and Perceval's sister; she declares what the knights must do, and the narrative is no longer anything but the realization of her words. We are then at the opposite pole from the folklore narrative, as it still appears in the first part, despite the presence of the ritual around Galahad.

The Quest of the Holy Grail is built on the tension between these two kinds of logic: narrative and ritual, or, one might say, the profane and the religious. We can observe both in the first pages; the ordeals, the obstacles (such as King Arthur's opposition to the beginning of the quest) derive from habitual narrative logic. On the other hand, Galahad's appearance and the decision to go on the quest—that is, the important events of the narrative—relate to ritual logic. The appearances of the Holy Grail are not in a necessary relation with the continuing ordeals of the knights.

The articulation of these two kinds of logic derives from two contrary conceptions of time (neither of which coincides with the one most habitual to us). Narrative logic implies, ideally, a temporality we might call the "perpetual present." Time here is constituted by the concatenation of countless instances of discourse; it is these latter which define the very idea of the present. We speak of the event occurring during the very act of speech; there is a perfect parallelism between the series of events one speaks of and the series of the instances of discourse. Discourse is never behind and never ahead of what it evokes. The characters, too, live in the present alone; the succession of events is governed by a logic proper to it, and is influenced by no external factor.

On the other hand, ritual logic is based on a conception of time which is that of the "eternal return." Here no event hap-

ens for the first or the last time. Everything has already been
foretold, and now one foretells what will follow. The origin of
the rite is lost in the origin of time; what matters is that the rite
constitutes a rule which is already present, already there. Con-
rary to the preceding case, the "pure" or "authentic" present,
experienced fully as such, does not exist. In both cases, time is
suspended, but conversely: in the first instance by the hyper-
trophy of the present, in the second by its disappearance.

The Quest of the Holy Grail acknowledges, like any narrative,
both kinds of logic—when an ordeal occurs and we do not know
how it will end; when we experience it with the hero moment
by moment and the discourse remains glued to the event, the
tale is obviously obeying narrative logic, and we inhabit the perpetual present. When, on the contrary, the ordeal begins and it
is stated that its outcome has been predicted for centuries, that
it is consequently no more than the illustration of the prediction, we are in the eternal return, and the narrative unfolds according to ritual logic. This second logic, as well as the temporality of the "eternal return" type, here emerges victorious in
the conflict between the two.

Everything has been foretold. At the moment the adventure
occurs, the hero learns he is merely fulfilling a prediction. The
accidents of his path lead Galahad to a monastery; the adventure of the shield occurs. Suddenly the celestial knight an-
nounces: everything has been foretold. " 'Here then is what you
must do,' Josephes said. 'Where Nascien will order that he be
buried, place the shield. It is there that Galahad will come, five
days after having received the order of knighthood.' Everything
has come to pass as was foretold, since on the fifth day you have
come to this abbey where the body of Nascien lies." There was
no accident, nor even any adventure; Galahad has simply played
his part in a pre-established rite.

Gawain receives a grievous blow from Galahad's sword; he
immediately recalls: "Thus is borne out what I heard on the day
of Pentecost, concerning the sword on which I set my hand. It
was foretold that before long I should receive a terrible blow,
and this is the very sword with which this knight has just
struck me. The thing has come to pass even as it was foretold to

me." The least gesture, the merest incident relate to the past and the present at the same time; the Knights of the Round Table live in a world made up of recalls.

This retrospective future, re-established at the moment a prediction is fulfilled, is completed by the prospective future, in which we are confronted with the prediction itself. The denouement of the plot is recounted, from the very first pages, with all the necessary details. Here is Perceval's aunt: "For we know well, in these countries as in other places, that in the end three knights will have, more than all others, the glory of the Quest: two will be virgin and the third will be chaste. Of the two virgin knights, one will be the knight you seek, and you the other; the third will be Bors of Gaunes. These three knights will complete the Quest." What could be clearer and more definitive? And just so that we do not forget the prediction, it is constantly repeated for us. Or again, Perceval's sister, who foresees where her brother and Galahad will die: "For my honor's sake, have me buried in the Spiritual Palace. Do you know why I ask this of you? Because Perceval shall rest there, and you beside him."

The narrator of the *Odyssey* permitted himself to declare, several books before an event occurs, how this event would take place. Thus, apropos of Antinous: "It is he who first tasted the arrows sped by the hand of noble Odysseus," and so forth. But the narrator of *The Quest of the Holy Grail* does precisely the same thing, there is no difference in the narrative technique of the two texts (on this precise point): "He took off his helmet; Galahad did the same, and they exchanged a kiss, for they loved each other with a great love—as was seen upon their death, for one did not long survive the other."

Finally, if the whole present was already contained in the past, the past remains present in the present. The narrative constantly, though surreptitiously, turns back on itself. When we read the beginning of *The Quest of the Holy Grail,* we imagine we understand the whole: here are the noble knights who determine to set off on the quest, and so forth. But the present must become past, memory, recall, so that another present can help us to understand it. This Lancelot whom we supposed powerful and perfect is an incorrigible sinner: he lives in adultery with

Queen Guinevere. This Gawain who has made the first vow to set off on the quest will never complete it, for his heart is hard and he does not think enough about God. These knights whom we admired at the beginning are inveterate sinners who will be punished, for years they have not said confession. What we naively observed in the first pages was no more than appearances, a simple present. The narrative will consist in an apprenticeship to the past. Even the adventures which to us appear to obey a narrative logic turn out to be signs of something else, parts of an enormous rite.

The reader's interest (and we read *The Quest of the Holy Grail* with a certain interest) does not come, as we see, from the question which habitually provokes such interest: what happens next? We know, from the beginning, what will happen, who will win the Grail, who will be punished and why. The interest is generated by a very different question: what is the Grail? These are two different kinds of interest, and also two kinds of narrative. One unfolds on a horizontal line: we want to know what each event provokes, what it *does*. The other represents a series of variations which stack up along a vertical line: what we look for in each event is what it *is*. The first is a narrative of contiguity, the second a narrative of substitutions. In our case, we know from the start that Galahad will complete the quest victoriously; the narrative of contiguity is without interest. But we do not know precisely what the Grail is, so that there is occasion for an enthralling narrative of substitutions, in which we slowly arrive at comprehension of what was given from the beginning.

This same opposition is to be found, of course, elsewhere. The two fundamental types of detective story, the mystery and the adventure, illustrate these same two possibilities. In the first case, the story is given in the very first pages, but it is incomprehensible. A crime is committed almost before our eyes, but we do not know its true agents nor the real motives. The investigation consists in returning to the same events over and over, checking and correcting the slightest details, until at the end the truth breaks out with regard to this same initial history. In the second case there is no mystery, no backward turn. Each event provokes another, and the interest we take in the story does not come from our expectation of a revelation as to the initial *données;* it is the expectation of their consequences which sustains the suspense. The cyclical construction of substitutions is again set in opposition to the one-directional and contiguous construction.

In a more general fashion, we can say that the first type of organization is most frequent in fiction, the second in poetry (it being understood that elements of both are always found together in the same work). We know that poetry is based essentially on symmetry, on repetition (in a spatial order), where fiction is constructed on relations of causality (in a logical order) and of succession (a temporal order). The possible substitutions represent so many repetitions, and it is no accident if an explicit avowal of obedience to this order appears precisely in the last part of *The Quest of the Holy Grail,* where narrative causality or contiguity no longer plays any part. Galahad seeks to take his companions with him; Christ refuses to let him, alleging as his reason repetition alone, not a utilitarian cause. "Ah, Sire," Galahad says, "why will you not permit them all to come with me?" "Because such is my will, and because this must be in the semblance of my Apostles. . . ."

Of the two principal techniques of plot combination, linking and embedding, it is the second which we must expect to discover here, and this is what occurs. The enclosed narratives are particularly abundant in the last part of the text, where they have a double function: to afford a new variation on the same theme and to explain the symbols which continue to appear in the story. Indeed, the sequences of interpretation, frequent in the first part of the narrative, disappear here; the complementary distribution of interpretations and enclosed narratives indicates that the two have a similar function. The narrative's "significance" is now realized through the enclosed stories. When the three companions and Perceval's sister step into the boat, every object present becomes the pretext of a narrative. Further, every object is the conclusion of a narrative, its last link in the chain. The enclosed stories produce a dynamism which is then lacking in the framing narrative—the objects

become heroes of the story, while the heroes become as motionless as objects.

Narrative logic is defeated throughout the tale. Some traces of
the combat remain, however, as though to remind us of its intensity: hence in that horrifying scene in which Lyonel, in a
frenzy, tries to kill his brother Bors; or in that other in which
the maiden, Perceval's sister, gives her blood to save a sick
woman. Such episodes are among the most moving of the book,
and yet it is difficult to discover their function in it. They serve,
of course, to characterize the figures, to reinforce "atmosphere."
But one also has the feeling that the narrative has here recov-
ered its powers, that it succeeds in emerging, through the
countless functional and signifying grids, into the nonsignifica-
tion which also happens to be beauty.

There is a kind of consolation in finding, in a narrative where
everything is organized, where everything signifies, a passage
which audaciously boasts its narrative non-sense and which
thereby forms the best possible eulogy of narrative. We are told,
for example: "Galahad and his two companions rode so well that
in less than four days they were at the sea's edge. And they
might have reached it even sooner, but not knowing the road
very well, they had not taken the shortest way." What is the importance here? Or again, about Lancelot: "He looked all about,
without managing to find his horse, but after having sought everywhere, he discovered his steed, saddled, and mounted." The
"unnecessary detail" is perhaps, of all details, the one most necessary to narrative.

The Quest of the Grail

What is the Grail? This question has provoked many commentaries; let us quote Pauphilet's answer: "The Grail is the fictive manifestation of God. The quest of the Grail, consequently,
is merely the search for God beneath the veil of allegory, the effort made by men of good will toward the knowledge of God."
Pauphilet asserts this interpretation in the face of another older
and more literal one which, based on certain passages of the
text, prefers to see in the Grail a simple material object (though
one linked to religious practice), a vessel for serving the mass.

But we already know that in *The Quest of the Holy Grail* the intelligible and the sensible, the abstract and the concrete, can combine in one; hence we shall not be surprised to find some accounts of the Grail as a material object and others as an abstract entity. On the one hand, the Grail equals Jesus Christ and all that Jesus symbolizes: "Then they saw emerging from the Holy Cup a naked man whose hands and feet and body were bleeding, and who said to them, 'My knights, my sergeants, my loyal sons, you who in this mortal life have become spiritual creatures and who have sought me out so diligently that I can no longer hide myself from your eyes.' " In other words, what the knights were seeking—the Grail—was Jesus Christ. On the other hand, a few pages further, we read: "When they gazed within the ship, they saw upon the bed the silver table which they had left with King Méhaignié. The Holy Grail was upon it, covered with a cloth of vermilion silk." It is obviously not Jesus Christ who is lying on the table covered with a cloth, but the chalice. The contradiction exists, as we have seen, only if we choose to isolate the palpable from the intelligible. For the tale, "the nourishment of the Holy Grail feeds the soul even as it sustains the body." The Grail is both at once.

Yet the very fact that these doubts exist as to the nature of the Grail is significant. This narrative recounts the quest of something; now those who are searching are ignorant of the nature of what they are searching for. They are obliged to search not for what the word designates, but for what it signifies; theirs is a quest for meaning ("the quest of the Holy Grail . . . will not cease before the truth is *known*"). It is impossible to establish who first mentions the Grail; the word seems to have been there always. But, even after the last page, we are not certain of having understood its meaning properly: the quest of what the Grail means is never over, and we are continually obliged to relate this concept with others which appear in the course of the text. From this relationship there results a new ambiguity, less direct than the first but also more revealing.

The first series of equivalences and oppositions links the Grail with God but also, by the intermediary of the quest, with narrative. The adventures are sent by God; if God does not manifest

Himself, there are no more adventures. Jesus Christ says to Galahad: "You must go then and accompany this Holy Chalice which will this night leave the realm of Logres where it will never be seen again and where no adventure will ever more occur." The good knight Galahad has as many adventures as he wishes. Sinners such as Lancelot and especially Gawain seek adventures in vain: "Gawain . . . passed many a day without the sign of an adventure." He meets Ywain: " 'Nothing,' he replied; he had met with no adventure." He sets out with Hector: "Eight days they rode without finding anything." The adventure is at once a reward and a divine miracle, as may be learned by asking a sage, who would immediately tell you the truth: "I beg you tell us," said the knight Gawain, "why we do not meet with so many adventures as once befell us." "Here is the reason," said the sage. "The adventures which now befall are the signs and the apparitions of the Holy Grail."

God, the Grail, and the adventures form, then, a paradigm, of which all the members have a similar meaning. But we know, further, that narrative can be generated only if there is an adventure to relate. This is what Gawain complains of: "The knight Gawain . . . rode long without meeting with any adventure worth the trouble to recall. . . . One day he came upon Hector des Mares who was riding alone, and they saluted each other with great joy. But also they lamented not having any wondrous exploit to tell." Hence narrative is situated at the other end of the series of equivalences which starts from the Grail and passes through God and the adventures; the Grail is nothing but the possibility of narrative.

Yet there exists another series in which narrative also participates and whose terms bear no resemblance to those of this first series. We have already seen that narrative logic was constantly in retreat before another logic—a ritual and religious logic; narrative is the vanquished party in this conflict. Why? Because narrative, as it exists at the period of *The Quest of the Holy Grail,* is attached to sin not to virtue, to the Devil not to God. The characters and the traditional values of the chivalric romance are not only contested but flouted. Lancelot and Gawain were the champions of these romances; here these knights are humiliated on each page and repeatedly told that the exploits of which they are capable no longer have any worth ("And do not believe that the adventures of these days are to slaughter men or to slay knights," the sage tells Gawain). They are defeated on their own ground: Galahad is a better knight than either, and he forces both from their horses. Lancelot is insulted even by the squires and beaten in the jousts; consider him in his humiliation: " 'You must hear me,' said the squire, 'and you can no longer hope for other gain. You were the flower of earthly chivalry! Caitiff! Now you are ensorceled by one who neither loves nor esteems you!' Lancelot answered nothing, so mortified was he that he wished indeed to die. The squire, however, continued to abuse and to offend him with every possible villainy. Lancelot heard him out with such confusion that he dared not raise his eyes to the fellow's face." Lancelot the invincible dares not raise his eyes to the man who insults him; the love he bears for Queen Guinevere, which is the symbol of the chivalric world, is dragged in the mud. Hence not only Lancelot is to be lamented, but the knightly romance itself. "As he rode, he began to think that never had he been in so wretched a state and that he had never yet taken part in a tournament wherein he was not the victor. At this thought he was aggrieved and knew that everything showed him to be the most sinful of men, since his faults and his misadventure had stripped him of strength and countenance."

The Quest of the Holy Grail is a narrative which rejects precisely what constitutes the traditional substance of narratives: adventures of love and battle, earthly exploits. A *Don Quixote* before its time, this book declares war on the romances of chivalry and, through them, on the fictive mode. Nor does narrative fail to take its revenge. The most enthralling pages are devoted to Ywain the sinner, whereas there cannot be, strictly speaking, a narrative about Galahad. Narrative is a switch-point, the choice of one track rather than another. With Galahad, hesitation and choice no longer have any meaning; the path he takes may divide, but Galahad will always take the "good" fork. The romance is made to tell earthly stories; but the Grail is a celestial entity. Hence there is a contradiction in the very title of this book: the word "quest" refers to the most characteristic method of narrative, and thereby to the terrestrial; the Grail is a transcendence of the terrestrial toward the celestial. Hence when Pauphilet says that "the Grail is the fictive manifestation of God," he juxtaposes two apparently irreconcilable terms: God does not manifest Himself in fictions; fictions refer to the realm of the Enemy, not to that of God.

But if the narrative refers to earthly values, and even directly to sin and the Devil (for this reason *The Quest of the Holy Grail* constantly seeks to combat him), we arrive at a surprising result: the chain of semantic equivalences, which started with God, has reached, by the link of narrative, His opposite, the Devil. But we are not entitled to regard this as some perfidy on the narrator's part; it is not God who is ambiguous and polyvalent in this world, it is narrative. An attempt has been made to use terrestrial narrative for celestial ends, and the contradiction has remained within the text. It would not be there if God were praised in hymns or sermons, nor if the narrative dealt with habitual knightly exploits.

The integration of narrative in these series of equivalences and oppositions has a special importance. What appeared as an irreducible and final signification—the opposition between God and the Devil, or between virtue and sin, or even, in our case, between virginity and lust—is not one, and this is because of narrative. It seemed at first glance that Scripture, the Sacred Book, constituted a halt in the perpetual reference from one layer of significations to the other; as a matter of fact this halt is illusory, for each of the two terms which form the basic opposition of the last network designates, in its turn, narrative, the text, that is, the very first layer. Hence the circle is closed and the retreat of the "final meaning" will never come to a halt again.

Thereby narrative appears as the fundamental theme of *The Quest of the Holy Grail* (as it is of all narrative, but always in a different way). Ultimately, the quest of the Grail is not only the quest of a code and a meaning, but also of a narrative. Significantly, the last words of the book tell its history: the last link of the plot is the creation of this very narrative we have just read.

"And when Bors had recounted the adventures of the Holy Grail even as he had seen them, they were set down in writing and preserved in the library at Salisbury, whence Master Walter Map took them; from them he made his book of the Holy Grail, for the love of King Henry, his lord, who had the story translated from Latin into French."

It might be objected that if the author had meant all this, he would have said so more clearly; and moreover are we not there attributing to a thirteenth-century author ideas which belong to the twentieth? One answer is already to be found in *The Quest of the Holy Grail:* the subject narrating this book is not any particular person, it is narrative itself, it is the tale. At the beginning and the end of each chapter we discover this subject, a traditional one for the Middle Ages: "But here the tale leaves off speaking of Galahad, and returns to the knight Gawain. The tale recounts that when Gauwain left his companions . . ." "But here the tale leaves off speaking of Perceval and returns to Lancelot who had remained with the sage . . ." Sometimes these passages are extended; their presence is certainly not a meaningless convention: "If it is asked of the book why man did not carry the branch out of paradise, rather than woman, the book replies that it was indeed her task, and not his, to bear this branch. . . ."

So that if the author could not quite understand what he was writing, the tale itself knew all along.

1968

10

The Secret of Narrative

i

French readers know—however insufficiently—the novels of Henry James better than the tales, which constitute a good half of his *oeuvre* (this is not an exceptional case: the public prefers novels to tales, long books to short texts, not because length is taken as a criterion of value, but because there is no time, in reading a short work, to forget it is only "literature" and not "life"). Almost all of James's major novels have been translated into French, but only a fourth of his tales. Yet it is not mere quantitative reasons which draw me to this part of his *oeuvre*. The tales play a special role; they stand as so many theoretical studies in which James poses the great esthetic problems of his work, and in which he solves them. Hence they constitute a privileged route which I have chosen for my journey into the author's complex and fascinating universe.

Many exegetes have been put off the track. Contemporary and later critics have agreed that James's art was perfect "technically," but they have agreed also that he lacked important ideas, that he was deficient in human warmth—his subjects were too insignificant (as if the first sign of a work of art were not, precisely, to make impossible the distinction between "techniques" and "ideas"). James has been ranked among the authors inaccessible to the common reader, and only professionals are "qualified" to appreciate his overcomplicated art.

A consideration of two tales will suffice to dissipate this misunderstanding. Rather than "defend" them, I shall try to situate them within the Jamesian universe, as it is defined in his tales.

ii

In a famous tale, "The Figure in the Carpet" (1896), James tells how a young critic who has just written an article on one of the authors he most admires—Hugh Vereker—happens to meet him soon afterwards. The author makes no secret that he is disappointed—not that the study lacks sublety, but it fails to name the secret of his work, a secret which is at the same time its motivating principle and its general meaning. "There's an idea in my work which I wouldn't have given a straw for the whole job. It's the finest, fullest intention of the lot, and the application of it has been, I think, a triumph of patience, of ingenuity. . . . It stretches, this little trick of mine, from book to book, and everything else, comparatively, plays over the surface of it." Pressed by his young interlocutor's questions, Vereker adds: "My whole lucid effort gives the clue—every page and line and letter. The thing's as concrete there as a bird in a cage, a bait on a hook, a piece of cheese in a mouse-trap. . . . It governs every line, it chooses every word, it dots every i, it places every comma."

The young critic commits himself to a fanatical investigation ("I was shut up in my obsession forever"); seeing Vereker again, he tries to obtain more details: "It was something, I guessed, in the primal plan, something like a complex figure in a Persian carpet. He highly approved of this image when I used it, and he used another himself. 'It's the very string,' he said, 'that my pearls are strung on!' "

Let us pick up Vereker's gauntlet as we approach Henry James's work (indeed the former said: "It's naturally the thing for the critic to look for. It strikes me . . . even as the thing for the critic to find.") Let us try, then, to find the figure in Henry James's carpet, that general plan which governs all the rest, as it appears in each of his works.

The search for such a constant can be made (as the characters in "The Figure in the Carpet" know so well) only by superimposing the various works in the manner of Galton's famous photographs—by reading them as if in transparency, one on top of the other. I have no desire, however, to quiz the reader and I shall tell the "secret" at once, thereby running the risk of being less convincing. The works we shall discuss will illustrate my hypothesis instead of obliging the reader to formulate it for himself.

The Jamesian narrative is always based on *the quest for an absolute and absent cause.* Let us consider the terms of this phrase one by one. There exists a cause: this word must here be taken in a very broad sense; it is often a character but sometimes, too, an event or an object. The effect of this cause is the narrative, the story we are told. It is absolute: for everything in this narrative ultimately owes its presence to this cause. But the cause is absent and must be sought: it is not only absent but for the most part unknown; what is suspected is its existence, not its nature. The quest proceeds; the tale consists of the search for, the pursuit of, this initial cause, this primal essence. The narrative stops when it is attained. On one hand there is an absence (of the cause, of the essence, of the truth), but this absence determines everything; on the other hand there is a presence (of the quest), which is only the search for an absence. Thus the secret of Jamesian narrative is precisely the existence of an essential secret, of something not named, of an absent and superpowerful force which sets the whole present machinery of the narrative in motion. This motion is a double and, in appearance, a contradictory one (which allows James to keep beginning it over and over). On one hand he deploys all his forces to attain the hidden essence, to reveal the secret object; on the other, he constantly postpones, protects the revelation—until the story's end, if not beyond. The absence of the cause or of the truth is present in the text—indeed, it is the text's logical origin and reason for being. The cause is what, by its absence, brings the text into being. The essential is absent, the absence is essential.

Before illustrating the diverse variations of this "figure in the carpet," we must deal with one possible objection—that not all of James's works conform to the same pattern. To speak of the tales alone, some do not participate in this movement, even if we discover it in most of them. We must therefore add two qualifications. First, that this "figure" is linked to a particular period in James's *oeuvre;* it dominates that *oeuvre* almost exclusively from 1892 to at least 1903 (when James was in his fifties): James wrote almost half his tales during these twelve years. What comes before may be considered, in the light of this hypothesis, as no more than a preparatory labor, as a brilliant but scarcely original exercise, which belongs to the context of the lessons James had learned from Gustave Flaubert and Guy de Maupassant. The second qualification is of a theoretical, not a historical order; we may assume, it seems to me, that an author comes closer in some works than in others to that "figure in the carpet" which epitomizes and sustains the totality of his writings. Whereby we may account for the fact that even after 1892 James continues writing tales which belong to the realm of his "realistic" exercises.

Let us add one comparison to those which Vereker proposed to his young friend in order to name the "fundamental element"—let us say that what we have just defined resembles the notational grid shared by the various instruments in a jazz group. The grid establishes certain points of reference, without which the piece could not be played. But this does not mean that the saxophone part becomes identical to the trumpet's. Similarly, in his tales James exploits very different timbres, tonalities which at first seem to have nothing in common, though the overall project remains the same. We shall try to observe these tonalities one by one.

iii

Let us begin with the most elementary case: that in which the tale is formed around a character or a phenomenon enveloped in a certain mystery which will be dissipated at the end. "Sir Dominick Ferrand" (1892) can be taken as our first example. It is the story of an indigent writer, Peter Baron, who lives in the same lodging house as a widowed musician, Mrs. Ryves. Baron buys an old desk and happens to discover that it contains a secret drawer. He is fascinated by this first mystery, which he manages to solve: he takes several bundles of old letters out of the drawer. A surprise visit from Mrs Ryves—with whom he is secretly in love—interrupts his scrutiny. Mrs Ryves has had an intuition that some danger threatens Baron, and catching sight of the bundles of letters, implores him never to look at them. This sudden action creates two new mysteries: what is the content of the letters? and how can Mrs Ryves have had such intuitions? The first will be solved in a few pages; the letters contain compromising revelations about Sir Dominick Ferrand, a statesman who had died several years before. But the second will last to the story's end, and its solution will be postponed by other developments, which concern Baron's hesitations as to the fate of the letters. He is tempted by the editor of a magazine to whom he has revealed their existence and who offers him large sums of money for them. Each time he is tempted—for he is extremely poor—he is halted by another "intuition" of Mrs Ryves, with whom he is falling more and more deeply in love. This second power prevails, and one day Peter Baron burns the compromising letters. Then follows the final revelation: Mrs Ryves, in a burst of frankness, confesses that she is Sir Dominick Ferrand's illegitimate daughter, the issue of the very liaison disclosed in the hidden letters.

Behind this melodramatic plot—distant characters turn out to be close relatives—looms the fundamental schema of the Jamesian tale: the secret and absolute cause of all the events was an absent figure, Sir Dominick Ferrand, and a mystery, the relation between him and Mrs Ryves. Her odd behavior is based (with hints of the supernatural) on the secret relationship; this behavior, moreover, determines Baron's. The intermediary mysteries (what is in the desk? what are the letters about?) were further causes where the absence of knowledge provokes the presence of the narrative. The appearance of the cause halts the narrative; once the mystery is disclosed, there is no longer anything to tell. The presence of the truth is possible, but it is incompatible with the narrative.

"In the Cage" (1898) takes another step in the same direction. Ignorance here is not due to a secret which can be revealed at the tale's end, but to the imperfection of our means of knowledge, and the "truth" that is arrived at in the final pages—contrary to the certain and definitive truth of "Sir Dominick Ferrand"—is merely a lesser degree of ignorance. The lack of knowledge is motivated by the main character's profession and by her center of interests: this young woman (whose name we are not told) is a telegraph operator, and her entire attention is focused on two persons whom she knows only through their telegrams: Captain Everard and Lady Bradeen.

The young telegraph operator possesses extremely sparse information about the fate of those who interest her. Indeed, she has only three telegrams on which her reconstructions are based. The first: "Everard, Hôtel Brighton,, Paris. Only understand and believe. 22nd to 26th, and certainly 8th and 9th. Perhaps others. Come. Mary." The second: "Miss Dolman, Parade Lodge, Parade Terrace, Dover. Let him instantly know right one, Hôtel de France, Ostend. Make it seven nine four nine six one. Wire me alternative Burfield's." And the last: "Absolutely necessary to see you. Take last train Victoria if you can catch it. If not, earliest morning, and answer me direct either way." On this meager canvas, the telegraph operator's imagination embroiders a novel. The absolute cause here is the life of Captain Everard and Lady Bradeen, but the operator knows nothing about it, shut up as she is in her post-office cage. Her quest is all the longer, all the more difficult, and at the same time all the more impassioned: "But if nothing was more impossible than the fact, nothing, on the other hand, was more intense than the vision" (James will write in another tale: "the echo had finally become more distinct than the initial sound").

The sole meeting she has had with Everard outside the office (between the second and third telegrams) does not shed much light on the latter's character. She can see what he is like physically, can observe his gestures, listen to his voice, but his "essence" remains quite as intangible as when the ground-glass cage separated them, perhaps more so. The senses retain only what is secondary—appearances; the truth is inaccessible to them. The only revelation—but one no longer dares apply this term to it—comes at the end, during a conversation between the telegraph operator and her friend Mrs Jordan. Mrs Jordan's

fiancé, Mr Drake, has been taken into Lady Bradeen's service,
so that Mrs Jordan can help her friend—however remotely—to
understand the fate of Lady Bradeen and Captain Everard. Understanding is rendered particularly difficult because the telegraph operator pretends to know much more than she does, in
order not to be humiliated in her friend's eyes; by her ambiguous replies, she frustrates certain revelations:

> "Why, don't you know the scandal?"
> She perched herself a moment on this. "Oh, there was nothing pub-
> lic." . . .
> Mrs Jordan hesitated. "Why, he was *in* something."
> Her comrade wondered. "In what?"
> "I don't know. Something bad. As I tell you, something was found."

There is no truth, there is no certainty—we are left with "something bad." Once the tale is finished, we cannot say that we
know who Captain Everard was; we are simply a little less ignorant about him than when the tale began. The essence has not
become present.

When the young critic of "The Figure in the Carpet" was
searching for Vereker's secret, he had asked the following question: " 'Is it something in the style or something in the thought?
An element of form or an element of feeling?' He indulgently
shook my hand again, and I felt my questions to be crude and
my distinctions pitiful." We understand Vereker's condescension, and if we were asked the same question apropos of the figure in James's carpet, we should have quite as many difficulties
in giving an answer. All aspects of the tale participate in the
same movement, as we shall prove.

Critics have frequently remarked (as had James himself)
upon a "technical" characteristic of these tales: each event is
described in them *as seen* by someone. We do not learn the
truth about Sir Dominick Ferrand directly, but through Peter
Baron's eyes; as a matter of fact, the reader never sees anything
but what is in Baron's consciousness. The same holds true for
"In the Cage": the narrator never sets the experiences of Captain Everard and Lady Bradeen before the reader, but only the
telegraph operator's image of them. An omniscient narrator

could have named the essence; the young woman is not capable of doing so.

James was particularly fond of this indirect vision, "that magnificent and masterly indirectness," as he calls it in a letter, and had taken his exploration of the method to considerable lengths. Here is how he himself describes his work: "I must add indeed that such as the Moreens were, or as they may at present incoherently appear, I don't pretend really to have 'done' them; all I have given in *The Pupil* is little Morgan's troubled vision of them as reflected in the vision, also troubled enough, of his devoted friend." We do not see the Moreens directly; we see the vision X has of the vision of Y who sees the Moreens. An even more complex case appears at the end of "In the Cage": we observe the perception of the telegraph operator, bearing on that of Mrs. Jordan, who herself tells what she has learned from Mr Drake, who in his turn knows Captain Everard and Lady Bradeen only from a distance!

Speaking of himself in the third person, James says further: "Addicted to seeing 'through'—one thing through another, accordingly, and still other things through *that*—he takes, too greedily perhaps, on any errand, as many things as possible by the way." Or in another preface: "It is not my fault if I am so put together as often to find more life in situations obscure and subject to interpretation than in the gross rattle of the foreground." Hence we shall not be surprised to see only the vision of someone and never the object of that vision directly, nor to find in James's pages such sentences as "He knew I really couldn't help him and that I knew he knew I couldn't."

But this "technique" of points of view, about which so much has been written, is no more technical than, say, the themes of the text. We see now that the indirect vision is, for James, inscribed within the same "figure in the carpet" established in our analysis of his plots. Never to show in broad daylight the object of perception, which provokes all the efforts of the characters, is nothing but a new manifestation of the general idea by which the narrative expresses the quest for an absolute and absent cause. "Technique" signifies as much as thematic elements; the latter, in their turn, are as "technical" (that is, organized) as the rest.

What is the origin of this idea of James's? In a sense, he has merely built up his narrative method into a philosophical concept. There are, by and large, two ways of characterizing a person in narrative. Here is an example of the first:

This broad-shouldered, brown-skinned priest, hitherto condemned to the austere chastity of the cloister, shivered and seethed at this love scene, occurring in voluptuous darkness before his eyes. The sight of a lovely disheveled girl surrendering to this ardent young man turned the blood in his veins to molten lead. Extraordinary impulses stirred within him. His gaze plunged with lascivious jealousy beneath all those unfastened laces. . . .   [*The Hunchback of Notre Dame*]

And here is an example of the second:

She noticed his nails, which were longer than was usual in Yonville. The clerk spent a great deal of time caring for them: he kept a special penknife in his desk for the purpose.   [*Madame Bovary*]

In the first case, the character's sentiments are named directly (in our example, this direct characterization is attenuated by rhetorical figures). In the second, the essence is not named. It is presented, on the one hand, through someone's vision; on the other, the description of character traits is replaced by that of one isolated habit. This is the famous "art of the detail," in which the part replaces the whole, according to the familiar rhetorical figure of synecdoche.

For some time James followed in Flaubert's wake; when we mentioned his "exercises" it was to evoke precisely those texts in which he perfects the use of synecdoche (we find such pages to the end of his life.) But in the tales which concern us here, James has gone a step further: he has become conscious of Flaubert's sensationalism (or antiessentialism), and instead of simply employing it as a means, he has made it the constructive principle of his *oeuvre*. We can see only appearances, and their interpretation remains suspect; only the pursuit of the truth can be present; truth itself, though it provokes the entire movement, remains absent (as in the case of "In the Cage").[1]

Now let us consider another "technical" element: composition. What is the classical tale, as we find it, for example, in Boccaccio? In the simplest case, and approaching the matter on the most general level, we might say that the tale recounts the transition from a state of equilibrium or disequilibrium to another similar state. In the *Decameron*, the initial equilibrium is often constituted by the conjugal ties of the two protagonists and is disrupted by the wife's infidelity; a second disequilibrium, at a second level, appears at the end. The two lovers escape the punishment with which the deceived husband threatens them; at the same time a new equilibrium is established, for adultery is raised to the status of a norm (see above, Chapter 8).

On the same level of generality, we may observe a similar design in James's tales. Take "In the Cage"; here the telegraph operator's stable situation at the beginning is disturbed by the appearance of Captain Everard; disequilibrium culminates in the meeting in the park; equilibrium is re-established at the tale's end by Everard's marriage to Lady Bradeen. The telegraph operator renounces her dreams, leaves her job, and soon gets married herself. The initial equilibrium is not identical to the final one; the first allowed dreams, hopes; the second did not.

But in such a summary of the plot of "In the Cage" we have traced only one of the lines of force which animate the narrative. The other line is of apprenticeship; contrary to the first, with its ebb and flow, the second obeys gradation. At the start, the telegraph operator knows nothing about Captain Everard; at the end, she possesses her maximum knowledge. The first movement is a horizontal one, composed of events which fill the telegraph operator's life. The second movement suggests rather a vertical spiral, composed of successive (but not temporally organized) glimpses into Captain Everard's life and personality. In the first, the reader's interest is oriented toward the future:

[1] Flaubert himself, in a letter to Maupassant dated August 15, 1878, wrote: "Have you ever believed in the existence of things? Isn't it all an illusion? Nothing is real but 'relations'—I mean, the way in which we perceive objects."

what will the relation between the captain and the young woman become? In the second, this interest is oriented toward the past: who is Everard? what has happened to him?

The narrative movement follows the resultant of these two lines of force: some events relate to the first, others to the second, still others to both at once. Thus the conversations with Mrs Jordan do nothing to advance the "horizontal" plot, whereas the encounters with Mr Mudge, the telegraph operator's future husband, serve this plot exclusively. Yet it is obvious that the pursuit of knowledge takes precedence over the unfolding of events, the "vertical" tendency is stronger than the "horizontal" one. And this movement toward the comprehension of events, which replaces that of the events themselves, leads us back to the same figure in the carpet: presence of the quest, absence of its object. The "essence" of the events is not given straightaway; each fact, each phenomenon first appears enveloped in a certain mystery; interest is naturally directed to "being" rather than to "doing."

Now let us turn to James's "style," which has always been said to be too complex, obscure, pointlessly difficult. In fact on this level too, James surrounds the "truth," the event itself (which the main proposition often epitomizes) with many subordinate clauses which are, in each case, simple in themselves but whose accumulation produces the effect of complexity. Yet these subordinate clauses are necessary, for they illustrate the many intermediary stages which must be passed through before the "core" is reached. Here is an example taken from the same tale: "There were times when all the wires in the country seemed to start from the little hole-and-corner where she plied for a livelihood, and where, in the shuffle of feet, the flutter of 'forms,' the straying of stamps and the ring of change over the counter, the people she had fallen into the habit of remembering and fitting together with others, and of having her theories and interpretations of, kept up before her their long procession and rotation." If we extract the basic proposition from this intricate sentence, we get: "There were times when the people kept up before her their long procession and rotation." But around this banal "truth" accumulate countless particularities, details, judgments, much more present than the core of the main sentence which, as absolute cause, has provoked this movement but nonetheless remains in a quasi absence. An American stylistician, Richard Ohmann, has suggested that much complexity in James's style is the result of this tendency to "self-embedding," the "embedded" elements having an infinitely greater importance than the main proposition. We may go further and say that the complexity of James's style derives entirely from this principle of construction and not from a referential (for instance, psychological) complexity. "Style," "feelings," "form," and "content" all say the same thing, all repeat the same figure in the carpet.

iv

This variant of the general principle allows us to penetrate the secret—at the end Peter Baron learns the information whose pursuit constituted the tale's mainspring; the telegraph operator could, strictly speaking, have learned the truth about Captain Everard—we are, therefore, in the realm of the *hidden*. Yet there exists another case in which "absence" cannot be conquered by means accessible to human beings: here the absolute cause is a *ghost*. Such a hero runs no risk of passing, as it were, unnoticed: the text is naturally organized around the search for him.

We might go further and say that in order for this ever-absent cause to become present, it *must* be a ghost. . . . For, curiously enough, Henry James always speaks of ghosts as *presences*. Here are a few phrases, chosen at random from various tales, all of which refer to a ghost: "I felt his presence as a strong appeal," "a perfect presence . . . a splendid presence," "the hideous plain presence . . ." "He was absolutely, on this occasion, a living, detestable, dangerous presence." "He had turned cold with the extinction of his last pulse of doubt as to there being in the place another presence than his own." "The image of the 'presence,' whatever it was, waiting there for him to go—this image had not yet been so concrete for his nerves as when he stopped short of the point at which certainty would have come to him." "Wasn't he now in the *most* immediate presence of some inconceivable occult activity?" "It gloomed, it loomed, it was something, it was somebody, the prodigy of a personal presence." And so on, to this lapidary and falsely tautological formula: "The presence before him was a presence." The essence is never present except if it is a ghost, that is, absence par excellence.

Any of James's fantastic tales can prove the intensity of this presence. "Sir Edmund Orme" (1891) tells the story of a young man who suddenly sees appear, at his beloved Charlotte Marden's side, a strange pale personage who is oddly unnoticed by everyone except our hero. The first time, this visible-invisible figure sits down beside Charlotte in church: "He was a pale young man in black, with the air of a gentleman." Here he is, next, in a parlor: "He held himself with a kind of habitual majesty, as if he were different from us. . . . He stood there without speaking—young, pale, handsome, clean-shaven, decorous, with extraordinary light blue eyes and something old-fashioned, like a portrait of years ago, in his head, his manner of wearing his hair. He was in complete mourning. . . ." He appears quite readily at the private meetings of the two young people: "He stood there as I had seen him . . . looking at me with the expressionless attention which borrowed its sternness from his sombre distinction." This leads the narrator to conclude: "Of what transcendent essence he was composed I knew not; I have no theory about him (leaving that to others), any more than I have one about such or such another of my fellow-mortals. . . ."

This "presence" of the ghost determines, of course, the development of the relations between Charlotte and the narrator, and more generally the development of the story. Charlotte's mother also sees the ghost and recognizes him—as that of a young man who had loved her and committed suicide when she rejected him. The ghost returns to make certain that feminine coquetry will not play the same tricks upon the daughter's suitor which caused the death of the mother's. In the end, Charlotte decides to marry the narrator, the mother dies, and the ghost of Sir Edmund Orme disappears.

The fantastic narrative (the ghost story) is a form which lends itself perfectly to James's project. Unlike the "marvelous" tale

(such as those of the *Thousand and One Nights*), the fantastic
text is not characterized by the simple presence of supernatural
phenomena or beings, but by the hesitation which is established
in the reader's perception of the events represented. Throughout the tale, the reader wonders (in the same way that a character often does, within the work) if the facts reported are to be
explained by a natural or a supernatural cause, if they are illusions or realities. This hesitation derives from the fact that the
extraordinary (hence potentially supernatural) event occurs not
in a marvelous world but in an everyday context, the one most
familiar to us. Consequently the tale of the fantastic is the narrative of a perception, and we have already seen why such a
construction fits so well within Henry James's "figure in the
carpet."

A tale such as "Sir Edmund Orme" conforms quite closely to
this general description of the fantastic genre. Most manifestations of the occult presence produce a hesitation in the narrator,
a hesitation which is crystallized in alternative phrases of the
"either—or" type. "It was either all a mistake or Sir Edmund
Orme had vanished." "Was the sound I heard when Chartie
shrieked—the other and still more tragic sound I mean—the
despairing cry of the poor lady's death-shock or the articulate
sob (it was like a waft from a great tempest), of the exorcised
and pacified spirit?"

Other characteristics of the texts are also shared with the fantastic genre as a whole. For instance, a tendency to allegory
(though this never becomes explicit, for if it did the allegory
would suppress the fantastic altogether): we may wonder if the
tale is not simply a morality. This is how the narrator interprets
the whole episode: "It was a case of retributive justice. The
mother was to pay, in suffering, for the suffering she had inflicted, and as the disposition to jilt a lover might have been
transmitted to the daughter, the daughter was to be watched, so
that *she* might be made to suffer should she do an equal
wrong."

Similarly, the tale follows the gradation—habitual in fantastic
narrative—of supernatural apparitions; the narrator is represented within the story, which facilitates the reader's integra-

ion into the universe of the text; allusions to the supernatural
re scattered throughout the text, preparing us for its accep-
ance. But alongside these features by which James's tales par-
icipate in the genre of the fantastic, there are other features
which distinguish these tales from it and which define them in
heir specificity. We may observe this phenomenon in another
example, the longest of the texts that can be called "tales" and
probably the most famous: *The Turn of the Screw* (1896).

The ambiguity of this tale is quite as important as that of the
others. The narrator is a young woman who takes a position as
governess of two children on a country estate. At a certain moment, she realizes that the house is haunted by two former servants, now dead, of depraved morals. These two apparitions are
all the more formidable for having made contact with the children, who pretend to know nothing about it. The governess has
no doubts as to their presence ("it was not, I am sure today as I
was sure then, my mere infernal imagination . . ." or "even
while she spoke the hideous plain presence stood undimmed
and undaunted"), and to support her conviction, she finds perfectly rational arguments: "Late that night, while the house
slept, we had another talk in my room; when she [the house-
keeper] went all the way with me as to its being beyond doubt
that I had seen exactly what I had seen. To hold her perfectly in
the pinch of that, I found, I had only to ask her how, if I had
'made it up,' I came to be able to give, of each of the persons ap-
pearing to me, a picture disclosing, to the last detail, their special marks—a portrait on the exhibition of which she had instantly recognized and named them." The governess then tries
to exorcize the children: one falls seriously ill, the other can be
"purified" only by death.

Yet this same series of events could be presented in an entirely different way, without any intervention of infernal powers.
The governess' testimony is continually contradicted by that of
the other characters ("What a dreadful turn, to be sure, Miss!
Where on earth do you see anything?" exclaims the housekeeper, and on the same occasion little Flora, one of the children, cries: "I don't know what you mean. I see nobody. I see
nothing. I never *have*"). This contradiction goes so far that ul-

timately a terrible suspicion occurs to the governess herself
"Within a minute there had come to me out of my very pity the
appalling alarm of his being perhaps innocent. It was for the in
stant confounding and bottomless, for if he *were* innocent, wha
then on earth was *I?*"

Nor is it difficult to find realistic explanations for the governess' hallucinations—she is an excitable and hypersensitive person. Moreover, imagining this disaster is the one way she has of
bringing to the estate the children's uncle with whom she is
secretly in love. She herself feels the need to defend herself
against an accusation of insanity: "She accepted without directly impugning my sanity the truth as I gave it to her," she
says of the housekeeper, and later on, "I go on, I know, as if I
were crazy; and it's a wonder I'm not." If we add to this the fact
that the ghosts always appear at twilight or even at night and
that moreover certain reactions of the children which might
otherwise seem strange are easily accounted for by the governess' own suggestive powers, there remains nothing supernatural
in the tale, and we are instead confronted with the description
of a neurosis.

This double possibility of interpretation has provoked endless
argument among its critics: do the ghosts in *The Turn of the
Screw* really exist, or not? Yet the answer is obvious: by maintaining the ambiguity at the tale's heart, James has merely
obeyed the rules of the genre. But not everything is conventional in this tale; whereas the canonical fantastic narrative, as
practiced by the nineteenth century, makes the character's hesitation its main and explicit theme, in James this represented
hesitation is virtually eliminated—it persists only in the reader:
hence both the narrator of "Sir Edmund Orme" and that of *The
Turn of the Screw* are convinced of the reality of their visions.

At the same time, we recognize in this text the features of the
Jamesian narrative we have already observed elsewhere. Not
only is the entire tale based on the two ghostly characters, Miss
Jessel and Peter Quint, but again, for the governess the essential question is, do the children *see* the ghosts? In the quest,
perception and knowledge replace the perceived object or the

bject to be perceived. The governess is less alarmed by her ision of Peter Quint than by the possibility that the children ave had such a vision as well. Similarly, Charlotte Marden's other, in "Sir Edmund Orme," was less afraid of the vision of e ghost than of its appearance to her daughter.

The source of evil (and also of the narrative action) remains idden: it is the depravities of the two dead servants which are ever named and which are transmitted to the children 'strange passages and perils, secret disorders, vices more than uspected"). The acute character of the danger derives precisely rom the absence of information about it: "What it was most im-ossible to get rid of was the cruel idea that, whatever I had een, Miles and Flora saw *more*—things terrible and unguessa-le and that sprang from dreadful passages of intercourse in the ast. . . ."

To the question as to what really happened at Bly, James ffers an oblique answer: he discredits the word "really," he as-erts the uncertainty of the experience when confronted with he stability—but also with the absence—of the essence. In fact, ve do not even have the right to say "the governess is . . ." or Peter Quint is not. . . ." In this world, the verb *to be* has lost ne of its functions, that of affirming existence and nonexis-ence. All our truths are no better founded than that of the gov-rness: the ghosts may have existed, but the effort to eliminate hat uncertainty costs little Miles his life.

In his last "ghost story," "The Jolly Corner" (1908), James re-urns once again to the same theme. Spencer Brydon, who has pent more than thirty years away from the country of his birth, eturns home with a haunting question: what would have be-ome of him had he remained in America—what could he have made of himself? At a certain moment of his life, he had a hoice between two incompatible solutions; he has chosen one ut now would like to discover the other, to effect an impossible nion of mutually exclusive elements. He treats his life like a narrative, in which one can trace actions backward and, at a fork in the path, take the alternative route. As we see once more, the tale is based on the impossible quest for absence: the character Spencer Brydon might have been, that alter ego of the conditional imperfect tense, materializes, so to speak, or in any case becomes a presence—which is to say, a ghost.

The game of the absent and absolute cause continues; yet it no longer takes the same role as before—this game is now no more than a background, tracing the same "figure in the carpet." But the story's interest is elsewhere. It is not so much the verb *to be* which is put in question here as the personal pronoun *I*. Who is Spencer Brydon? So long as the ghost does not appear, Brydon seeks him eagerly, convinced that even if he does not belong to himself, he must find the phantom to understand who he himself is. That Other is and is not himself ("rigid and conscious, spectral yet human, a man of his own substance and stature waited there to measure himself with his power to dismay"). But the moment the Other becomes present, Brydon realizes he is totally alien to himself: "Such an identity fitted his at *no* point, made its alternative monstrous." Absent, this "I" of the conditional imperfect tense belonged to him; present, he does not recognize himself in it.

His old friend Alice Staverton has also seen the ghost—in a dream. How could she? "Because, as I told you weeks ago, my mind, my imagination, had worked so over what you might, what you mightn't have been." So this stranger is not so strange as Brydon might have wished, and there is a dizzying play of personal pronouns in the conversation of the two characters:

"Well, in the cold dim dawn of this morning I too saw you."
"Saw *me*—?"
"Saw *him*. . . ."
"He had come to you. . . ."
"*He* didn't come to me."
"You came to yourself."

Yet the last sentence reaffirms the difference: "And he isn't—no, he isn't— *you!*" Alice Staverton murmurs. The decentering is generalized, *selfhood* is as uncertain as *being*.

v

The first variant of our figure in the carpet postulated a natural and relative absence: the secret was of such a nature that it

vas not inconceivable to penetrate it. The second variant, on
he other hand, described the absolute and supernatural absence of a ghost. A third variant confronts us with an absence
both absolute and natural, with pure absence: *death*.

We may observe it first in a tale which is very close to the
"ghostly" variant, "The Friends of the Friends" (1896). A man
has seen the ghost of his mother at the moment she died; a
woman has had the same experience with her father. Their mutual friends, especially the narrator, struck by this coincidence,
try to arrange a meeting, but every effort to bring the two
together collapses, each time for quite insignificant reasons
moreover. The woman dies; the man (who is engaged to marry
the narrator) claims to have met her on the eve of her death. As
a living woman or as a ghost? No one will ever know, and this
meeting will result in the breaking-off of the engagement between the man and the narrator.

So long as both were alive, their meeting (their love) was impossible. Physical presence would have slain life. Not that they
know this in advance: they try—always vainly—to meet. But
after a final effort (which fails because of the narrator's appre-
hensions), the woman resigns herself: "I shall never, never see
him." A few hours later she is dead, as if death were necessary
for the meeting to occur (just as each of the pair met a parent at
the moment of that parent's death). At the moment when life—
an insignificant presence—ends, occurs the triumph of that essential absence which is death. According to the man, the
woman paid him a visit between ten and eleven at night, without speaking a word; at midnight she was dead. The narrator
has to decide whether this meeting "really" occurred or if it is of
the same nature as the meetings with the dying parents. She
would rather opt for the first solution ("it is remarkable that for
a moment, though only for a moment, I found relief in the more
personal, as it were, but also the more natural of the two odd
facts"). Yet this relief does not last; the narrator realizes that
this version is too easy, for it fails to explain the change that has
taken place in her friend.

We cannot speak of death "in itself"; we always die for someone. "She's buried, but she's not dead. She's dead for the

world—she's dead for me. But she's not dead for *you*," the narrator says to her friend, and again: "My unextinguished jealousy—that was the Medusa-mask. It hadn't died with her death, it had lividly survived, and it was fed by suspicions unspeakable." Justifiably, for this meeting which had never occurred in life has here given birth to an incredible love. We know nothing about it except what the narrator believes, but she manages to convince us: "How *can* you hide it when you're abjectly in love with her, when you're sick almost to death with the joy of what she gives you? . . . You love her as you've never loved, and, passion for passion, she gives it straight back!" He dares not deny this, and the engagement is broken off.

The final stage is reached very quickly; since death alone affords him the conditions of love, he will take refuge in it himself. "When six years later, in solitude and silence, I heard of his death I hailed it as a direct contribution to my theory. It was sudden, it was never properly accounted for, it was surrounded by circumstances in which—for oh, I took them to pieces!—distinctly read an intention, the mark of his own hidden hand. It was the result of a long necessity, of an unquenchable desire. To say exactly what I mean, it was a response to an irresistible call."

Death makes a character become the absolute and absent cause of life. Further: death is the source of life, love is born from death instead of being interrupted by it. This romantic theme (that of Théophile Gautier's "Spirite") is fully developed in "Maud-Evelyn" (1900), which tells the story of a young man named Marmaduke who falls in love with Maud-Evelyn, a young girl who died fifteen years before he learns of her existence (it will be noted how often the tale's title emphasizes the absent and essential character: "Sir Dominick Ferrand," "Sir Edmund Orme," "Maud-Evelyn," and also in other tales, such as "Nona Vincent").

Marmaduke's love—and therefore Maud-Evelyn's "reality"—pass through all the phases of a gradation. At the start, Marmaduke merely admires the girl's parents, who behave as if she were not dead. Then he begins thinking as they do, to conclude at the end, in the words of his old friend Lavinia: "He thinks he

new her." A little later on, Lavinia declares: "He *was* in love
with her." There follows their "marriage," after which Maud-
Evelyn "dies" ("He has lost his wife," Lavinia says, to explain
the fact that he is in mourning). Marmaduke dies in his turn,
but Lavinia will preserve his belief.

As is usual in James, the central and absent character of
Maud-Evelyn is not observed directly, but through many reflections. The tale is told by a certain Lady Emma, who draws her
impressions from conversations with Lavinia, who in her turn
meets Marmaduke. Yet Marmaduke knows only Maud-Evelyn's
parents, the Dedricks, who evoke the memory of their daughter;
hence the "truth" is distorted four times over! Further, these
visions are not identical, but also constitute a gradation. For
Lady Emma, the case is pure folly ("Was he altogether silly or
was he only altogether mercenary?"); she lives in a world where
the real and the imaginary form two separate and impermeable
blocks. Lavinia obeys the same norms but she is ready to accept
Marmaduke's action, which she finds beautiful: "It's self-decep-
tion, no doubt, but it comes from something that . . . is beautiful when one does hear of it." For Marmaduke himself, death is
not a venture into nonbeing; on the contrary, death merely
gives him the possibility of having the most extraordinary of all
experiences ("the moral appeared to be that nothing in the way
of human experience of the exquisite could again particularly
matter"). Finally the Dedricks take Maud-Evelyn's existence
quite literally: they communicate with her through mediums,
and so forth. Here we have an exemplification of four possible
attitudes toward the imaginary or, one may say, toward the figurative meaning of an expression: the realistic attitude of rejection and condemnation, the estheticizing attitude of admiration
mingled with incredulity, the poetic attitude which admits the
coexistence of being and nonbeing, and finally the naive attitude which consists of taking the figurative literally.

We have seen that in their composition James's tales were
turned toward the past: the quest for an essential, always
evanescent secret implied that the narrative was an exploration
of the past rather than a progression into the future. In "Maud-
Evelyn," the past becomes a thematic element, and its glorifica-

tion one of the tale's main affirmations. Maud-Evelyn's secon[
life is the result of this exploration: "It's the gradual effect [
brooding over the past; the past, that way, grows and grows.
There are no limits to this enrichment by the past, which is wh[
the girl's parents choose this path: "You see, they couldn't d[
much, the old people—and they can do still less now—with th[
future; so they had to do what they could with the past." An[
Marmaduke concludes: "The more we live in the past, the mor[
things we find in it." To "limit" oneself to the past signifies t[
reject the originality of events, to believe one lives in a world [
recall. If we trace back the chain of reactions in order to dis[
cover the initial motive, the absolute beginning, we suddenl[
come up against death, the end par excellence. Death is the ori[
gin and essence of life, the past is the future of the present, th[
answer precedes the question.

And the narrative will always be the story of another narra[
tive. Let us take another tale in which a dead person constitute[
the mainspring, "The Tone of Time" (1900). Just as in "Th[
Friends of the Friends" there was an effort to reconstitute th[
impossible narrative of a love beyond death, or in "Maud[
Evelyn" that of the life of a dead woman, the attempt in "Th[
Tone of Time" is to reconstruct a story which has taken place i[
the past and whose chief protagonist is dead. Though not for ev[
eryone. Mrs Bridgenorth cherishes the memory of this man[
who was her lover, and one day decides to commission his por[
trait. But something alters her decision, and she commission[
not *his* portrait but that of a distinguished gentleman, of anyon[
at all, of no one. The painter who is to execute the commission[
Mary Tredick, happened, by coincidence, to know this sam[
man; he lives for her too, but in a different way: in the resent[
ment and the hatred which have followed his abandonment o[
her. The splendidly successful portrait not only continues th[
life of this man, who is never named, but also permits him to re[
cover a kind of movement. Mrs Bridgenorth triumphs; sh[
thereby possesses him doubly. "It vibrated all round us that sh[
had gone out to the thing in a stifled flare, that a whole clos[
relation had in the few minutes revived." She has only one fear[

that Mary Tredick (about whom she knows nothing) will become jealous.

Her fear turns out to be well founded. In an impulsive gesture, Mary takes back the portrait and refuses to give it up.
Henceforth this man belongs to her once again: she has taken
her revenge on her successful rival of the past. In order to
possess him more completely, that rival had commissioned his
portrait. But once objectified in the picture, his memory can be
taken away. Once again, death is that absolute and absent
cause which determines the movement of the narrative.

James wrote another tale, a veritable requiem, which certainly deserves pride of place among these explorations of the
life of the dead: "The Altar of the Dead" (1896). Nowhere else is
the power of death, the presence of absence affirmed so intensely. Stransom, the tale's main character, lives in the cult of
the dead. He knows only absence and prefers it to anything
else. His fiancée died before the first "bridal embrace," yet
Stransom's life has not suffered as a result, and he rejoices in
his being "for ever widowed." His life "was still ruled by a pale
ghost, it was still ordered by a sovereign presence," it is perfectly poised upon its "central hollow."

One day he meets a friend, Paul Creston, whose wife has died
some months earlier. Suddenly he notices beside him another
woman whom his friend, in some slight embarrassment, introduces as his wife. This substitution of a vulgar presence for
the sublime absence deeply shocks Stransom. "That new
woman, that hired performer, Mrs Creston? Mrs Creston had
been more living for him than any woman but one. . . . He felt
quite determined, as he walked away, never in his life to go near
her. She was perhaps a human being, but Creston oughtn't to
have shown her without precautions, oughtn't indeed to have
shown her at all." For Stransom, the wife-as-presence is a su-
pernumerary, a forgery, and to substitute her for the memory of
the absent woman is nothing short of monstrous.

Gradually, Stransom elaborates and enlarges his cult of the
dead. He wants to perform "some material act," and decides to
dedicate an altar to them. Each dead person he had known (and

there are many, "he had perhaps not had more losses than most men, but he had counted his losses more") receives a candle, and Stransom "plunges" into a trance of admiration before them: "The enjoyment became even greater than he had ventured to hope." Why this enjoyment? Because it permits Stransom to recuperate his past: "Half the satisfaction of the spot for this mysterious and fitful worshipper was that he found the years of his life there, and the ties, the affections, the struggles, the submissions, the conquests, if there had been such, a record that adventurous journey in which the beginnings and the endings of human relations are lettered milestones."

But also because death is purification ("the fellow had only had to die for everything that was ugly in him to be washed out in a torrent"), because death permits the establishment of that harmony toward which life tends. The dead represented by candles are infinitely close to him: "Various persons in whom his interest had not been intense drew closer to him by entering this company." And as a natural consequence "he almost caught himself wishing that certain of his friends would now die, that he might establish with them in this manner a connection more charming than, as it happened, it was possible to enjoy with them in life."

One step remains to be taken, nor does it stop Stransom: the step of envisaging his own death. He dreams already of this "rich future" and declares: " 'The chapel will never be full till a candle is set up before which all the others will pale. It will be the tallest candle of all.' 'What candle do you mean?' 'I mean, dear lady, my own.' "

Suddenly a false note is sounded in this encomium of death. Stransom has become acquainted, at his altar, with a lady in mourning who attracts him precisely by her dedication to the dead. But when this acquaintanceship deepens, he learns that the lady mourns only one dead man, and this dead man is none other than Acton Hague, once an intimate of Stransom's with whom he has quarreled bitterly and who is the only dead man for whom Stransom has never lit a candle. The woman realizes this as well, and the charm of their relationship is broken. The dead man is present: "Acton Hague was between them, that was the essence of the matter; and he was never so much between them as when they were face to face." Thus the woman is led to choose between Stransom and Hague (preferring Hague), as is Stransom, between his resentment of Hague and his affection for the woman (his resentment prevails), which results in this moving dialogue: " 'Will you give him his candle?' she asked. . . . 'I can't do that!' he declared at last. 'Then goodbye.' " The dead man disposes of the lives of the living.

And at the same time the living continue to act upon the life of the dead (interpenetration is possible in both directions). Once abandoned by his friend, Stransom suddenly discovers that his affection for the dead has vanished. "All the lights had gone out—all his Dead had died again."

One further step then remains to be taken. After suffering a serious illness, Stransom returns to the church, having made up his mind to forgive Acton Hague. His friend finds him there, a symmetrical transformation having occurred in her own heart: she is ready to forget her one dead man and to consecrate herself to the cult of all the dead. Hence this cult undergoes a final sublimation: it is no longer love, friendship, or resentment which determines it; death is glorified in its pure state, without regard for those it has touched. Forgiveness abolishes the last barrier on the road to death.

Then Stransom can entrust to his friend his own life in death, and he expires in her arms, while she feels a great terror seize her heart.

vi

We now come to the last variant of this same figure in the carpet: the one in which the place successively occupied by the hidden, the ghost, and the dead man, is now taken by the *work of art*. If in a general way the tale tends to become, more than the novel, a theoretical meditation, James's tales about art represent veritable treatises on esthetic doctrine.

"The Real Thing" (1892) is a rather simple parable. The narrator, a painter, is visited one day by a couple who show every sign of belonging to the nobility. They ask if they can pose for any book illustrations he might be doing, for they are reduced to a state of extreme destitution. They are certain they can meet the artist's requirements, for the narrator is in fact supposed to be portraying people of the leisure class to which they once belonged. "We thought," the husband says, "that if you ever have to do people like us, we might be something like it. *She,* particularly—for a lady in a book, you know."

The couple are in fact "the real thing," but this property makes the painter's task no easier. Quite the contrary, his illustrations become worse and worse, until one day a friend remarks that the problem may be the models he is working from. On the other hand, there is nothing authentic about the painter's other models, but they allow him to create his most successful illustrations. A certain Miss Churm was "only a freckled cockney, but she could represent everything, from a fine lady to a shepherdess"; and a vagabond Italian named Oronte is ideal for the illustrations of princes and gentlemen.

The absence of "real" qualities in Miss Churm and Oronte is what confers upon them this essential value necessary to the work of art; the presence of these same qualities in the "distinguished" models can only be insignificant. The painter accounts for this by his "innate preference for the represented subject over the real one: the defect of the real one was so apt to be a lack of representation. I liked things that appeared; then one was sure. Whether they *were* or not was a subordinate and always a profitless question." So that at the end of the tale we find the two uncultivated and low-born characters playing their noble parts to perfection whereas the "noble" models are doing the housework—in accord with "the perverse and cruel law by virtue of which the real thing could be so much less precious than the unreal."

Art, then, is not the reproduction of a "reality," art does not follow after reality by imitating it. Art requires quite different qualities, so that being "real" can even, as in the case just cited, be disastrous. In the realm of art, there is nothing which is antecedent to the work, nothing which is its origin. The work of art itself is original; the secondary is the sole primary. This accounts for a tendency of James's comparisons to explain "nature" by "art," for example: "a pale smile that was like a moist sponge passed over a dimmed painting," or "she bore a singular resemblance to a bad illustration." Or again: "That was the way many things struck me at that time, in England—as reproductions of something that existed primarily in art or literature. It was not the picture, the poem, the fictive page, that seemed to me a copy; these things were the originals and the life of happy and distinguished people was fashioned in their image."

Several other tales, especially "The Death of the Lion" (1894), deal with the problem of "art and life," but from another perspective, that of the relation between an author's life and his work. A writer becomes famous toward the end of his days; yet the public's interest is focused not so much on his work as on his life. Journalists eagerly ask for the details of his personal existence, admirers prefer to see the man rather than read his texts. The entire end of the tale testifies, by its both sublime and grotesque movement, to the profound indifference to the work felt by the very persons who claim to admire it, while admiring only the author. And this misunderstanding produces disastrous consequences: not only is the writer unable to write since his "success," but he is ultimately (and literally) killed by his adorers.

"The artist's life's his work, and this is the place to observe him," says the narrator, himself a young writer. And again: "Let whoever would represent the interest in his presence. . . . I should represent the interest in his work—in other words in his absence." These words deserve some reflection. Psychological criticism (here called into question after "realistic" criticism) regards the work as a presence—though unimportant in itself—and sees the author as the work's absolute and absent cause. James reverses this relation: the author's life is merely appearance, contingency, accident; it is an unessential presence. The work of art, though, is the truth to be sought out—even without the hope of attaining it. In order to understand the work better, it is no use to know its author; indeed this second knowledge destroys both the man (Paraday's death) and the work (the loss of the manuscript).

The same problematics inspires the tale "The Private Life" (1892), in which the configuration of absence and presence is articulated in all its details. Two characters form an opposition. Lord Mellifont is the man of the world, entirely present, entirely unessential. He is the most agreeable of companions, his conversation is rich, relaxed, and instructive. But it would be useless to try to find anything deep or personal about him: he exists only in terms of others. He has a splendid presence but it is one that conceals nothing—to such a degree that no one manages to observe him *alone*. "He's there from the moment he knows somebody else is," someone says about him. Once he is alone, he vanishes, "reabsorbed into the immensity of things."

Opposite him, Clare Vawdrey illustrates the other possible combination of absence and presence—possible because he is a writer, because he creates works of art. This great author has a nondescript, mediocre presence, his behavior in no way corresponds to his works. The narrator reports, for instance, a mountain storm during which he is alone with the writer: "Clare Vawdrey was disappointing. I don't know exactly what I should have predicated of a great author exposed to the fury of the elements, I can't say what particular Manfred attitude I should have expected my companion to assume, but it seemed to me somehow that I shouldn't have looked to him to regale me in such a situation with stories (which I had already heard) about the celebrated Lady Ringrose." But this Clare Vawdrey is not the "real" one: at the same time that the narrator is gossiping with him, another Clare remains sitting at his desk, writing magnificent pages: "The world was vulgar and stupid, and the real man would have been a fool to come out for it when he could gossip and dine by deputy."

The opposition is thus a perfect one—Clare Vawdrey is double, Lord Mellifont is not even single: "Lord Mellifont was all public and had no corresponding private life, just as Clare Vawdrey was all private and had no corresponding public one." These are the two complementary aspects of the same movement: presence is empty (Lord Mellifont), absence is a plenitude (the work of art). In the paradigm in which we have inscribed it, the work of art has a special place—more essential than the hidden, more accessible than the ghost, more material than death, it affords the one means of experiencing essence.

That other Clare Vawdrey, sitting in the dark, is secreted by the work itself, is the text writing itself, the most present absence of all.

The perfect symmetry on which this tale is based is characteristic of the way in which Henry James conceives the plot of a narrative. As a general rule, coincidences and symmetries abound in his fictions. We are reminded of Guy Walsingham, a woman who writes under a man's name, and of Dora Forbes, a man who writes under a woman's, in "The Death of the Lion"; of the unheard-of coincidences which resolve "The Tone of Time" (it is the same man whom the two women happen to have loved) or "The Altar of the Dead" (it is the same dead man who has determined the behavior of the two characters); of the denouement of "Sir Dominick Ferrand." We know that for James the narrative interest does not reside in its "horizontal" movement but in the "vertical" exploration of a single event, and this is what accounts for the conventional and quite predictable aspect of the anecdote.

"The Birthplace" (1903) resumes and develops the theme of "The Death of the Lion," the relation between the work and its author's life. This tale tells of the public idolatry of the greatest national poet, now dead for many centuries, through the experience of a couple, Mr and Mrs Gedge, keepers of the museum set up in the poet's "birthplace." An authentic interest in the poet would lead one to read and admire his work; by supposedly dedicating oneself to his cult, one replaces the essential absence by an insignificant presence: "None of Them care tuppence about Him. The only thing They care about is this empty shell—or rather, for it isn't empty, the extraneous, preposterous stuffing of it."

Morris Gedge, who had been so happy to obtain his position as keeper of the museum (because of his admiration for the poet), realizes the contradiction on which his situation is based. His public functions oblige him to affirm the poet's presence in this house, in these objects; his love for the poet—and for the truth—leads him to contest this presence ("I'll be hanged if He's *here!*"). First of all, almost nothing is known about the poet's life, nothing exists but a vast uncertainy as to even its most elementary events. "Well, I grant you there was somebody, but the details are naught. The links are missing. The evidence—in particular about that room upstairs, in itself our Casa Santa—is *nil*. It was so awfully long ago." No one knows whether he was born in that room, or even if he was born at all. . . . So Gedge suggests "modalizing" the speeches he is supposed to make to the public, as a guide to the museum. "Couldn't you adopt . . . a slightly more *discreet* method? What we can say is that things have been *said;* that's all *we* have to do with."

Even this effort to replace the reality of *being* by that of *saying*, by that of discourse, does not go far enough. We need not regret the lack of information about the author's life, we must rejoice in it. The poet's essence is his work, not his house; hence it is preferable that the house show no trace of him whatever. As the wife of one visitor remarks: " 'It's rather a pity, you know, that He *isn't* here. I mean as Goethe's at Weimar. For Goethe *is* at Weimar.' " To which her husband replies: " 'Yes my dear; that's Goethe's bad luck. There he sticks. *This* man isn't anywhere. I defy you to catch him.' "

One step remains to be taken, and Gedge does not hesitate: "Practically . . . there *is* no author; that is for us to deal with. There are all the immortal people—*in* the work; but there's nobody else." Not only is the author a product of the work, he is also a useless product. The illusion of *being* must be dissipated: "There *is* no such Person."

The plot of this tale deals with this same idea (which we found till now in Gedge's remarks). At the beginning, the museum keeper had tried to tell the public the truth; as a consequence he was threatened with dismissal from his post. So Gedge chooses another means: instead of reducing his discourse to the minimum which the facts warrant, he amplifies it to absurdity, inventing nonexistent but lifelike details about the poet's life in his birthplace. "It was a way like another, at any rate, of reducing the place to the absurd"; exaggeration has the same meaning as discretion. Yet the two means are distinguished, nonetheless, by an important characteristic: whereas Gedge's first method was merely the statement of the truth, his second has all the advantages of art. Gedge's discourse is admiable, a work of art in itself. And the reward soon follows; instead of being dismissed, Gedge finds his salary doubled at the tale's end—because of all he has done for the poet.

James's very last tales avoid so categorical a formulation of any opinion whatever. They remain indecisive, ambiguous, their nuances dim the bold colors of the earlier work. "The Velvet Glove" (1909) deals with the same problem of the relation between "art" and "life," but the answer it affords is much less specific. John Berridge is a successful writer; in a fashionable salon he meets two splendid characters, the Lord and the Princess, who, like Olympians come down to earth, incarnate all he has always dreamed of. The Princess flirts with Berridge, and he is about to lose his head when he realizes that she wants only one thing from him: a preface for her latest novel.

At first sight, this tale is a panegyric of "life" in contrast to writings. From the beginning of the reception Berridge tells himself: "What was the pale page of fiction compared with the intimately personal adventure that, in almost any direction, he [the young Lord] would have been all so stupidly, all so gallantly, all so instinctively . . . ready for?" As for the Princess, he notes "the really 'decadent' perversity, recalling that of the most irresponsibly insolent of the old Romans and Byzantines, that could lead a creature so formed for living and breathing her Romance, and so committed, up to the eyes, to the constant fact of her personal immersion in it and genius for it, the dreadful amateurish dance of ungrammatically scribbling it, with editions and advertisements and reviews and royalties and every other futile item. . . ." Imagining himself an Olympian too, Berridge rejects as vehemently as he can everything that has to do with writing: "He would leave his own stuff snugly unread, to begin with; that would be a beautiful start for an Olympian career. He should have been as unable to write those works in short as to make anything else of them; and he should have had no more arithmetic for computing fingers than any perfectheaded marble Apollo mutilated at the wrists. He should have consented to know but the grand personal adventure on the grand personal basis: nothing short of this . . . would begin to be, on any side, Olympian enough."

But the moral Berridge draws is not necessarily the moral of the tale. First of all, the famous writer's attitude might be usefully paralleled with that of the Princess: both want to become what they are not. Berridge writes fine novels but sees himself in his imagination, as a "prepossessing young shepherd"; the Princess participates in the life of the gods, while longing to be a successful novelist. Or as James himself puts it: "The mysterious values of other types kept looming larger before you than the doubtless often higher but comparatively familiar ones of your own, and if you had anything of the artist's real feeling for life the attraction and the amusement of possibilities so projected were worth more to you, in nineteen moods out of twenty, than the sufficiency, the serenity, the felicity, whatever it might be, of your stale personal certitudes."

Moreover, in order to describe the "life" which is being affirmed in contrast to writing, Berridge (and James) has only one word: "romance." The young Lord's rendezvous must be "of a high 'romantic' order," and the young Lord himself resembles "far-off romantic and 'plastic' figures"; the Princess' adventures could exist only if they had "the absolute attraction of romance." Supposing that she loves him, Berridge can compare his own emotion only to something in books: "It was ground he had ventured on, scenically, representationally, in the artistic sphere, but without ever dreaming he should 'realize' it thus in the social." So it is not "life" which is affirmed in contrast to fiction, but rather the role of a character in relation to that of an author.

Besides, John Berridge is as unsuccessful in becoming a "prepossessing shepherd" as the Princess in becoming a popular novelist. Just as Clare Vawdrey in "The Private Life" could not be both a great writer and a brilliant man of the world, here Berridge must return to his unromantic condition of a novelist—after a romantic gesture (he kisses the Princess) whose purpose is precisely to prevent her from behaving like a novelist! Art and life are incompatible, and it is with a serene bitterness that Berridge exclaims, at the tale's end: "You *are* Romance . . . so what more do you want?" James leaves it to the reader to decide which side of the argument will win his allegiance. Here we begin to perceive a possible reversal of the "figure in the carpet."

The essential secret is the motive force of Henry James's tales, it determines their structure. But more than this—such a principle of organization becomes the explicit theme of at least two of them. These are, as it were, metaliterary tales, tales devoted to the constructive principle of the tale.

The first of these tales, "The Figure in the Carpet," we discussed at the very beginning of this study. The secret whose existence Vereker had revealed becomes a motive force in the narrator's life, then in the life of his friend George Corvick, of the latter's friend and fiancée Gwendolen Erme, and finally, of Gwendolen's second husband, Drayton Deane. A moment comes when Corvick declares that he has plumbed the secret, but he dies soon afterwards. Gwendolen has learned the solution before her husband's death but without telling it to anyone else: she keeps silent until her own death. Hence at the tale's end we are as ignorant as we were at its beginning.

Yet this identity is only apparent, for between the beginning and the end occurs the entire narrative, that is, the search for the secret. We now know that Henry James's secret (and doubtless Vereker's) resides precisely in the existence of a secret, of an absent and absolute cause, as well as in the effort to plumb this secret, to render the absent present. Vereker's secret was therefore told to us, and this in the only way possible. If it had been named, it would no longer have existed, for it is precisely its existence which constitutes the secret. This secret is by definition inviolable, for it consists in its own existence. The quest for the secret must never be ended, for it constitutes the secret itself. Critics have already interpreted "The Figure in the Carpet" in this sense; for instance, R. P. Blackmur speaks of "the exasperation of the mystery without the presence of mystery," and Blanchot evokes that "art which does not decipher but which is the cipher of the undecipherable"; with greater precision, Philippe Sollers describes it thus: "The solution of the problem which is expounded to us is nothing other than the very exposition of this problem."

In a darker tonality, and once again, with more nuances, "The Beast in the Jungle" deals with the same answer. John Marcher believes that some unknown and essential event is to occur in his life; he organizes that life entirely in terms of this future moment. Here is how his friend, May Bartram, describes Marcher's feeling: "You said you had had from your earliest time, as the deepest thing within you, the sense of being kept for something rare and strange, possibly prodigious and terrible, that was sooner or later to happen to you, that you had in your bones the foreboding and the conviction of, and that would perhaps overwhelm you."

May Bartram decides to participate in Marcher's expectation. He greatly appreciates her solicitude and on occasion even wonders if this strange thing is not related to her. Thus when she moves into a house nearer him, "perhaps the great thing he had so long felt as in the lap of the gods was no more than this circumstance, which touched him so nearly, of her acquiring a house in London." Similarly, when she falls sick, "he caught himself—for he *had* so done—*really* wondering if the great accident would take form now as nothing more than his being condemned to see this charming woman, this admirable friend, pass away from him." After her death, this doubt turns into what is nearly a conviction: "Her dying, her death, his consequent solitude—*that* was what he had figured as the beast in the jungle, that was what had been in the lap of the gods."

Yet this supposition never becomes an utter certainty, and Marcher, while valuing May Bartram's effort to help him, spends his life in an endless state of expectation, in which everything is reduced to the single condition of waiting. Before she dies, May declares that the Thing is no longer to be waited for—that it has already happened. Marcher has the same feeling but vainly tries to understand what this Thing consists in. Until one day, at May's grave, the revelation comes: "All the while he had waited the wait was itself his portion." The secret was the existence of the secret itself. Horrified by this revelation,

Marcher flings himself, sobbing, onto the grave, and with this image the tale ends.

"It wouldn't have been failure to be bankrupt, dishonoured, pilloried, hanged; it was failure not to be anything." Marcher could have avoided this failure: it would have been enough to have paid a different kind of attention to May Bartram's existence. She was not the sought-for secret, as he had sometimes supposed, but loving her would have let him escape the moral despair which overwhelms him at the sight of the truth. May Bartram had understood this: in loving him she had found the secret of her own life; helping Marcher in his quest was her "essential thing." "What else does one ever want to be," she asks Marcher, "but interested?" And she has her reward: "I'm more sure than ever my curiosity, as you call it, will be but too well repaid." And Marcher does not know how right he is when he exclaims, dismayed by the idea of her death, that her absence will be "the absence of everything." The search for the secret and the truth is never anything but a search, without any content; May Bartram's life has for its content her love for Marcher. The figure we have observed throughout our inspection of the tales here assumes its supreme, ultimate form—which is at the same time its dialectical negation.

If Henry James's secret, the figure in the carpet of his work, the string which unites the pearls of the separate tales, is precisely the existence of a secret, how does it come about that we can now name the secret, render absence present? Am I not thereby betraying the fundamental Jamesian precept which consists in this affirmation of absence, this impossibility of designating truth by its name? But criticism too (including mine) has always obeyed the same law: it is the search for truth, not its revelation, a treasure hunt rather than the treasure itself, for the treasure can only be absent. Once this "reading of James" is over, we must then begin reading James, set out upon a quest for the meaning of his *oeuvre*, though we know that this meaning is nothing other than the quest itself.

viii

Henry James was born in 1843 in New York. He lived in Europe after 1875, first in Paris, then in London. After several brief visits to the United States, he became a British citizen and died in Chelsea in 1916. No event characterizes his life; he spent it writing books: some twenty novels, tales, plays, essays. His life, in other words, is perfectly insignificant (like any presence): his work, an essential absence, asserts itself all the more powerfully.

1969

The Ghosts of Henry James

Ghost stories stud the whole of Henry James's long literary career. "De Grey: A Romance" was written in 1868, when its author was just twenty-five; "The Jolly Corner" (1908) is one of James's last tales. Forty years separate them, during which James published some twenty novels, over a hundred tales, as well as plays, criticism, and travel essays. Let us add straightway that these ghost stories are far from constituting an image that is simple and easy to grasp.

A certain number of them seem to conform to the general formula of fantastic narrative, characterized not by the simple presence of supernatural events but by the way in which the reader and the characters perceive them. An inexplicable phenomenon occurs; to obey his determinist mentality, the reader finds himself obliged to choose between two solutions: either to reduce this phenomenon to known causes, to the natural order, describing the unwonted events as imaginary, or else to admit the existence of the supernatural and thereby to effect a modification in all the representations which form his image of the world. The fantastic lasts as long as this uncertainty lasts; once the reader opts for one solution or the other, he is in the realm of the uncanny or of the marvelous.

"De Grey: A Romance" already corresponds to this description. Paul De Grey's death can be explained in two ways—according to his mother, he died of a fall from his horse; according to Father Herbert, a curse hangs over the De Grey family: if one of the sons marries his first love, he must die. The girl who loves Paul De Grey, Margaret, is plunged into uncertainty; she will end in madness. Further, uncanny episodes occur which may be coincidences but which may also testify to the existence of an invisible world: for example, Margaret suffers a sudden pain and utters a piercing shriek—heard by Paul who is out riding some three miles away.

"The Ghostly Rental" (1876) seems at first to be a tale of the supernatural explained. Every three months, Captain Diamond visits an abandoned house to collect a sum of money left there by the ghost of his daughter, whom he had unjustly cursed and driven from the house. One day when the captain falls gravely ill, he asks a young friend (the narrator) to collect the money in his place. The young man does so, with a pounding heart; he discovers that the ghost is no ghost but the daughter herself, still alive, who in this fashion supports her father. At this moment, the fantastic reasserts its claims: the young woman leaves the room a moment but suddenly returns, "with parted lips and dilated eyes"—she has just seen her father's ghost! The narrator subsequently investigates and learns that the old captain gave up his ghost at precisely the moment when his daughter saw it.

The same supernatural phenomenon will be evoked in another tale written twenty years later, "The Friends of the Friends" (1896). Here two persons have symmetrical experiences: each sees a parent of the opposite sex at the moment the latter dies hundreds of miles away. Yet it is difficult to categorize this tale as fantastic. Each text possesses a dominant element which engrosses the others and becomes the generating principle of the whole. Now in "The Friends of the Friends" this dominant element is thematic: death, an impossible communication. The supernatural incident plays a secondary part: it contributes to the general atmosphere and justifies the narrator's doubts as to a postmortem meeting of these same two characters. Hence the hesitation is absent from the text (it was not represented in "The Ghostly Rental" but remained perceptible there), which thereby escapes the norm of the fantastic.

Other structural aspects of the tale may also affect its fantastic character. Habitually ghost stories are told in the first person. This allows an easy identification of the reader with the
character (the latter plays the part of the former); at the same
time, the speech of the narrator-character possesses double
characteristics; it is beyond the test of truth as the narrator's
speech, but it must be subject to that test as the speech of the
character. If the author (that is, a nonrepresented narrator) tells
us he has seen a ghost, hesitation is no longer legitimate. If a
mere character tells us the same thing, we can attribute his
words to madness, to a drug, to illusion, and uncertainty, once
again, has no title to its claim. In a privileged position with
regard to the two, the narrator-character facilitates our hesitation: we want to believe him but we are not obliged to do so.
"Sir Edmund Orme" (1891) illustrates the latter case nicely.
The narrator-character sees a ghost himself, several times in a
row. Yet nothing else contradicts the laws of nature, as they are
commonly known. The reader is caught in a hesitation with no
way out: he sees the apparition along with the narrator, and at
the same time cannot permit himself to believe in it. Quite similar visions will produce a different effect when they are reported
by characters other than the narrator. Thus in "The Solution"
(1890), two characters, a man and a woman (just as in "Sir Edmund Orme") see the latter's deceased husband, who does not
want the newcomer to undertake to write his biography. But the
reader feels much less prompted to believe, for he sees these
two persons from outside and can readily explain their visions
by the woman's hypernervous state and by the influence she
wields over the other man. The same is true of "The Third Person" (1900), a humorous ghost story, in which two cousins, old
maids smothered by a life of idleness and boredom, begin seeing
a smuggler-relative who had died some centuries ago. The
reader feels the distance between narrator and characters is too
great to be able to take the latter's visions seriously. Last, in a
tale such as "Maud-Evelyn" (1900), the hesitation is reduced to
zero: the narrative is given in the first person but the narrator
puts no trust in the assertions of another character (whom she
knows only indirectly, moreover), who claims to live with a

young girl dead for fifteen years. Here we leave the supernatural in order to enter the description of a so-called pathological case.

Allegorical interpretation of the supernatural event represents another threat to the genre of the fantastic. Already in "Sir Edmund Orme," we could read the entire story as the illustration of a certain moral lesson. Moreover the narrator does not fail to formulate it: "It was a case of retributive justice. The mother was to pay, in suffering, for the suffering she had inflicted, and as the disposition to jilt a lover might have been transmitted to the daughter, the daughter was to be watched, so that *she* might be made to suffer should she do an equal wrong." Obviously if we read the tale as a fable, as the staging of a moral lesson, we can no longer experience the "fantastic" hesitation. Another tale, "The Private Life" (1892), comes still closer to pure allegory. The writer Clare Vawdrey leads a double life: one of his incarnations gossips about mundane matters with friends, while the other writes, in silence, inspired pages. "The world was vulgar and stupid, and the real man would have been a fool to come out for it when he could gossip and dine by deputy." The allegory is so obvious that the hesitation is once again reduced to zero.

"Owen Wingrave" (1892) would have been a pure example of the fantastic had the supernatural event played a more important part in the tale. In a haunted house, a young woman puts the courage of her suitor to the test: she asks him to spend the night in a place said to be dangerous. The consequence is tragic: "On the threshold of an open door, Owen Wingrave, dressed as [Spencer Coyle] had last seen him, lay dead on the spot on which his ancestor had been found." Was it the ghost or fear which killed Owen? We do not know, but in fact the question is not very important. The core of the tale is the drama lived by Owen Wingrave, who on the one hand seeks to defend his principles but on the other seeks to keep the trust of those who love him (these two aspirations being contradictory). Again, the fantastic has a subordinate, secondary function. The fact remains that the supernatural event is not explicitly presented as such—contrary to what occurred in a tale of James's youth, "The Romance of Certain Old Clothes" (1868), in which precisely the same scene permitted the reader no hesitation. Here is the description of the body: "Her lips were parted in entreaty, in dismay, in agony; and on her bloodless brow and cheeks there glowed the marks of ten hideous wounds from two vengeful ghostly hands." In such a case, we leave the fantastic for the marvelous.

There exists at least one example among James's tales where the ambiguity is maintained throughout the text and where it plays a dominant part: the celebrated *Turn of the Screw* (1898). Here the author has been so successful that subsequent critics have formed two distinct schools: those who consider the estate of Bly to be in fact haunted by evil spirits and those who explain everything by the neurosis of the governess who tells the story. Of course it is not necessary to choose between the two contrary solutions; the rule of the genre implies that the ambiguity be maintained. Nonetheless, the hesitation is not represented within the tale—the characters believe or do not believe, they do not hesitate between the two options.

The attentive reader, by this time, will have experienced a certain irritation: why should we try to persuade him that all these works belong to a single genre when each of them obliges us to consider it chiefly as an exception? The center around which we are attempting to arrange the individual tales (though we do so with little success) may quite simply not exist. Or in each case, it is to be found elsewhere, as is proved by the fact that to fit these tales into the mold of the genre, we are obliged to mutilate them, to adjust them, to accompany them with explanatory notes.

If this reader is thoroughly familiar with James's *oeuvre* he might go further and say: the proof that in James the genre of the fantastic has no homogeneity and hence no relevance is that the tales mentioned so far fail to constitute a clearly isolated group which would be differentiated from all the other texts. On the contrary, many intermediary tales exist, which make imperceptible the transition from fantastic works to nonfantastic ones. In addition to those already cited which speak in praise of death or of a life with the dead ("Maud-Evelyn" but also "The Altar of the Dead," (1895), there are those which evoke superstitions. For example "The Last of the Valerii" (1874) is the story of a young Italian count who believes in the old pagan gods and who allows his life to be organized around this belief. Are we to regard this as a supernatural phenomenon? Or "The Author of Beltraffio" (1885), where the wife of a famous writer believes that her husband's presence is destroying the health of their own son; in her efforts to prove the fact, she ends by provoking the child's death. Merely a strange occurrence, or the intervention of occult forces?

Nor are these the only unwonted phenomena which James offers us. The intuitions of Mrs Ryves in "Sir Dominick Ferrand" (1892) afford a further example: how is it possible that this young woman should be "warned" each time her fellow lodger Peter Baron is in danger? What are we to say of those prophetic dreams of Allan Wayworth, who sees the heroine of his play at the very moment when the heroine's prototype visits the actress who is to play the part ("Nona Vincent," 1892)? Moreover is this dream so different from that of George Dane in that Jamesian utopia "The Great Good Place" (1900), a dream sustaining strange relations with the waking state? And such questions can be multiplied—as is evidenced moreover by the choices editors make when they collect "the ghost stories of Henry James": they never arrive at the same result.

The disorder ends, however, if we give up looking for the ghost of the fantastic genre and turn to the project which unifies all of James's *oeuvre*. This author grants no importance to the raw event but concentrates all his attention on the relation between the character and the event. Further, the core of a story will often be an absence (the hidden, the dead, the work of art) and its quest will be the only possible presence. Absence is an ideal and intangible goal; the prosaic presence is all we have to work with. Objects, "things" do not exist (or if they exist, do not interest James); what intrigues him is the experience his characters can have of objects. There is no "reality" except a psychic one; the material and physical fact is normally absent, and we never know anything about it except the way in which various persons can experience it. The fantastic narrative is necessarily centered upon a perception, and as such it serves Henry James, especially since the object of perception always has a phantasmal existence for him. But what interests James is the exploration of this "psychic reality," the scrutiny of every variety of the possible relations between subject and object. Whence his attention to such special cases as hallucination, communication with the dead, telepathy. Here James makes a fundamental thematic choice: he prefers perception to action, relation with the object to the object itself, circular temporality to linear time, repetition to difference.

We might go further and say that James's project is fundamentally incompatible with that of the fantastic tale. By the hesitation which the latter sustains, it raises the questions: is this real or imaginary? is it a physical fact or merely a psychic one? For James, on the contrary, the only reality is imaginary, there are no facts but psychic ones. Truth is always a special case, someone's truth; consequently, to ask "does this ghost really exist?" has no meaning the moment it exists for someone. We never reach absolute truth, the gold standard is lost, we are doomed to abide by our perceptions and by our imagination—which moreover is not much different.

At this point an even more attentive reader may object once again. All you have done so far, he will say, is replace the formal genre (fantastic narrative) by the genre of author (Jamesian narrative) which also has, moreover, a formal reality. But thereby we lose no less of the specificity of each of James's texts. To attempt to reduce the *oeuvre* to a variant of the genre is a false notion at the outset; it is based on a vicious analogy between the facts of nature and the works of the mind. Each particular mouse can be considered a variant of the species "mouse"; the birth of a new specimen in no way modifies the species (or in any case such a modification is negligible). A work of art (or of science), on the contrary, cannot be presented as the simple product of a pre-existing combinatorial system; it is that too, but at the same time it transforms the system of elements, it establishes a new code of which it is the first (the only) message. A work which would be the pure product of a *pre-existing* system does not exist; or more exactly, does not exist for the history of literature. Unless, of course, we reduce literature to a marginal case—say, mass literature: the murder mystery, the thriller, the spy novel belong to literary history; any particular book, which can only exemplify, only illustrate the pre-existing genre, does not. To signify in history is to proceed from difference not merely from repetition. Hence the work of art (or of science) always involves a transforming element, an innovation of the system. The absence of difference equals non-existence.

Take for instance James's last and densest ghost story, "The Jolly Corner." All we know about the fantastic narrative and about the Jamesian narrative is insufficient for our comprehension of this tale, for a satisfactory account of it. Let us consider the text a little more closely, in order to observe what is *unique* and *specific* about it.

Spencer Brydon's return to America, after an absence of thirty-three years, is accompanied by a singular discovery: he begins doubting his own identity. Hitherto his existence seemed to him the projection of his own essence; in America once more he realizes that he might have been a different man. He has talents as an architect and builder which he has never utilized; now, during the years of his absence, New York has experienced a veritable architectural revolution. "If he had but stayed at home he would have anticipated the inventor of the sky-scraper. If he had but stayed at home he would have discovered his genius in time really to start some new variety of awful architectural hare and run it till it burrowed in a gold-mine." These past conditionals begin to obsess Brydon: not because he regrets not having become a millionaire, but because he discovers he might have had another existence. And would that existence, then, have been the projection of the same essence, or of another? "He found all things come back to the question of what he personally might have been, how he might have led his life and 'turned out,' if he had not so, at the outset, given it up." What is his essence? And does one exist? Brydon believes in the existence of an essence, at least with regard to others, for example his friend Alice Staverton: "Oh, you're a person whom

othing can have altered. You were born to be what you are,
nywhere, anyway. . . ."

Then Brydon decides to rediscover himself, to know himself
o encounter his authentic identity, and he sets out on a difficult
quest. He succeeds in localizing his alter ego thanks to the exis-
ence of two houses, each corresponding to a different version of
Spencer Brydon. He returns, night after night, to the house of
his ancestors, coming ever closer to that *other* self. Until one
night . . . he finds a door shut which he had left open; he realizes that the apparition is there; his impulse is to flee, but he no
onger can; the apparition blocks his path, becomes present,
discloses its countenance. . . . And Brydon is overcome by a
remendous disappointment: the *other* is a stranger. "The waste
of his nights had been only grotesque and the success of his adventure an irony. Such an identity fitted his at *no* point." The
quest was futile, the other is no more his essence than he himself is. The sublime essence-as-absence does not exist, the life
Brydon has led has made him a man who has nothing to do
with the man whom a different life would have produced. This
does not keep the apparition from advancing upon him in a
threatening way, and Brydon has no solution but to vanish into
nothingness—into unconsciousness.

When he comes to, he realizes that his head is no longer rest-
ing on the cold tiles of his deserted house, but on Alice Staverton's lap. She had realized what was happening, she had come
looking for him in his house, to help him. Two things then
become clear to Brydon. First that his quest was vain. Not because its result is disappointing, but because the quest itself
had no meaning: it was the quest for an absence (his essence,
his authentic identity). Such a quest is not only fruitless (this is
not so serious), but it is also, in a profound sense, a selfish act.
He himself characterizes it as "a selfish frivolous scandalous
life" and Alice Staverton confirms him: "You don't care for anything but yourself." This investigation, postulating one's essence, excludes the other's existence. Here occurs Brydon's second discovery, the discovery of a presence: Alice Staverton.
Halting the fruitless quest for his essence he discovers another

existence, and he asks for only one thing more: " 'Oh keep me
keep me!' he pleaded while her face still hung over him: i
response to which it dropped again and stayed close, clingingl
close." Having set out in search of a profound *I*, Brydon ends b
discovering a *you*.

This text thereby signifies the reversal of the figure we see re
curring throughout the Jamesian *oeuvre*. The essential absenc
and the insignificant presence no longer dominate his universe
the relation with another, even the humblest presence, is af
firmed against the selfish (solitary) quest for absence. The sel
does not exist outside its relation with others, with another; es
sence is an illusion. Thus James pivots, at the end of his *oeuvre*
to the other side of the great thematic dichotomy we evoked ear
lier: the problematics of man alone confronting the world gives
way to another, that of the relation of human being to humar
being. *To be* is supplanted by *to have*, *I* by *you*.

This reversal of the Jamesian project had already beer
heralded by several previous works. "The Altar of the Dead" is
at first sight, a veritable encomium of death. Stransom, the
main character, spends his life in a church where he has
lighted candles to the glory of all the dead he has known. He
openly prefers absence to presence, the dead to the living, and
ends by desiring the death of those close to him: "There were
hours at which he almost caught himself wishing that certain of
his friends would now die, that he might establish with them in
this manner a connection more charming than, as it happened,
it was possible to enjoy with them in life." But gradually a presence is introduced into this life: the presence of a woman who
comes to the same church. Imperceptibly, this presence becomes so important that when the woman disappears one day,
Stransom discovers that his dead no longer exist for him—they
have died a second time. Stransom will achieve a kind of recon-
ciliation with his friend but it will be too late; the hour has come
when he himself must enter the realm of the dead. Too late—
this same conclusion is reached in "The Beast in the Jungle"
(1903), in which the narrative presents a character, Marcher,
who has spent his life searching for absence, without valuing
the presence at his side of May Bartram, who lives within pres-

ence: "What else does one ever want to be but interested?" she asks Marcher. It is only after her death that Marcher understands the bitter lesson he has been taught. But it is too late and he must accept his failure, the failure which consists in "being nothing." Thus "The Jolly Corner" is the least despairing version of this new Jamesian figure—thanks to the ghost, the lesson is learned before death. The great, the difficult lesson of life consists precisely in refusing death, in accepting the conditions of life (one has to learn this). Death's presence makes us understand—too late!—what its absence signified; we must try to live out death in advance, to understand before we are caught short by time.

No mistake about it, our exigent reader will say at this point, you got off on the wrong track, only to get on it once again. You were to speak about a tale, about what is specific and unique in it, and here you are again, constituting a genre, closer to this tale than the earlier genres perhaps, but a genre all the same, of which it is merely one of the possible illustrations!

And whose fault is that, if not the fault of language itself, essentialist and generic by nature. As soon as I speak, I enter the universe of abstraction, of generality, of concepts, and no longer of things. How to name the individual, when the names themselves, as we all know, do not belong to the individual himself? If the absence of difference equals nonexistence, pure difference in unnamable: it is nonexistent for language. In language the individual, the specific is only a ghost, that ghost which produces speech, that absence which we try in vain to apprehend, which we have grasped as little before as after discourse, but which produces, in its void, discourse itself.

Or else, for the individual to be heard, the critic must fall silent. That is why, discussing "The Jolly Corner," I have said nothing of the pages which form its center and which constitute one of the peaks of Henry James's art. I let them speak for themselves.

1969

12

Number, Letter, Word

It may come as a surprise to find a series of studies on the functioning of narrative interrupted by an essay in the reconstruction of a theory of language: here Khlebnikov's, earlier Constant's, later Artaud's. Is the accident of chronology entirely responsible? For me, the meaning of this alternation, which I should prefer to regard as a synthesis, is to be found elsewhere. In one of this book's early chapters, I asserted that language encompasses and explains literature; in another, that the structure of narrative becomes intelligible through the structure of language. But of which language?

From Homer to Artaud, literary works have asserted something very different on this point from what was proposed formerly by philosophers and today by linguists. If we take literary works seriously, the perspective must be inverted: it is literature which encompasses and explains language, literature is a theory of language we can no longer ignore if we are to understand literary functioning with the help of linguistic categories. Whence this absolute necessity: if we would make language into a theory of literature, we must read literature, attentively, as a theory of language.

To "discover" an author of the past, to translate his theories into a contemporary vocabulary, to relate them to current ideas,

he endeavor is both seductive and unattractive—by its very fa-
cility. Such an activity provides a faithful, though caricatural,
image of all interpretation and of all reading. Unless we let the
author's sentences speak for themselves (but in what language?), we merely tend to relate them to ourselves, by contrast
or likeness. If I feel the need to introduce such texts, it is doubtless because I want to make their author into one of my own
predecessors.

With Velemir Khlebnikov, leader of the Russian futurists, in-
spirer of the Formalists and of several generations of Soviet
poets, the temptation is great indeed. The main themes of his
theoretical writings are all very much a la mode: numbers, writing (*écriture*), the sovereignty of the signifier (this last term already marks an effort toward rapprochement . . .). But suppose
it were true that his sole merit was to be the precursor of one or
another Parisian critic—would that be a sufficient reason to attempt to rescue him from oblivion?

The realization that one of today's commonplaces was already
articulated some fifty years ago is of no interest unless you are
a historian of ideas, particularly since commonplaces themselves are yesterday's truths, not today's. When Khlebnikov
compares the opposition between practical language and "autonomous" language to the opposition between reason and feelings; when he says that "the nature of song is in the release
from the self"; or even when he presents the life of language as
a permanent conflict between "pure sound" and "reason," between signifier and signified, between the intelligible and the
sensible, we feel somewhat frustrated. The very familiarity of
these notions has made us suspicious about them.

Awareness of the risks we are running may help us shift our
objective, though without changing it altogether. If Khlebnikov
did not have something to say to the present, we could not read
him today. But instead of considering his *oeuvre* as a series of
heterogeneous quotations, we might try to reconstruct the system of the text. This would be the one means of not reducing
him to the already-known, of not confining him in a present
tense so narrow that it already, and always, smells stale. So we
shall try to perform a series of displacements in the Khlebnikov-

ian text (rather than translation-substitutions), to arrange the elements of the game so that its rules will be apparent.

Certainly the strangest part of Khlebnikov's doctrines is the one consecrated to numbers. At first glance, it appears to have something to do with the myth of the eternal return: similar events, Khlebnikov says, are separated by identical intervals of time, or at least by intervals reducible to each other with the help of a few simple formulas. Here is his proof.

The beginnings of states are separated by $(365 + 48)n = 413n$. For example, England 827, Germany 1,240, Russia 1,653. Or another series: Egypt 3,643 B.C., Rome 753 B.C., France 486, Normandy 899.

Major wars are separated by $(365-48)n = 317n$. "The struggle for control of the seas between an island and the mainland, England and Germany in 1915, was preceded at an interval of 317×2 by a major war between Japan and China under Kublai Khan in 1281. The Russo-Japanese War of 1905 occurred 317 years after the war between England and Spain in 1588."

The same is true of the events in the life of an individual, though here we are to count days, not years. Hence in Pushkin's case: "His wedding occurred on the 317th day after his betrothal to Natalia Goncharova, and the first manifestation of his Anacreontic series . . . occurred $317 \times n$ days before his marriage."

The same is also true for the birth of famous men, which form homogeneous series. Here are the logicians: Aristotle 384 B.C., John Stuart Mill 1804, that is, 365×6. Or Aeschylus 525 B.C., Mohammed 570, Firdausi 935, Hafiz 1300: the intervals separating them are all divisible by 365. Or the "founders of classicism": Confucius 551 B.C. and Racine 1639—the difference is 365×6 (Khlebnikov comments, "We imagine France's smile of disgust and her *Fi donc:* she has no use for China").

So far, all the regularities concern time, and Khlebnikov explicitly links the law of numbers to temporality. The texts which deal with it are entitled, "Time the Measure of the World," "The Mathematical Conception of History," and one of his "Proposi-

ions" insists: "Everywhere the concept of time must replace
he concept of space."

But one does not get rid of space so readily. First of all, this
concept of time—circular, repetitive—already evokes a "spa-
tialized" temporality; "pure" time would be a time in which the
present moment is pure difference, without any resemblance to
the preceding or following moments: repetition rigidifies, irre-
versibility consists of differences. Moreover, Khlebnikov shows
that the law of numbers rules not only the temporal intervals
but space as well. Thus for the distance between planets: "The
surface of a rectangle, one side of which is equal to the radius of
the earth and the other side to the distance traversed by light in
one year, equals the surface described by the straight line con-
necting the sun to the earth during a period of 317 days." Or
again: "The surface of the blood corpuscle equals the surface of
the terrestrial globe divided by 365 to the tenth power."

Further, these same laws, this same number 365 ($\pm$48) govern not only periods and distances, but also many other kinds of
countable homogeneous groups. Thus a man's body contains
317×2 muscles, Petrarch wrote 317 sonnets to Laura, "the
number of persons graduating from the Bestujev Institute over
a twenty-five-year period was 317×11, the Astrakhan Sokol in
1913 had 317 members; the number of vessels entering and
leaving British ports during six months of submarine warfare,
divided by the number of vessels sunk, yields a quotient of 317."
"According to the law of June 14, 1912, Germany would have
317 combat units afloat. In 1911, there were 317×95 Finns
and Norwegians in Sweden." "The Japanese guard on the
southern Manchurian line was composed of $617 + 17$
men $= 317 \times 2$. During the Franco-Prussian war one man was
killed for every 365 bullets fired."

The important thing, then, is not time or space but, as Khlebnikov puts it, "proportion, order, and harmony." His first goal is
to denounce "so-called chance," to show that there is nothing
fortuitous, that the arbitrary is merely a relationship not yet understood. A universal harmony prevails; man must honor it by a
generalized calculus which will reveal its rules: "The laws of
the world coincide with the laws of the calculus." Number itself

is merely the best way of formulating these regularities, it is no
an end in itself, and sometimes it may fail to intervene. Henc
the observations concerning the rhythm of wars are accom
panied by others concerning the geographical disposition of cap
ital cities. "If we draw a line linking the cities (1) Byzantiun
(Constantinople), (2) Sofia, (3) Vienna, (4) St. Petersburg, (5
Tsaritsyn, Kiev appears situated at the center of a spiderwe
whose identical radii spread toward the four capitals." Or again
these reflections on the fact that one and the same initial lette
occurs in the name of the most famous men of a country—
hence for Germany the key letters are Sch- and G-: Schille
Schlegel, Schopenhauer, Schelling; Goethe but also Heine
Heise, Hegel, Habsburg, Hohenzollern, names which in Rus
sian transcription appear as Geine, Geise, Gegel. . . .

The generalized calculus will give meaning to the past; at th
same time, it will enable us to foresee the future: "Capitals an
cities will arise around the old ones according to the arc of
circle whose radius is $R \div 2\pi$ in which R is half the earth's di
ameter." In 1912, Khlebnikov writes a text in which he asks
following a calculation: "Is not the fall of some state to be ex
pected in 1917?" Just as we have been able to deduce the exis
tence of unknown planets, of chemical elements never yet ob
served, we should be able to describe the future works of th
mind. It suffices for this to observe their laws in already exist
ing works. Hence, in the first strophe of one of his poems
Khlebnikov notes the presence of four letters, each repeated fiv
times. Consequently, "the island of thought within autonomou
discourse, like the hand which has five fingers, must be con
structed on five radii of sound, vocalic or consonantal, which
pierce the world like a hand." "We must construct our verse
according to Darwin's law."

Nothing is arbitrary; everything must be motivated, and th
best motivation is nature. The number 365 is not selected arbi
trarily, for it is the "natural" duration of the year. One of Khleb
nikov's first targets will be the units of measurement: "Establish
a new system of units on the following principles—the dimen
sions of the terrestrial globe in time, space, and force are to be
acknowledged as the initial unit, and the series of decreasing

mounts by a power of 365, as derived units: $a,\ a \div 365,$
$\div 365^2$. Thus the stupid seconds and minutes will have disap-
eared, but the twenty-four hours will remain, divided into 365
arts; the 'daytime of the day' will be equal to 237 seconds, the
ext unit being 0.65 seconds. The surface unit will be 59
m² $= K \div 365^7$, in which $K =$ the surface of the earth. The unit
f length will be $R \div 365^3 = 13$ cm, in which $R =$ the radius of
he earth." "To calculate all labor in heartbeats, the monetary
nit of the future in which each living being is equally
ich. . . ."

On the horizon of this superrationalist system appears—
owever vaguely—the shadow of a theology. If the events of this
vorld obey a regular rhythm, it is because the principle of this
hythm comes from somewhere else. For Khlebnikov, this abso-
ute principle is that of the stellar world. "Terrestrial science
»ecomes a chapter of celestial science." And in another "propo-
ition" he recommends: "Gradually transmit power to the starry
leavens."

The Khlebnikovian conception of language is merely a special
:ase of this theory of universal harmony and generalized cal-
:ulus (need we add that it must be read at a different level from
he one on which we receive current linguistic theories?). Here
s the initial observation: graphically, all the worlds in a lan-
;uage are the product of a combination-system based on the 28
etters of the alphabet (once again, Khlebnikov is "naturaliz-
ng"—28 is the number of days in a month, while the Russian
alphabet of the time contains 35 letters); the same method is
followed with sounds. An analogous operation on the level of
meaning must then be performed, and the "elementary names"
of the language discovered, which correspond to Mendeleyev's
chemical elements and whose combinations produce the apparent variety of significations. "The entire plenitude of language
must be decomposed into fundamental units of *primary truths,*
and we can then elaborate for sono-substances a kind of Mendeleyev's or Moseley's law, that pinnacle of chemical thought."

To undertake this analysis, Khlebnikov advances three successive hypotheses.

First of all, there are as many "elementary names" as letters of the alphabet, that is 28.

Second, the meaning of such a name is the common denominator of the meaning of all the words which have the same initial letter. All words beginning with M have something in common in their meaning, and this "something" is the signification of the "elementary name" (of the letter) M.

We have not attempted to look for Khlebnikov's successors, but we cannot fail, at this point, to point out the existence of a precursor (even if Khlebnikov knew nothing about him). In his treatise, *Les Mots anglais,* Stéphane Mallarmé had already formulated this second hypothesis. "In it (=the initial consonant), he writes, "lies the radical virtue, something like the word's fundamental meaning." And he proceeds to describe the signification of each letter when it comes at the beginning of the word.

The first hypothesis, the one which permits the system's closure, is not present in Mallarmé; yet it is this hypothesis which establishes Khlebnikov's third proposition, already bearing on the very nature of the meaning of the "elementary nouns": "The elementary bodies of the language—the sounds of the alphabet—are the names of the various forms of space, the enumeration of the cases of its life."

This is the final stage of Khlebnikov's thought as to the meanings of the letters. Earlier he had not yet found the unity of all meanings, and he attempted various solutions. In a text entitled "On the Elementary Names of Language," he analyzes four consonants and proposes the following interpretation: M = division, V = subtraction, K = addition, S = multiplication. The letter V affords a good illustration of the development of his thought. At first, he interprets it as "the penetration of the great by the small," then comes "the act of subtraction." "The name-V begins the names of the animals which caused damage to the agrarian life of early man. . . . What was protected . . . also begins with the name-V." And then the final version (which recurs in several texts): "V in all languages indicates the rotation of one point around another."

Khlebnikov's analysis thus becomes increasingly abstract. Mallarmé's remains close to the individual significations of

ords. It is interesting to compare these two interpretations on
nother point as well: to the degree that Khlebnikov claims uni-
ersality, we might attempt to discover whether the two poets'
ntentions are similar. The coincidences are rare; we find them,
r approach them, it would seem, only apropos of the letters T
nd G. Mallarmé writes of the former—"This letter . . . repre-
ents, more than all the rest, arrest"; and Khlebnikov—"T in-
icates the direction where a motionless point has created an
bsence of movements oriented in the same direction, the nega-
ve path and its direction behind the motionless point." But the
ivergence between Khlebnikov and Mallarmé is not always sig-
ificant either, precisely because of the difference of level on
hich the two analyses are located.

Mallarmé takes his analysis further in another direction: he
tudies not only the total signification of the initial letter but
lso the modifications it undergoes because of the other conso-
ants present in the word. For instance: "Words beginning with
C, a consonant with a prompt and decisive attack, appear in
reat numbers, receiving from this initial letter the signification
f vigorous actions such as clasp, clear, climb, thanks to the ad-
ition of an *l*, and with *r*, of cracking and crashing . . ."; this
ermits him to speak of "those terminal consonants which add a
ind of secondary meaning to the notion expressed by those of
he word's beginning." Khlebnikov is content in this regard with
a comparison, without going into detail: "A separate word re-
embles a small labor force in which the word's first sound is in
effect the president of the union controlling the totality of the
word's meanings."

Here is how Khlebnikov discovers the meaning of each letter:
"L is the shift in the movements of points on a straight line to
he movement over the surface passing through this line. For
the raindrop (*liven'*) has fallen, then has become part of the
puddle (*luzha*). And the puddle is a liquid body in the form of a
plank, transverse to the direction of the drop. The meadow (*lug*)
and the ravine (*log*) are puddle-sites (*luzhi*). The plane of the
foot (*lapa*), of skis (*lyzhi*), of the boat (*lodka*) is transverse to the
direction of a man's weight."

Starting here, it becomes possible to gain a clearer understanding of the meaning of other words beginning with the same letter and remaining, at first glance, independent; this is the calculus of the meaning of words: "Then would it not be suitable to give the following definition: L is the shift of the points of a one-dimensional body to a two-dimensional body under the influence of the arrest of movement, it is the transition point, the meeting-point of the one-dimensional world and the two-dimensional world. Is not the word *lyubit'* (to love) thus accounted for? In it a man's consciousness was following a single dimension in its fall: a one-dimensional world. But a second consciousness appears and we see created the two-dimensional world of two human beings, transverse to the first, as the plane of the puddle is transverse to the falling rain."

Hence it is no accident if a word begins with L and its meaning includes that of the "elementary name" L. The relation between signifier and signified is not arbitrary but necessary (Mallarmé, too, wrote: "So perfect a link between signification and the form of a word that a single impression seems to be made, that of its success, on the mind and on the ear—this is frequent . . ."). This motivation is still due to nature: "According to all appearances, language is as wise as nature." "Language is wise because it belongs itself to nature."

Since the relation between the letter and the letter's meaning is the same for all languages (contrary to the relation between a word and its meaning), it becomes possible to eliminate the diversity of languages. "The goal of a single scientifically elaborated universal language becomes increasingly clear to humanity." Here is how we are to proceed: "By comparing the words which begin with SH we see that they all signify one body within the envelope of another; SH signifies envelope. . . . If it appears that SH has the same signification in all languages, the problem of a universal language is then solved—every kind of shoe will be called SH of the foot; every kind of cup, SH of water—it is as clear and simple as can be." (We may indicate here the existence of another representative of the same poetic family. Alfred Jarry was writing some ten years earlier: "For anyone who knows how to read, the same sound or the same syllable always has the same meaning in every language.")

The universal language is possible because it would be nothing but the rediscovery of a pre-Babel language, ideal and mute, which has always existed—an archlanguage. "We may remark in passing that beyond the language of words there is the mute language of concepts constituted from units of the mind (a texture of concepts orienting the language of words)." The only means of materializing this archlanguage today is writing. The analogy Khlebnikov proposes is a striking one, as much for what it says as for what it suggests. Current spoken languages resemble the currency of each country; "like original exchange-sounds permitting the barter of rational products, they have divided polyglot humanity into tariff-war camps, into a series of verbal markets, beyond whose limits no one language has any currency. Each system of money-sound claims supremacy, and hence languages as such serve to divide humanity and wage ghost wars." Writing, on the other hand, can correspond only to gold, that universal equivalent which has currency in every country: "The mute graphic signs will reconcile the polyphony of languages."

Khlebnikov's concern for motivation impels him to go further. It is not enough that the relation between signifier and signified be necessary, it must be analogical: "In life, it has always been so: initially the sign of the concept was the simple outline of this concept." We must discard letters as signifiers (though they have allowed the organization of the signified) and replace them by drawings of concepts, by ideograms. V signifies rotation: "For me V assumes the form of a circle with a point at the center."

If letters have a signification independent of the words in which they are included (though a function of the meaning of these words), it then becomes possible to form combinations of letters which will be endowed with meaning without their being words of the language. Such is the origin of *zaum'*, the transrational language and the most famous invention of Khlebnikov and his futurist friends (especially Alexei Kruchenykh). We find transrational words in the earliest of Khlebnikov's futurist poems, and he writes: "The language developed naturally from certain fundamental units of the alphabet. . . . If we take the combinations of these sounds in a free order—for instance, *bo-beobi*, or *dyr bul shchil*, or *mantch! mantch!*, or *chi breo zo!*—the words of this type belong to no language but at the same time say something indefinable which nonetheless exists."

They belong to no language but they say something: such are the narrow limits within which the transrational words function. Khlebnikov seeks to make these limits explicit in a reflection upon the language of magic, which affords the purest example of transrational discourse. We must distinguish what is *comprehensible* to reason from what is *significative*. Incantations and magic formulas are not comprehensible but they signify nonetheless: "These incomprehensible words are endowed with a superior power over man. . . . They are assigned the power of administering good and evil, and of governing the hearts of lovers. . . . We do not understand them for the time being. We recognize it clearly. But there is no doubt whatever that these series of sounds are a series of universal truths advancing into the twilight of our soul." Moreover, "the prayers of many peoples are written in a language incomprehensible to those who utter them."

A metaphor again gives the best description of this transrational intellection: "Does the earth understand the characters of the seeds the ploughman sows within it? No. Yet the autumn fields flourish in answer to these seeds."

Transrational language is jeopardized by serious dangers. The first is overpowerful reason, the generalized calculus, and it is Khlebnikov himself who destroys what he has just constructed. This language is transrational only in incantations, in the primitive state; once we have discovered the "elementary names" of the language, the "alphabet of reason," then reason recovers its powers: "Hence transrational language ceases to be transrational. It becomes an alphabet game of which we are quite conscious, a new art on whose threshold we are standing."

The other great adversary of the transrational is one of the basic principles of language itself, the principle of repetition. In order to belong to language, an entity must possess the capacity for repetition; otherwise it risks being not only incomprehensible but also nonsignifying. Khlebnikov discerns the danger in his "notebooks": "What has been written with the help of new words exclusively does not touch the consciousness." And he observes apropos of some of his own transrational words: "At the moment they were written, the transrational words of the dying Akhnaton *mantch! mantch!* in *Ka* provoked something like suffering; I could not read them, seeing flashes of light between them and me; now they are nothing to me. Why—I do not know, myself." The incapacity of reproduction transforms transrational discourse into "nothing"; such discourse can by definition exist only as a limit-condition.

We cannot write "with the help of new words exclusively." The existing language must continue to serve, though it is not so rational as the one based on the "alphabet of reason," though it does not so perfectly obey the laws of universal harmony. And moreover, with the help of a particular analysis, we can discover these laws even within real languages. Khlebnikov develops this analysis apropos of what he calls the "declension of roots" (in his book on Khlebnikov, Jakobson speaks of the method of "poetic etymology" as analogous to popular etymology).

Declension is a feature of the Russian language. A word with zero-desinence in the nominative takes *a* in the genitive, *u* in the dative, and so forth. Khlebnikov presumes that a similar alternation also occurs within roots; in other words, "different" words appear as cases of each other. Further, their signification is in direct or inverse relation to the general meaning of the case whose desinence alternates in the root.

The genitive answers the question "whence?"; the accusative, the question "whither?" Here is how the roots are declined according to these cases: "If we take the pair *vol* (ox) and *val* (wave), the action of leading is oriented *toward* the domestic ox which leads man and proceeds *from* the wave which leads man and boat upon the stream." Or again: "*Beg* (flight) is provoked by fear, and *bog* (god) is the creature toward which fear is to be directed."

Alongside this declension of roots appears a "derivation of roots." *Sem'* in Russian signifies "seven," and *semja* "family." Khlebnikov concludes from this that the primitive family was composed of seven persons ("five children and two parents") and that the number "seven" is a truncated form of the word "family." *Eda* signifies "meal," *edinica* "one"(this is because primitive man ate by himself, he "had no need of external assistance during meals." Mallarmé had discovered similar relations concerning English; he had preceded Khlebnikov in this Cratylic form of linguistic analysis: "What discovery could be more delightful, for instance, and indeed likely to compensate many a disappointment, than the fact that there is an acknowledged link between such words as *house* and *husband, who is its head; between loaf* and *lord,* whose function is to distribute it; between *spur* and *spurn;* between *glow* and *blood;* between *well* and *wealth;* and between the *threshing* ground and *threshold,* the ground packed together like a pavement? . . .* The shift in signification can become absolute moreover to the point of affecting us as a real analogy: thus *heavy* seems suddenly to be rid of all sense of the burden it suggests in order to give us *heaven,* high and ethereal, considered as a spiritual abode." Khlebnikov, moreover, discerns precisely the same relation in Russian between *ves* (weight) and *vys'* (height)! Similarly, Jarry analyzes the word *industry* on the model of the word *alphabet: "in-dus-tria,* one, two, three, in every language."

The discovery of root declension leads logically to an activity which exploits its results and which Khlebnikov calls the creation of words, "verbocreation." Why be content with only the "cases" present in the language, when one might decline all roots and obtain new words whose meaning will have been deduced? Why be confined to only the combinations of letters and affixes which the language exploits and not forge new ones? Such neologisms will remain comprehensible for everyone, since their creation will have obeyed the already existing laws of the language. Hence will be created not only new sound-combinations, but also new concepts. Here is an example—"Such *direction* as is based solely on the fact that it is morally *pleasing* could thus be called a *plirection. . . .* Or *plirect* or *plirecting:* you have noticed how by replacing the *d* by the letters *pl* we have shifted from the field of the verb 'to direct' to the field of the possessions of the verb 'to please.' "

Hence a generalized calculus, worthy of Leibniz, reasserts its

owers. As usual, Khlebnikov starts from the law and inquires
into its particular realizations only after the fact. Certain words
re invented without his having had time to think of their
meaning: "The word 'flowers' (*cvety*) allows the construction of
mlowers' (*mlety*), a word unforeseeably rich." The same impulse is to be found in his "Propositions": "Recalling that n^0 is
he sign of the point, n^1 the sign of the straight line, n^2 and n^3
he signs of surface and volume, seek the spaces of the frac-
ional powers: n^{12}, n^{23}, n^{13}—where are they?"

This poet never speaks of poetry, nor of literature; the opposi-
ion between literature and nonliterature does not seem to have
any meaning for him. His conception of language culminates
however in a different opposition: that of practical language and
autonomous language (*samovitaya rech'*). In practical language, the word is not perceived in itself but as a substitute for
he object it designates:

Like a child who during his play can imagine that the chair on which
he is sitting is a real thoroughbred, and just as the chair replaces the
horse for him, in the course of oral and written discourse the little word
"sun" replaces, in the conventional world of human conversation, the
magnificent and majestic star. The heavenly body, calmly resplendent,
replaced by a verbal toy, is readily put in the dative and the genitive,
cases applied to its substitute in language. But this equality is conventional: if the real star were to vanish and only the word "sun" were left,
it could no longer shine in the sky and warm the earth, the earth would
freeze, and turn into a snowflake in the fist of universal space. . . .
The sonorous doll "sun" allows us, in our human play, to pull the ears
and tug the moustaches of the august star without pitiable mortal
hands, all those datives which the real sun would never have approved. . . .

At the same time that we bring signifier and signified closer
together, we must show the difference between sign and referent. More to the point, Khlebnikov proposes no longer using
words in this referential and communicative function, for they
perform it badly and we elsewhere possess a much more adequate instrument—numbers: "The most perspicacious minds
cannot define thought by means of words, except as an imperfect measurement of the world. . . . Verbal reflection does not
offer the basic condition permitting measurement, that is, the

constancy of the measuring unit, and the Sophists Protagoras and Gorgias are the first audacious pilots who have shown the danger in navigating on the waves of the word. Each noun is merely an approximative measurement, the comparison of several sizes, of kinds of signs of equality. Leibniz exclaiming, 'the time will come when men will replace offensive arguments by calculus' (will shout *calculemus*), Novalis, Pythagoras, Amenophis IV have anticipated the victory of number over word as a technique of thought."

Words must be liberated from a function which numbers can fulfill better than they—that of being a "technique of thought." Then they can resume their own function—to be autonomous words: "Failing weapon of thought, the word will nonetheless remain for the arts." "Languages will remain for art and will be liberated from an offensive burden. The ear is weary." On one side there is mathematics, on the other metaphors; there is nothing between the two.

Khlebnikov's thought, as we see, admits of no compromise. Nor does his life, which is why it can be read as a text; instead of seeking literary glory, he lives his ideas. Hence we are scarcely surprised to read his "propositions" on the social organization of the universe in which his linguistic extremism is transformed into a Fourierism just as pure: "Introduce an innovation into the possession of land by recognizing that the owned surface each individual can enjoy cannot be less than the surface of the entire globe. Thus are resolved the quarrels between states."

And again: "Transformation of rental rights, the right to be the owner of a room in any city with the right to change location at any time (right to private lodgings of spatial determination). Humanity on the move does not limit its property rights to a single site."

And finally: "To require of armed alliances of men that they contest the futurians' opinion which says that the entire terrestrial globe belongs to them."

1969

I3

Art according to Artaud

Artaud said what he "meant" so well and so abundantly that one might wonder if it is not superfluous to interpose an exegesis between his text and his readers—past or still to come. To ask this question is to raise at the same time the whole problematics linked to the status of what we call these days "a reading."

Indeed a docile commentary, whose limit is paraphrase, is scarcely justified with regard to a text whose initial comprehension does not raise excessive difficulties. But the converse danger is still more disturbing: by avoiding the very specific, we risk encountering the too general, risk depriving the glossed text of its particularity; the text then turns into a simple example of an abstract and anonymous schema. This danger is elicited, in the form of a characteristic denial, in the two best commentaries on Artaud. In *Le Livre à venir*, Maurice Blanchot writes: "It would be tempting to compare what Artaud tells us with what we are told by Hölderlin and Mallarmé. . . . But we must resist the temptation of too-general assertions. Every poet speaks the same, yet it is not the same but the unique that we hear." And Jacques Derrida, in *L'Ecriture et la différence*, examines at length what he calls "the violence of exemplification" and begins his reading by a refusal to "constitute Artaud as an example of what he teaches us"; yet he ends his reading by testifying to a certain failure ("the violence of exemplification, that very violence we were unable to avoid precisely when we had hoped to protect ourselves against it").

A reading can be constituted only by avoiding this double danger, paraphrase and exemplification. It will be respectful of the text, in its very literality, but at the same time will not be content with its apparent order, striving rather to re-establish the textual system. It will proceed by choice, displacement, superposition—all operations which upset the immediately observable organization of a discourse. In order to articulate this system, we shall be led to translate into different terms certain elements which constitute it. We shall seek a fidelity not to the letter, nor moreover to a hypothetical "spirit," but to the principle of the letter. In doing so, however, we shall know that a reading succeeds in averting one of the symmetrical dangers jeopardizing it only by making itself vulnerable with regard to the other; for us, a reading is a boundary line rather than a territory.

I shall confine myself, here, to a less complex substance than Artaud's writings as a whole; it is the theoretical texts I am concerned with, those he produced between 1931 and 1935, in other words *The Theatre and Its Double* and the texts which accompany it. This is already an extremely important choice: first because the texts of this period are relatively homogeneous and therefore keep us from raising any problem of development. Second, and more serious, this period is probably the only one in which we can isolate the "theoretical texts" from the "remainder" or, one might say, the "work" from the "life." For it is precisely Artaud who makes this division (and so many others) impossible. In him, the split between the flesh and the Word does not exist. Imprisoned by our traditional categories, we are puzzled by his writings, which we would read, sometimes, as "documents" of his life," sometimes as a "theory," sometimes as "works." The text of *The Theatre and Its Double,* however, allows us to put the other aspects of this production between provisional parentheses, and to consider it solely as theory. We shall question it from the perspective of that ambiguous concept (called into question by Artaud himself) which seems to us to have a strategic utility here: *Art.*

Artaud's reflection on the theatre can be summarized in a formula much more accessible today than forty years ago, but which teaches us nothing if we are satisfied by its brevity: the theatre must be considered as a language. This assertion constantly recurs throughout *The Theatre and Its Double;* from that text I shall quote only one formulation, to be found in the description of the Balinese theatre: "from their labyrinth of gestures, attitudes, sudden cries, their articulation of sweeping gestures which leave no part of the stage space unused, emerges the meaning of a new physical language based on signs and no longer on words." The theatre is a different language from the one we use every day; to circumscribe this difference is to understand the meaning of Artaud's formula—theatre and language enter into a relation not of analogy but of contiguity. A certain language, verbal language, has caused the death of the theatre; another language, *symbolic*[1] language, can effect its rebirth.

We must therefore begin by interrogating verbal language or, more precisely, "Occidental Ideas about Speech." The principal charge—of which the others are merely ramifications—is as follows: this language is the result of an action, instead of being the action itself. Verbal language, as we conceive it in the Occident, is merely the conclusion of a process, as the corpse is the conclusion of a life, and we must get rid of this cadaverous conception of language: "By nature, and because of their determined character, being fixed once and for all, [words] arrest and paralyze thought instead of permitting and favoring its development." The creation of language is cut off from its result, words. In the theatre, this "cutting" is symbolized by the role given to the *written* word—a thing which even in its signifier is only an immutable result and not an action: "For the theatre, as it is practiced today, a written word has as much value as the same word spoken. . . . Everything which concerns the specific utterance of a word, the vibration which it can send through space, escapes us." If we can thus readily reduce the difference which

---

[1] This term is not to be found in Artaud, who prefers to speak of "spatial" language, "concrete" language.

exists between a present and an absent speech-act (speech-act being, moreover, only a part of the creation of language), it i because we are accustomed to identify language with the iso lated and fixed utterance.

Interrogation of verbal language defines, *a contrario*, sym bolic language (of which the theatre is the best example): a lan guage not separated from its becoming, from its own creation Whereas verbal language is content to be the final point in a process, symbolic language will be a trajectory between the necessity to signify and its result: "Theatre occurs precisely a the point where the mind *needs* a language in order to produce its manifestations." This new "language starts from the *neces sity* of speech rather than from an already formed speech. . . . It re-creates poetically the trajectory which has concluded in the *creation of language*." We now see that we must under stand creation in a much broader sense than the *speech-act* which creates a sentence, in an already existing language; cre ation is the constitution of language itself. Hence the first char acteristic of symbolic languages—and especially of the theatre— is that they possess no system of pre-established signs; speaking a symbolic language signifies precisely inventing it, hence repe tition will be the limit of art.

Nonetheless the speech-act mimics creation and derives a privilege from such mimicry. Whence the attention Artaud pays to the spoken word; whence too his preference for what—by the explicit intervention of two interlocutors—in writing comes clos est to speech: the letter addressed to someone. A remarkable number of writings in Artaud's *oeuvre* take the form of letters, from the "Correspondence with Jacques Rivière" to the "Letters from Rodez." And Artaud explains this preponderance: "Let me send you an article in the form of a letter. It is the only means I have of combating an absolutely paralyzing feeling of futility and of formulating what I have to say, though I've been think ing about it for more than a month. . . ."

This first constitutive feature of symbolic language (that "the signs will be invented as they are needed") may surprise those who use the term language in its classical meaning. Its pole of attraction is no longer Order but Chaos: "Stage language, if it exists and if it is to be formed, will be by nature destructive, threatening, anarchic, it will evoke chaos." Now verbal language is a principle of organization and classification, as a consequence of what subtends its functioning: repetition. It will therefore be upon repetition, specifically, that Artaud's severest condemnation falls: "Let us leave the criticism of texts to the schoolmasters, the criticism of forms to the esthetes, and realize that what has been said is to be said no longer; that an expression has no validity more than once; that any uttered speech is dead and acts only at the moment of its utterance, that a utilized form no longer serves, and only obliges the search for another, and that the theatre is the only place in the world where a gesture once made is never made again."

It might be thought that this virulent rejection of repetition is equivalent to a praise of improvisation, especially since Artaud will also say: "This language . . . derives its effectiveness from its spontaneous creation on the stage." Moreover, he denies that supremacy of the author in the theatre whose result is that the spectacle becomes a mere reflection of the text (and the reflection of a dead man is not alive either): "The author is the one who possesses the language of speech and . . . the director is his slave. . . . Hence we renounce the theatre's superstition of the text and the writer's dictatorship." In other words, no prewritten text. But improvisation finds no favor in Artaud's eyes either: "My productions will have nothing to do with Copeau's improvisations. However deep they plunge into the concrete, into the external, however powerfully they take root in an open-air nature and not in the closed rooms of the brain, they are not for all that surrendered to the actor's ignorant and irresponsible inspiration." We must not confuse "ignorant inspiration," which is nothing but the projection of an unconscious text, with the freedom Artaud is seeking.

This apparent contradiction can be found within the limits of a single sentence: "The spectacles will be created directly on the stage . . . which does not mean that they will not be rigorously composed and established once and for all before being acted." The spectacle must be neither spontaneous nor prewritten: here is another opposition which loses its pertinence in Artaud's eyes. A language which invents itself as it proceeds is irreconcilable with the notion of a pre-text; but for it to be a language, its functioning must be governed by a mathematical precision. This precision can be achieved only through a slow onstage elaboration which, once completed, must be notated: "These images, these movements, these dances, these rites, this music, these truncated melodies, these broken-off dialogues will be carefully notated and described, as much as is possible in words and chiefly in the nonspoken parts of the performance, the principle being to notate or encode, as in a musical score, what cannot be described in words." Thus a *post*-text will cut short any attempt at improvisation.

Now let us return to the description of symbolic language and attempt to indicate its specific features. And first of all its signifier, particularly rich in the theatre (it is in this regard, among others, that the theatre is privileged in relation to the other arts); Artaud has listed, on several occasions, its elements: "All the means of expression usable on the stage, such as music, dance, pantomime, mimicry, gesticulations, intonations, architecture, lighting, and setting." The theatre must make use of this multiple signifier; "the theatre's fixation within *one* language—written words, music, light, noises—indicates its imminent death, the choice of a language proving one's taste for the expediency of that language." But—a new dichotomy canceled by Artaud—this multiplicity of signifiers does not signify a plurality of languages; quite the contrary, theatre-as-language can be constituted only if, within it, music ceases to be music, painting, painting, dance dance: "It would be pointless to say that theatre-as-language calls upon music, dance, or pantomime. Obviously it uses movements, harmonies, rhythms, but only insofar as they contribute to a kind of central expression, without benefit to any particular art." The signifier must be simultaneously various and single; we might describe the specific feature of symbolic language as the *overflow* off the signifier, a superabundance (and an overdetermination) of what signifies in relation to what is signified.

To attain a "mathematical calculation" in the use of symbolic anguage, we must inventory it, that is, scrupulously account for ach of its signifying layers. Artaud has already sketched out uch a program. Hence for pantomime and gesture: "Those housand and one expressions of the face, caught in the form of nasks, can be labeled and catalogued with a view to partici-ating directly and symbolically in this concrete language of the tage." Hence for lighting: "In order to produce qualities of par-icular tones, we must reintroduce into light an element of ten-ousness, of density, of opacity, with a view to producing varmth, cold, anger, fear, and so forth." Hence above all for reathing, to which he devotes several texts: "It is clear that to ach feeling, each movement of the mind, each impulse of uman affectivity corresponds an appropriate kind of breath-ng."

The signifier of symbolic language is different from that of erbal language; the same is true of the signified: neither one peaks of the "same thing." "The thoughts expressed by [this hysical, concrete language] escape articulate speech"; "in the ealm of thought and of intelligence [there are] attitudes which vords are unable to assume and which gestures and everything articipating in spatial language achieves with more precision han words are capable of."

What are these two distinct signifieds? That of verbal lan-guage is well known: it is irreplaceable in order to "elucidate a characteristic, to recount the human thoughts of a character, to et forth clear and specific states of consciousness"; in short, it s everything we can designate as "psychology." Obviously des-gnation of the signified of symbolic language in words is much more difficult, and Artaud several times evokes this difficulty ("I onfess it has been difficult for me to specify *in words* the kind of extraverbal language I want to create"). This is why we must be content here with general indications, such as the "things of the intelligence," "feelings, moods, metaphysical ideas," or again "ideas, attitudes of the mind, aspects of nature." We shall not betray Artaud's thought if we say that this signified is rather of a "metaphysical" order. Two semantic networks seem to be woven into this opposition: repetition, psychology, verbality in one, alternating with difference, metaphysics, nonverbality in the other. We shall elsewhere encounter an inverted distribution of repetition and difference.

The relation between signifier and signified is not the same in verbal language and in symbolic language. In verbal language this relation is purely abstract or, as we say today, arbitrary: there is no particular reason for certain sounds, certain graphic signs to evoke one idea rather than another. In symbolic language, on the other hand, the ideas evoked must "set up a whole system of natural analogies." What is a natural analogy? Here is the example Artaud gives: "This language represents night by a tree in which a bird that has already closed one eye begins to close the other." Night represented by the sleeping bird is, in rhetorical terms, a synecdoche; the relation between the two is motivated (the part for the whole). Or again, here is the evocation of Balinese actors: "The actors with their costumes compose a series of living and moving hieroglyphs." The actor ceases to be a complete presence, he is the sign which refers to an absence; nor is this absence a word—just as night an appellation for the sake of convenience, was not a word in the preceding case. The characteristic property of the hieroglyph is altogether different: it is the relation of analogy between the signifier and the signified, between the graphic image and the idea.

Artaud does not use the term *metaphor* (probably associating it with a gratuitous estheticism); but resemblance (analogy) and contiguity (synecdoche) form the matrix of all rhetorical figures. These would then be nothing but an inventory of the possible relations between signifiers and signifieds in symbolic languages. This, in any case, is Artaud's postulate: "I take objects, things in space, as images, as words which I assemble and which I make correspond to one another according to the laws of symbolism and living analogies. Eternal laws which are those of all poetry and of all viable language; and among other things those of Chinese ideograms and ancient Egyptian hieroglyphs." Rhetorical figures are the code of symbolism, according to Artaud.

The analogical principle explains Artaud's efforts to discover the theatre's "doubles" (especially in the articles at the beginning of *The Theatre and Its Double*): the plague, the painting of Lucas van Leyden, alchemy. "The theatre . . . like the plague . . . re-establishes the link between what is and what is not"; "this painting is what the theatre should be"; "further, there is a higher resemblance between the theatre and alchemy." This principle seems so essential to him that it determines the title of his book: "This title will account for all the theatre's doubles which I believe I have found over the years: metaphysics, the plague, cruelty."

We must not confuse the relation between signifier and signified with the relation between sign and referent. Whereas the former must be reinforced by analogy, the latter must, on the contrary, be denaturalized; we must break down the automatism which makes us take the word for the thing, makes us consider one as the natural product of the other. The relation, Artaud reminds us, is purely arbitrary: "We must admit that everything, in the intended purpose of an object, in the meaning or use of a natural form, everything is a matter of convention. Nature, when it has given a tree the form of a tree, might just as well have given it the form of an animal or of a hill, we would have thought *tree* in the presence of the animal or the hill, and the trick would have been played." The function of symbolic language is to make this arbitrariness evident: "Whereby it may be understood that poetry is anarchic insofar as it calls into question every relation between objects and between forms and their significations." Thus from another angle symbolic language again verges upon Chaos. The analogy established within the sign destroys the false analogies outside it: "Poetry is a dissociative and anarchic power which by analogy, associations, images lives entirely on the destruction of known relations."

A language which is not isolated from the process of its creation; a signifier which is multiple, "overflowing," and concrete; a metaphysical signified, which cannot be designated by words; an analogical relation between signifier and signified—such as the main characteristics of "symbolic language," more precisely of the arts, still more particularly of the theatre. All these properties are revealed by an opposition to verbal language. Yet, as Artaud observes elsewhere, it is not impossible to use verbal language *like* a symbolic language. There is less difference, as we have already seen, between two independent types of language than between two conceptions of language ("Oriental" and "Occidental"), and consequently between two uses (or functions) of language. Artaud will write: "Alongside this logical meaning, words will be taken in an incantatory, truly magical sense—for their form, for their sensuous emanations, and no longer for their meaning alone." Hence it is enough to accentuate the *magical* rather than the logical function of verbal language for it to have its place among the other symbolic systems.

How is this transformation brought about? By instituting all the properties we have just listed, and also by *concretizing* the signifier. Language used in its logical function tends to efface the signifier, to replace real sounds by abstract ones. In order to make the magical function appear,[2] we must "return to some degree to the active, respiratory sources of language, we must once again link words to the physical movements which once generated them, and the logical and discursive aspect of speech must give way to its physical and affective aspect, that is, words, instead of being taken for what they mean grammatically, must be understood in their phonic aspect, must be perceived as movements." Here the signifier regains an autonomy of which it has been stripped by the logical use of language: "Sounds, noises, cries are sought first of all for their vibratory quality, and subsequently for what they represent." This is why, in his descriptions of the actor's work, Artaud always insists on the elaboration of pure sound: "He trains his voice. He uses vibrations, different registers. He mutilates rhythms, he mashes sounds."

Thus a double process is instituted. On the one hand, actor, decor, gesture lose their opaque materiality, cease being a

---

[2] But to restore to language its "magical efficacy" is at the same time to renounce another "Occidental" conception according to which language is opposed to action. Yet as Artaud says, "The magical state is what leads to action." This would be the last specific feature of symbolic languages: they recover, "in a material, immediately effective mode, the meaning of a certain ritual and religious action." Language is action.

present substance in order to become a sign. On the other hand—but in this same movement—the sign ceases to be abstract, it is not a simple reference but becomes a substance whose physicality arrests our attention. Nothing is more precious to Artaud in this vision of theatrical language than "the revelatory aspect of matter which seems suddenly to explode into signs in order to teach us the metaphysical identity of the concrete and the abstract." Symbolic language (theatre) abolishes the opposition of these two categories, it must become "a kind of experimental demonstration of the profound identity of the concrete and the abstract."

This is not the first dichotomy which Artaud's text renders null and void. The man and the work, the one and the many, the prescribed and the improvised, the abstract and the concrete—all are oppositions which his thought refuses to admit. This is no accident; oppositional structure characterizes verbal language and the logic it engenders. "This" and "the opposite" are no longer pertinent, on the other hand, for symbolic language; the laws of identity and of the excluded middle do not function here. Further, it is in the very nature of symbolic language to combat oppositional logic, incessantly to reiterate the oxymoron, "to resolve by conjunctions unimaginable and alien to our still waking minds, to resolve or even to annihilate every conflict produced by the antagonism of matter and spirit, of idea and form, of the concrete and the abstract. . . ."

A similar dichotomy is pulverized in the answer Artaud gives to another great question: why art? (whereas all the preceding can be considered as the answer to what is art?). Art for art's sake, art outside of life, is a purely "Occidental" and limited notion; "we have reached the point where we attribute to art no more than a recreational value, where we oblige it to abide by a purely formal utilization of forms." This absurd limitation of art must cease; "we are all sick and tired of the purely digestive forms of the today's theatre, which is no more than a kind of futile toying"; "if there remains anything hellish and truly accursed in this day and age, it is to dally artistically with forms instead of being something like victims who are to be burned and who make signs above their pyres." Note moreover that the realistic conception (art as imitation of life) is merely a variant of the model of art for art's sake: both maintain the isolation of art from "life."

But the converse attitude, which subjects art to specific goals, is just as untenable: "We need authentic action, but without practical consequences. It is not on the social level that the theatre's action has its effect. Still less on the moral and psychological level." To make the theatre subservient to political objectives is to betray both the theatre and politics. Here is a text of Artaud's which leaves no doubt as to his position on this problem: "I believe in the authentic action of the theatre, but not on the level of life. It is needless to say, then, that I consider futile all the recent experiments in Germany, Russia, or America, to make the theatre *serve* certain immediate social and revolutionary ends. However novel the methods employed, because they consent to and *desire* subservience to the strictest *données* of dialectical materialism, because they turn their backs upon metaphysics which they scorn, such efforts remain a mise-en-scène in the crudest and most literal sense of the phrase." This action—to produce a subservient theatre—is charged with an ideology independent of (and more powerful than) the ideology which such a theatre seeks to defend. To make the theatre *serve* (whatever goal) is to produce a mise-en-scène, a staging in the limited and narrow sense which Occidental tradition has given this expression; it is thereby to accept all the presuppositions of that tradition, which in fact crush the very thing the theatre was supposed to serve.

At the time of *The Theatre and Its Double,* moreover, this idea was not a new one for Artaud. Some years earlier he had vehemently broken with the Surrealists, reproaching them precisely for subordinating art to immediate political objectives and thereby keeping it a prisoner of an oppressive metaphysical tradition: "Surrealism surely died the day Breton and his adepts decided to join the Communists and seek in the realm of facts and immediate substance the fulfillment of an action which normally could occur only in the intimate confines of the brain," Artaud wrote in 1927.

Art is to be neither gratuitous nor utilitarian; the two terms of this false alternative are to be discarded, and we must become aware of art's essential function—which is, Artaud writes, metaphysical. Far from being satisfied by a pure play of forms or by a modification in the external material conditions of mankind, the theatre must strive to affect and to change human beings at their deepest levels: "The theatre must pursue, by every means, a questioning, not only of all aspects of the objective and descriptive external world, but of the internal world, that is, of man considered metaphysically." The theatre "must strive to reach the deep regions of the individual and to produce there a kind of real, though hidden alteration, of which he will perceive the consequences only afterward." Art is not to *represent* life; in what is most essential about life, art must *be* life.

This then is the trajectory: art must tend toward a total autonomy, toward an identification with its essence. But once the limit is reached, this essence itself vanishes, and the term *art* no longer has any meaning. To reach the center is to make it disappear; the highest art is nothing but "life" or "metaphysics" (in the sense Artaud gives the word). The way which leads to the greatest effectiveness passes through the most extreme disinterestedness.

The "center" is also undermined in another manner—by the necessary relation existing between symbolic systems and becoming (and, through becoming, chaos): "The highest art is the one which brings us closest to Chaos." Art as a symbolic system rejects the very notion of a stable, hence dead essence; once fixed, such an essence becomes alien to art, which is defined by a renunciation of repose: "Clear ideas are dead ideas." Art is a permanent questioning of its own definition, or again, if we prefer, art is nothing but a desperate quest for its own essence.

1969

14

Narrative Transformations

The knowledge of literature is constantly threatened by two contrary dangers: either we construct a coherent but sterile theory, or we limit ourselves to describing "facts," assuming that each little stone will find its place in the great edifice of science. Take the case of genres. Either we describe the genres "as they have existed" or, more exactly, as critical (metaliterary) tradition has hallowed them—the ode and the elegy "exist" because we find these appellations in the critical discourse of a certain period. But then we abandon all hope of constructing a system of genres. Or else we start from the fundamental properties of the literary phenomenon and declare that their different combinations produce the genres. In this case, we must either remain within a disappointing generality and be content, for instance, with the division into lyric, epic, and dramatic; or else we are faced with the impossibility of explaining the absence of a genre which would have the elegy's rhythmic structure combined with a thematics of joy. Now the aim of a theory of genres is to account for the system of *existing* genres: why these, and not others? The distance between theory and description remains irreducible.

The same is true of the theory of narrative. Up to a certain moment, we possessed no more than observations, sometimes penetrating and invariably chaotic, as to the organization of one narrative or another. Then came Vladimir Propp: starting from one hundred Russian fairy tales, he postulated the structure of narrative (at least this is how his endeavor was understood, for the most part). In the works which followed this essay, much has been done to improve the internal coherence of his hypothesis, much less to fill the gap between his generality and the diversity of particular narratives. The time has come when the most urgent task of the analysis of narrative is to be found precisely between the two: in the *specification* of the *theory,* in the elaboration of "intermediate" categories which no longer describe the general but the generic, no longer the generic but the specific.

I propose, in what follows, to introduce into the analysis of narrative a category—*narrative transformation*—whose status is, precisely, "intermediary." I shall proceed by three stages. By a *reading* of already existing analyses I shall try to show both the absence and the necessity of this category. In a second stage, I shall *describe,* following a systematic order, its functioning and its varieties. Last, I shall briefly evoke, by a few examples, the possible utilizations of the notion of narrative transformation.

But first a few words about the more general context in which this study is to be placed. I maintain the distinction of the verbal, syntactic, and semantic aspects of the text; the transformations discussed here refer to the syntactic aspect. I further distinguish the following *levels* of analysis: predicate (or motive, or function), proposition, sequence, text. The study of each level can be made only in relation to the level hierarchically above it: for example, the study of predicates, in the context of the proposition; that of propositions, in the context of the sequence, and so forth. This rigorous delimitation concerns the analysis and not the object analyzed; it is even possible that the literary text is defined by the impossibility of maintaining the autonomy of the levels. The present analysis deals with narrative, not literary narrative.

Reading

Boris Tomashevsky is the first to have attempted a typology of narrative predicates. He postulates the necessity of "classifying motifs according to the objective action they describe," and he proposes the following dichotomy: "Motifs which change the situation are called dynamic motifs, those which do not change it, static motifs." The same opposition is adopted by A.-J. Greimas, who writes: "We must introduce a division in the class of predicates by postulating a new classificational category, one which takes account of the "static" vs. "dynamic" opposition. According to whether they include the "static" seme or the "dynamic" seme, predicative sememes can supply information about either the state or the processes concerning the agents."

I note here two other similar oppositions, though they are not pertinent on the same level. Propp (following Joseph Bédier) distinguishes constant motifs from variable motifs and calls the former *functions*, the latter *attributes*: "The appellations (and also the attributes) of the characters change, their actions or functions do not change." But the constancy or the variability of a predicate can be established only within a genre (in Propp's case, the Russian fairy tale); it is a generic and not general distinction (here, propositional). As for Roland Barthes's opposition between function and index, it is located on the level of the sequence and therefore concerns propositions, not predicates ("two large classes of functions, distributional and integrative").

The only category we have for describing the variety of predicates is consequently that of static/dynamic, which adopts and makes explicit the grammatical opposition between adjective and verb. We should search in vain for other distinctions, on this same level: it seems that all we can assert about predicates, on the syntactic level, is exhausted by this characteristic: "static/dynamic," "adjective/verb."

Yet if we turn not to theoretical assertions but to analyses of texts, we find that a refinement of predicative typology is possible; further, that it is suggested (though not explicitly formulated) by these very analyses. We shall illustrate this assertion by the reading of a part of Propp's analysis of the Russian fairy tale.

Here is the summary of the primary narrative functions, as analyzed by Propp. "1. One of the members of a family is away from home. 2. A prohibition is imposed upon the hero. 3. The prohibition is violated. 4. The aggressor seeks to gain information. 5. The aggressor receives information about his victim. 6. The aggressor seeks to deceive his victim in order to seize him or his goods. 7. The victim falls into the trap and thereby involuntarily helps his enemy. 8. The aggressor harms one of the members of the family or causes a lack. 9. The harm or lack is announced, and the hero is presented with a demand or an order, is sent away, or is allowed to depart. 10. The searcher agrees to react, or determines to do so. 11. The hero leaves the house," and so forth. As we know, the total number of these functions is thirty-one, and according to Propp each of them is indivisible and incomparable to the others.

Yet if we compare these propositions two by two, we find that the predicates often possess common and opposed features; hence that it is possible to discern underlying categories which define the combination-system of which Propp's functions are the products. Thus we shall turn against Propp himself the reproach he addressed to his precursor A. Veselovsky: the failure to carry the analysis as far as the smallest units (though the reproach will doubtless be turned against us, eventually). This requirement is not a new one; Claude Lévi-Strauss has already written: "It is not impossible that this reduction can be taken still further, and that each part, taken in isolation, is analyzable into a small number of recurrent functions, so that several functions distinguished by Propp would in reality constitute the transformation group of one and the same function." We shall follow this suggestion in the present analysis, but we shall see that the notion of *transformation* here assumes a somewhat different meaning.

The juxtaposition of 1 and 2 already shows us a first difference. Function 1 describes a simple action which has really taken place; 2, on the other hand, evokes two actions simultaneously. If someone in the tale says: "Say nothing to Baba Yaga, should she come" (Propp's example), there is, on the one hand, the possible but not real action of informing Baba Yaga; on the other hand, there is the immediate action of prohibition. In other words, the action of informing (or speaking) is not presented in the indicative mood but as a negative obligation.

If we compare 1 and 3, another difference appears. The fact that one of the members of the family (father, mother) is away from home is different in nature from the fact that one of the children violates the prohibition. The former describes a state which lasts an indefinite time; the latter, a punctual action. In Tomashevsky's terms, the former is a static motif, the latter a dynamic motif: one constitutes the situation; the other modifies it.

If we now compare 4 and 5, we find another possibility of carrying the analysis further. In the former proposition, the aggressor seeks information; in the latter, he obtains it. The common denominator of the two propositions is the action of gaining information, but in the first case it is described as an intention, in the second as a fait accompli.

Functions 6 and 7 present the same case: first there is an effort to deceive, then the deception is effected. But here the situation is more complex, for at the same time that we shift from intention to realization, we slip from the aggressor's viewpoint to the victim's. The same action can be presented from different perspectives—"the aggressor deceives" or "the victim falls into the trap"—it remains nonetheless a single action.

Function 9 permits us another particularization. This proposition does not designate a new action, but the fact that the hero becomes aware of it. Moreover 4 described a similar situation: the aggressor seeks *information*. But to be informed, to learn, to know is a second-degree action, it presupposes another action (or another attribute)—precisely what is learned or discovered.

In 10 we encounter another form already noted: before leaving the house, the hero decides to leave the house. Once again, we cannot put the decision on the same level as the departure, since one presupposes the other. In the first case, action is a desire, an obligation, or an intention; in the second, it actually occurs. Propp also adds that what is involved here is the "beginning of the reaction"; but "to begin" is not an action in and of itself, it is the (inchoative) aspect of another action.

It is not necessary to continue in order to illustrate the principle we are defending. One already glimpses the possibility, in each case, of taking the analysis further. Yet we may note that this criticism emphasizes different aspects of narrative, of which we shall concern ourselves with just one. We shall spend no more time on the failure to distinguish between static and dynamic motifs (adjectives and verbs). Claude Bremond has insisted on another category neglected by Propp (and by Dundes): we must not confuse two different actions with two perspectives of the same action. The *perspectivism* proper to narrative cannot be "reduced," it constitutes, on the contrary, one of narrative's most important characteristics. Or as Bremond writes: "The possibility and the obligation to shift, by conversion of viewpoints, from the perspective of one agent to that of another, are crucial. . . . They imply the disclaimer, on the level of the analysis where we are working, of the notions of 'Hero,' 'Villain,' and so forth, conceived as labels assigned once and for all to the characters. Each agent is his own hero. His partners are described from his perspective as allies, adversaries, and so forth. These qualifications are inverted when we shift from one perspective to another." And in another study: "The same sequence of events admits of different structurations, depending on whether it is construed according to the interests of one or another of its participants."

But it is another viewpoint that I want to consider here. Propp rejects any paradigmatic analysis of narrative. This rejection is formulated explicitly: "It might have been expected that function A would exclude certain other functions, belonging to other tales. It might have been expected that several pivots be obtained, but the pivot is the same for all tales of the marvelous." Or again: "If we read all the functions straight through, we see that one function derives from the previous one by a logical and artistic necessity. We see in fact that no function excludes the other. All belong to the same pivot, and not to several pivots."

It is true that in the course of his analysis, Propp is led to contradict his own principle, but despite a few "wild" paradigmatic remarks, his analysis remains fundamentally syntagmatic. This is what has provoked a reaction—equally inadmissible, as we see it—from certain of his commentators (Lévi-Strauss and Greimas) who deny any pertinence to the syntagmatic order, to succession, and enclose themselves in an equally exclusive paradigmatism. We need quote only one sentence of Lévi-Strauss, "The order of chronological succession is reabsorbed into an atemporal matrical structure," or one of Greimas, "Our reduction has required a paradigmatic and achronic interpretation of the relations among functions, . . . this paradigmatic interpretation, the very condition for grasping the signification of narrative in its totality. . ." For our part, we refuse to choose between one or the other of these perspectives; it would be a pity to deprive the analysis of narrative of the double benefit it can gain from both Propp's syntagmatic studies and Lévi-Strauss' paradigmatic analyses.

In the case which concerns us here, and in order to identify the category of *transformation,* fundamental for a grammar of narrative, we must oppose Propp's rejection of any paradigmatic perspective. Without being identical, the predicates we encounter throughout the syntagmatic chain are comparable, and analysis has everything to gain by emphasizing the relations they sustain among themselves.

Description

I shall note first, for purposes of terminology, that the word "transformation" appears in Propp, with the meaning of a semantic, not a syntactical transformation; that it is to be found in Lévi-Strauss and in Greimas, in a similar but, as we shall see, much more restricted sense; that we find it, finally, in current linguistic theory in a technical sense which is not precisely our own.

Two propositions may be said to be in a relation of transformation when one predicate remains identical on both sides. We shall find ourselves immediately obliged to distinguish between two types of transformations. Let us call the first *simple transformations* (or *specifications*): they consist in modifying (or adding) a certain operator specifying the predicate. The basic predicates can be considered as being endowed with a zero operator. This phenomenon suggests, in language, the process of auxiliation, understood in the broad sense: that is, the case where a verb accompanies the main verb, specifying its sense

("X begins to work"). Yet we must not forget that we are adopting the perspective of a logical and universal grammar, not that of a particular language; we shall not consider ourselves hampered by the fact that in English, for example, this operator might be designated by various linguistic forms: auxiliary verbs, adverbs, or other lexical terms.

The second type will be that of the *complex transformations* (or *reactions*) characterized by the appearance of a second predicate which is grafted on the first and cannot exist independently of it. Whereas in the case of simple transformations there is only one predicate and consequently only one subject, in the case of complex transformations the presence of two predicates permits the existence of one or two subjects. "X thinks he has killed his mother" is—as is "Y thinks X has killed his mother"—a complex transformation of the proposition "X has killed his mother."

We may note here that the derivation described is purely logical, not psychological: we may say that "X decides to kill his mother" is the transformation of "X kills his mother," although psychologically the relation is the converse. "Psychology" intervenes here as an object of knowledge, not as a working tool; complex transformations designate, as we see, psychic operations or the relation between an event and its representation.

The transformation has, apparently, two limits. On the one hand, there is not *yet* a transformation if the change of operator cannot be clearly established. On the other, there is no *longer* a transformation if instead of two "transforms" of one and the same predicate we find two autonomous predicates. The closest case of transformed predicates, and one which we must carefully distinguish, will be that of actions which are *consequences* of each other (a relation of implication, motivation, presupposition). Take the propositions "X hates his mother" and "X kills his mother"; they no longer have a predicate in common, and the relation between the two is not one of transformation. An apparently still closer case is that of actions we designate by causative verbs: "X incites Y to kill his mother," "X makes Y kill his mother." Although such a sentence evokes a complex transformation, we are here dealing with two independent predicates, and with a consequence; the confusion comes from the fact that the first action is entirely bypassed and only its finality is retained (we are not told how X "incites" or "makes").

In order to enumerate the different kinds of transformations, I shall adopt a double hypothesis. First, I shall limit the actions considered to those which the English lexicon codes in the form of completive verbs. Second, in the description of each kind I shall use terms which often coincide with grammatical categories. These two suppositions could be modified without jeopardizing the existence of narrative transformation. The verbs grouped within one type of transformation are united by the relation between the basic predicate and the transformed predicate. They are separated, however, by the presuppositions implied in their meaning. For example, "X confirms that Y has killed his mother" and "X reveals that Y has killed his mother" perform the same transformation of description but "to confirm" presupposes that this fact was already known, "to reveal" presupposes that X is the first to assert it.

Simple transformations

1. *Transformations of mode.* Language expresses these transformations concerning the possibility, the impossibility, or the necessity of an action by modal verbs such as *ought* and *may,* or by one of their substitutes. Prohibition, very frequent in narrative, is a negative necessity. An example of the action will be: "X must commit a crime."

2. *Transformations of intention.* In this case, we indicate the intention of the subject of the proposition to perform an action, and not the action itself. This operator is formulated in language by the intermediary of such verbs as: *try, intend, premeditate.* Example: "X plans to commit a crime."

3. *Transformations of result.* Whereas in the preceding case the action was seen in the nascent state, the present type of transformations formulates the action as already accomplished. In English we designate such action by verbs like *succeed in, manage to, obtain;* in the Slavic languages, the perfective aspect of the verb denotes the same phenomenon. It is interesting to note that the transformations of intention and of result,

preceding and following the same zero-operator predicate, have already been described by Bremond as "triads"; but this author regards them as independent actions—causally linked—and not as transformations. Our example becomes: "X succeeds in committing a crime."

4. *Transformations of manner*. All the other groups of transformations in this first type might be characterized as "transformations of manner": we specify the manner in which an action occurs. Even so I have isolated two more homogeneous subgroups, uniting under the present rubric rather varied phenomena. Language designates this transformation mainly by adverbs, but we shall frequently find auxiliary verbs performing the same function: thus *dare, excel in, strive*. A relatively coherent group will be formed by the indices of intensity, one form of which is found in the comparative and the superlative. Our example will here become: "X is eager to commit a crime."

5. *Transformations of aspect*. Greimas has already indicated the proximity between adverbs of manner and the aspects of the verb. In English, the aspect finds its least ambiguous expression in auxiliary verbs such as *begin, be in the act of, finish* (inchoative, progressive, terminative). We may note the referential proximity between the inchoative and terminative aspects, and the transformations of intention and of result, but the categorization of the phenomena is different, the ideas of finality and of will being absent here. Other aspects are the durative, the punctual, the iterative, the suspensive.

The example here becomes: "X is beginning to commit a crime."

6. *Transformations of status*. Taking the term "status" in Whorf's sense, we may thus designate the replacement of the positive form of a predicate by the negative form or by the contrary form. As we know, English expresses negation by "not," and opposition by a lexical substitution. This group of transformations was already pointed out, very briefly, by Propp; it is to the same type of operation that Lévi-Strauss in particular refers when he speaks of transformations ("we may treat 'violation' as the converse of 'prohibition,' and the latter as a negative transformation of 'injunction' "); he is followed by Greimas, who

relies on the logical models described by Brøndal and Blanché. Our example becomes: "X does not commit a crime."

Complex transformations

1. *Transformations of appearance.* We turn to the second major type of transformations, those which produce not a specification of the initial predicate but the adjunction of a derived action upon the first action. The transformations which I call "of appearance" indicate the replacement of one predicate by another, this latter being able to pass for the former without actually being it. In English, we designate such a transformation by the verbs *feign, pretend, claim;* such actions are based, as we see, on the distinction between being and seeming, absent in certain cultures. In all these cases, the action of the first predicate is not realized. Our example will be: "X (or Y) pretends that X is committing a crime."

2. *Transformations of knowledge.* Alongside these deceptions, we can conceive of a type of transformations which in fact describe gaining consciousness of the action denoted by another predicate. Verbs such as *observe, learn, guess, know, ignore* describe the different phases and modalities of knowledge. Propp had already noted the autonomy of these actions, but without granting it much importance. In this case, the subject of the two verbs is habitually different. But it is not impossible to keep the same subject, as in stories about a loss of memory, unconscious actions, and so on. Our example thus becomes: "X (or Y) learns that X has committed a crime."

3. *Transformations of description.* This group is also to be found in a complementary relation with the transformations of knowledge; it unites the actions destined to provoke knowledge. In English a subgroup of "verbs of speech" most often appears in this function: constative verbs, performative verbs signifying autonomous actions, such as *to recount, to say, to explain.* The example will then be: "X (or Y) reports that X has committed a crime."

4. *Transformations of supposition.* A subgroup of descriptive verbs refers to actions not yet performed, hence *foresee, anticipate, suspect, expect.* Here we are dealing with prediction; in

opposition to the other transformations, the action designated by the main predicate is located in the future, not in the present or in the past. We may note that various transformations can denote common elements of situation. For example, the transformations of mode, intention, appearance, and supposition all imply that the event denoted by the main proposition has not occurred, but each time a different category is employed. Here the example has become: "X (or Y) foresees that X will commit a crime."

5. *Transformations of subjectivation.* Here we move into another sphere—whereas the four preceding transformations dealt with relations between discourse and object of discourse, knowledge and object of knowledge, the following transformations relate to the attitude of the subject of the proposition. Transformations of subjectivation refer to actions denoted by such verbs as *believe, think, consider.* Such a transformation does not really modify the main proposition, but attributes it, as an observation, to some subject: "X (or Y) thinks that X has committed a crime." We may note that the initial proposition can be true or false: I can believe in something which has not actually occurred. We are thereby introduced to the problematics of the "narrator" and of the "point of view:" Whereas "X has committed a crime" is a proposition which is not presented in the name of any particular person (but of the omniscient author—or reader), "X (or Y) thinks X has committed a crime" is the trace left by the same event in an individual.

6. *Transformations of attitude.* I refer by this term to descriptions of the state provoked in the subject by the main action in the course of its duration. Close to the transformations of manner, transformations of attitude are distinguished from them by the fact that here the additional information concerns the subject, whereas in the case of the transformations of manner it concerns the predicate. In the present case, then, we are concerned with a new predicate and not with an operator specifying the first one. This is what is expressed by such verbs as *delight, loathe, despise.* Our example becomes: "X enjoys committing a crime" or "Y is disgusted that X should commit a crime." The transformations of attitude, like those of knowledge

or of subjectivation, are particularly frequent in what we conventionally call the "psychological novel."

Three remarks before concluding this brief enumeration:

First, it is extremely common, we observe, that conjunctions of several transformations are designated by a single word in the lexicon of a language; from this we must not be led to assume the indivisibility of the operation itself. For example, the actions of *condemning* or *congratulating* can be decomposed into a judgment of value and an act of speech (transformations of attitude and of description).

Second, it is nonetheless impossible at present to explain the existence of these particular transformations, and the absence of all others; nor would this be even desirable before further observations are accumulated. The categories of truth, knowledge, utterance, futurity, subjectivity, and judgment, which permit us to delimit the groups of complex transformations, are certainly not independent of one another; additional constraints doubtless govern the functioning of the "trans-forms." We can here merely suggest these directions of investigation and hope they will be followed.

Third, a methodological problem of primary importance, which we have deliberately avoided, is that of the transition between the observed text and our descriptive terms. This problem is particularly acute today in literary analysis, where the substitution for a part of the present text by a term which does not figure there always provokes accusations of sacrilege. A similar split seems to be forming here between two tendencies in the analysis of narrative: one, a propositional or semic analysis, elaborates its units; the other, a lexical analysis, finds them ready-made in the text. Here again, only further investigations will prove the greater utility of one method or the other.

Application

The application of the notion of transformation in the description of narrative predicates seems to me to require no commentary. Another obvious application is the possibility of characterizing texts by the quantitative or qualitative predominance of one or another type of transformations. We often criticize the analysis of narrative for being incapable of accounting for the complexity of literary texts. Now the notion of transformation permits us both to surmount this objection and to establish the bases of a typology of texts. I have tried to show, for example, that *The Quest of the Holy Grail* was characterized by the role which two types of transformations played in it: on the one hand, all events which occur are announced in advance; on the other, once they have occurred they receive a new interpretation, in a particular symbolic code. In another example, the tales of Henry James, I have tried to indicate the role of transformations of knowledge: they dominate and determine the linear movement of the narrative. In speaking of typology, we must, of course, realize that a typology of texts will be multidimensional, and that the transformations correspond to a single dimension.

We can take as another example of application a problem of the theory of narrative already discussed: the definition of the narrative sequence. The notion of transformation permits us to cast some light upon this problem, if not to solve it.

Several representatives of Russian Formalism have attempted to define the sequence. Shklovsky does so in his study "The Construction of the Story and of the Novel." He asserts first of all the existence, in each of us, of a faculty of judgment (we might say, today, of a competence) permitting us to decide if a narrative sequence is complete or not. "A simple image, a mere parallel, or even the description of an event is not enough to give the impression that we are reading a story. . . . It is clear that the passages quoted are not stories; this impression does not depend on their dimensions. . . . We have the impression that the story is not finished." This "impression" is thus incontestable, but Shklovsky does not succeed in making it explicit and declares his failure from the start: "I cannot yet say what quality should characterize the motif, nor how the motifs must combine in order that we obtain a subject [that is, a plot]." If we nonetheless turn to the particular analyses he makes after this declaration, we shall see that the solution, though not formulated, is already present in his text.

In effect, following each example analyzed, Shklovsky formulates the rule which seems to him to function in the specific case. Thus: "The tale requires not only action but also reaction, it requires a lack of coincidence." "The motif of a false impossibility is also based on a contradiction. In a prediction, for instance, this contradiction is established between the intentions of the characters who strive to avoid the prediction and the fact that it comes true (the motif of Oedipus)." "We are first presented with an inescapable situation, then with a witty solution. The tales in which a riddle is proposed and solved belong to the same case." "This kind of motif implies the following sequence: the innocent is capable of being accused, is accused, and is finally acquitted." "This completed character derives from the fact that after we have been deceived by a false recognition, the true situation is revealed. Hence the formula is respected." "This new motif appears parallel to the preceding narrative, as a result of which the tale seems completed."

We may summarize these six particular cases, analyzed by Shklovsky, in the following way; a complete sequence requires the existence of two elements. We may transcribe them as follows:

(1) relation of characters —relation of characters inverted
(2) prediction —realization of the prediction
(3) riddle proposed —riddle solved
(4) false accusation —accusation dismissed
(5) distorted presentation of the facts —correct presentation of the facts
(6) motif —parallel motif

We now see what notion would have allowed Shklovsky to unify these six particular cases into a "formula": it is, precisely, transformation. A sequence implies the existence of two distinct situations each of which can be described with the help of a small number of propositions; between at least one proposition of each situation there must exist a relation of transformation. We can in fact recognize the groups of transformations identified above. In case (1), it is a transformation of status: positive/negative; in (2), a transformation of supposition: prediction/realization; in (3), (4), and (5), a transformation of knowledge: ignorance or error are replaced by correct knowledge; in (6), finally, we are dealing with a transformation of manner: more or less intense. We may add that there also exist narratives of zero-transformation: those in which the effort to modify the preceding situation fails (though its presence is necessary for us to be able to speak of a sequence, and of narrative).

Such a formula is obviously very general: its usefulness is that it proposes a context for the study of all narrative. It allows us to unify narratives, not to distinguish them; in order to proceed to this latter task, we must inventory the various means which narrative possesses of varying this formula. Without going into detail, let us say that this specification functions in two ways: by addition and by subdivision. On the functional level, this same opposition corresponds to *optional* and *alternative* propositions: in the first case, the proposition appears or does not; in the second, at least one of the alternative propositions must be found in the sequence. Of course, the very nature of the transformation already specifies the type of sequence.

Finally we might inquire if the notion of transformation is purely a descriptive artifice or if it allows us, more essentially, to understand the very nature of narrative. I incline to the second answer, and here is why. Narrative is constituted in the tension of two formal categories, difference and resemblance; the exclusive presence of one of them brings us into a type of discourse which is not narrative. If the predicates do not change, we are not yet within narrative, but in the immobility of psittacism; yet if the predicates do not resemble each other, we find ourselves beyond narrative, in an ideal reportage entirely consisting of differences. The simple relation of successive facts does not constitute a narrative: these facts must be organized, which is to say, ultimately, that they must have elements in common. But if all the elements are in common, there is no longer a narrative, for there is no longer anything to recount. Now, transformation represents precisely a synthesis of differences and resemblance, it links two facts without their being able to be identified. Rather than a "two-sided unit," it is an operation in two directions: it asserts both resemblance and difference; it engages and suspends time, in a single movement; it permits discourse to acquire a meaning without this meaning becoming pure information; in a word, it makes narrative possible and yields us its very definition.

1969

15

How to Read?

By an endeavor which contradicts my title only in appearance, I should like to discuss here the modalities and means of
writing when writing takes the literary text as its object. Rather
than a general theory of understanding and of exegesis, it is the
description of a praxis, making and unmaking itself from day to
day, which I shall undertake. The description will be organized,
like any other, according to the requirements of an order, this
one nonetheless prejudices the answer I can reach only at the
end of this text. The answer thus precedes the question, and to
write on "how to read?" implies that we renounce any return to
an absolute beginning.

To begin, let us rehearse a few commonplaces.
I shall call *projection* a "first" activity upon the literary text
(the quotation marks signify that this activity is first in my order
only), which has been strongly and frequently attacked for over
a century, especially outside of France, but which continues to
dominate institutions, in France as elsewhere. The projective
attitude is defined by a conception of the literary text as a transposition starting from an original series. The author has given a
first transition, from the original to the work; it is now up to the
critic to conduct us along the inverse path, to come full circle by
returning to the original. There will be as many projections as

here are acceptations of what constitutes the origin. If we believe it is the author's life, we obtain a biographical or (primitive) psychoanalytic projection: the work is a means of gaining
access to "the man." If we postulate that the original is constituted by the social reality contemporary with the appearance of
the book or with the events represented in it, we are dealing
with sociological criticism (or projection), in all its varieties. Finally, when the presumed point of departure is "the human
mind" in its atemporal properties, we are dealing with a philosophical or an anthropological projection (though there are
many more than one!). But whatever such a reader's idea of the
nature of the original, he always participates in the same reduc-
tionist and instrumentalist attitude toward the text.

Let us designate by the word *commentary* a second attitude,
complementary and opposed to the first. Stemming from the difficulties raised by the immediate comprehension of certain
texts, commentary is defined by its interiority to the work discussed: it seeks to illuminate meaning, not to translate. The
commentator refuses to omit anything from the text-as-object,
just as he banishes any addition which may have been grafted
upon it; fidelity is both his guiding principle and the criterion of
his success. The limit of commentary is paraphrase (whose limit
is reiteration), commentary is infinitely specific, whence, probably, the absence of a theory of commentary (in this sense of the
word). Under the name *explication de texte*, it has constituted
the fundamental exercise of literary instruction in France, for
many decades. Its limited ambitions assure it a relative invul-
nerability—relative, but paid for at a very high cost.

We mount one step when we approach a third type of work
on the text, which we may call *poetics*. The object of poetics is
constituted by the properties of literary discourse. Particular
works are instances exemplifying these very properties. Poetics
is—distantly—related to projection. Both regard the individual
work as a product, but the resemblance ends there: in the case
of projection, the text is produced by a heterogeneous series
(the life of the author, social conditions, the properties of the
human mind). For poetics, on the other hand, the text is the
product of a fictive and yet existing mechanism, literature. Thus

the object of Aristotle's *Poetics* is not a certain poem by Homer or a certain tragedy by Aeschylus, but tragedy or epic.

The discourse of *poetics* is no newer than that of projection or commentary; yet our century has witnessed a renaissance of studies in poetics, linked to several critical schools: Russian Formalism, the German morphological school, Anglo-American New Criticism, structural studies in France (in the order of their appearance). These critical schools (whatever the divergences among them) are situated on a level qualitatively different from that of any other critical tendency, insofar as they do not seek to name the meaning of the text, but to describe its constitutive elements. Thereby, the procedure of poetics is related to what we may one day call "the science of literature." In 1919 Jakobson summarized in a concise formula what constitutes the point of departure for poetics: "If literary studies seek to become a science, they must acknowledge the device as their sole personage." Much more than by works, the object of poetics will be constituted by literary "devices"—which is to say, by concepts which describe the functioning of literary discourse.

The end point of a study in poetics is always the "general," that is, literature or one of its subdivisions (genres): whether it starts from the analysis of a particular work, or whether it stays within the field of theoretical discourse, and independent of the fact that the very course of the study will most often consist in a continual oscillation between the analyzed text and theory. Indeed, as is readily seen, a converse endeavor, from the general to the particular, can have only a didactic interest. By locating the universal features of literature within an individual work, we merely illustrate, to infinity, premises we will have already posited. A study in poetics, on the contrary, must come to conclusions which complete or modify the initial premises.

Poetics has been reproached for its inattention to the specificity of the individual text and for its concern to define and study abstract concepts which have no perceptible existence. This objection participates, historically, in an attitude which has already wrought considerable havoc upon literary criticism and which we shall call, for lack of a better term, the ostrich attiude. To deny the legitimacy of a general theory of literature has never been equivalent to the absence of such a theory, but only to the prejudice which leads to not making such a theory explicit, not inquiring as to the status of the concepts employed. The moment we produce a discourse on literature, we rely, willy-nilly, on a general conception of the literary text; poetics is the site where this conception is elaborated. On the theoretical level, this reproach echoes a confusion very familiar to the history of science: that between the real object and the object of knowledge.

But if we would avoid incurring the objection that there is no longer any place for the study of the particular work, we must posit, alongside poetics, a different activity which it will be convenient to call *reading*. A reading's object is the singular text; its goal, to dismantle the system of that text. A reading consists in relating each element of the text to all the others, these being inventoried not in their general signification but with a view to this unique usage. In theory, of course, such a reading verges upon the impossible. It strives, with the help of language, to grasp the work as pure difference, whereas language itself is based on resemblance and names the generic, not the individual. The expression "system of the text" is an oxymoron. It remains possible precisely to the degree that difference (specificity, singularity) is not pure. The task of a reading always consists, to a greater or lesser degree, not in obliterating difference, but in taking it apart, in presenting it as an *effect of difference* whose functioning can be known. Without ever "reaching" the text, a reading infinitely approaches it: it is an asymptotic activity.

Let us distinguish reading from the other types of activity we have just described. In relation to projection, the difference is double: projection denies both the autonomy of the work and its particularity. The relation with commentary is more complex: commentary is an atomized reading; reading, a systematic commentary. But if system is our goal, we must renounce the principle of literal fidelity which, as we have seen, is the basis of the commentator's activity. In the work of reading, the critic will tend to put certain parts of the text provisionally between parentheses, to reformulate others, to complete or to add where he feels there is a significant absence. Derrida, who has recently produced several exemplary philosophical readings, remarks "Reciprocally, the man prevented by 'methodological discretion,' 'norms of objectivity,' and 'the guardrails of knowledge' from putting himself into the text will not even be reading." We do not gain direct access to fidelity, we conquer it; it implies frequent, but not irresponsible desertions.

Nor is the relation between reading and poetics a simple one: neither one is the converse or the symmetrical complement of the other. Reading presupposes poetics; in poetics it finds its concepts, its instruments. At the same time, reading is not the simple illustration of these concepts, for its object is different: a text. The apparatus of poetics ceases to be a goal in itself in order to become an (indispensable) instrument in the investigation and description of the individual system.

The context I have just sketched still remains rather broad: in order to particularize it, we must distinguish a reading from its closest relatives. To do this, I shall contrast it with two other activities which I shall call—limiting the meaning of the words—*interpretation* and *description*.

The term *interpretation* here refers to any substitution of another text for the present text, to any endeavor which seeks to discover, through the apparent textual fabric a second more authentic text. It is interpretation which has dominated our western tradition from the allegorical and theological exegeses of the Middle Ages down to contemporary hermeneutics. The conception of the text as a palimpsest is not alien to reading, but instead of replacing one text by another, reading describes the relation of the two. For reading, the text is never *another*, it is multiple.

This denial of substitution is radical, and it also covers psychoanalytical interpretations. A certain, now superseded doctrine held that the work's system was constituted by the author's conscious intentions; today, by a much too symmetrical reversal, we are told that it is this same author's unconscious desires which form such a system. The reading of a literary text cannot be "symptomal," that is, it cannot attempt to reconstitute a second text articulated on the lapses of the first; a reading cannot privilege the unconscious (any more than the conscious) by obligatorily seeking a system "unperceived" by the writer. The opposition between conscious and unconscious refers to an extratextuality with which a reading has nothing to do.

We must not deduce, from this refusal to privilege the unconscious (or conscious) elements of a system, a general refusal to privilege any part of the work whatever; we must not assume that there is only a monotonous reading which attributes an equal importance to every sentence of the text, to every part of the sentence. There are points of focalization—axes and nodes—which, strategically, dominate the rest. But in order to discover them, we cannot apply a procedure based on external criteria. Such points, axes and nodes, will be chosen as a consequence of their role in the work, not of their place in the author's psyche. This very choice locates one reading in relation to another, and this preferential attention determines the existence of an indefinite number of readings. If a reading did not privilege certain points of the text, it could be rapidly exhausted: the "right" reading of each work would be settled once and for all. The choice of axes and nodes, which can vary infinitely, produces in return the variety of our readings; it is this choice which makes us speak of a more or less rich reading (and not simply of a true or false one), of a more or less appropriate strategy.

On the other hand, we distinguish reading from *description*, a term by which I refer to the linguistic-oriented studies essentially concerned with the analysis of poetry. Description differs from reading not in its general direction of study, but in the choice of particular methodological presuppositions. Let us list the main ones:

1. For description, all categories of literary discourse are given in advance, once and for all, and the particular work is located in relation to them the way a new chemical product is located in relation to Mendeleyev's periodic system, which is achronic. Only the combination is new, the combination-reservoir always remains the same; or again, the rules remain as they are, only the order of their application changes. In the perspec-

tive of reading, the text is both the product of a system of pre-existing literary categories, and the transformation of this same system; the new text modifies the very combination-reservoir of which it is the product, it changes not only the order of application of the rules, but their nature. The only exception—though one which merely confirms the rule—are works which belong to so-called "mass literature" and which can be entirely deduced from their genre, pre-existing the individual work. Since it does not acknowledge the means of describing how the work transforms the system of which it is the product, description implicitly affirms the adherence of all works to "mass literature."

2. For description, the linguistic categories of a text are automatically pertinent on the literary level, in the exact order of their organization in the language. In its very course, description follows the stratification of the linguistic object: it proceeds from distinctive features to phonemes, from grammatical categories to syntactic functions, from the rhythmic organization of the line of verse to that of the strophe, and so on. Because of this, all grammatical categories, for instance, will signify on the same level, each in relation to the others (as Riffaterre had already observed). Reading, however, adopts another postulate: the literary work effects a systematic short-circuiting of the autonomy of linguistic levels. Here a grammatical form is made contiguous with a certain theme of the text, the phonic or graphic constitution of a proper noun will engender the remainder of the narrative. The organization of the literary text has a pertinence which belongs only to itself; automatically to accept the pertinence of language is to subject the text if not to an extratextuality, at least to a pretextuality.

3. For description, the order of appearance of the textual elements, the syntagmatic or temporal course has virtually no importance. As Lévi-Strauss writes, "The order of chronological succession is reabsorbed into an atemporal matrical structure." In practice, the description of a poem should lead to a diagram which represents the text's system in the form of a spatial organization. Reading, as we have seen, starts from the principle that no part of the work can be declared a priori to lack signification, neither the syntagmatic order nor any particular

theme. Any other position would be equivalent to a re-establishment of the form/content dichotomy, a pairing in which one term is essential, whereas the other, being superficial, can be discarded without any great damage.

These distinctions between reading and its doubles—interpretation and description—must not lead us to suppose that an abyss separates them, and that nothing links them together. We must, precisely, *read* the interpretations and descriptions, and not reject or accept them en bloc. Without the practice of description, for example, we should not be able to respond to the text's phonic and grammatical aspects.

This negative description of reading has already familiarized us with certain of its practices; now let us attempt to consider them in some detail.

The inaugural act of any reading is a certain destruction of the text's apparent order. In its surface linearity, the work presents itself as pure difference: difference of this work from others, difference of a part of the work compared to the rest. The task of reading begins by comparison, by the discovery of resemblance. In this sense, there is an analogy between reading and *translation,* which is also based on the possibility of finding an equivalent for a part of the text. But whereas in translation we orient the text toward another series, toward an extratextuality, in reading we seek an intratextuality—we are always concerned with an intratextual or intertextual resemblance (the word *resemblance* is here taken in a very general sense, close to that of "relation"; we shall specify it below).

A *certain* destruction, we said: for to destroy does not mean to ignore. The apparent order is not the only one, and our task will be to make evident *all* the orders of the text and to specify their interrelations. A literary reading cannot, therefore, be modeled on the image of the reading of myths, concerning which Lévi-Strauss observes: "Considered in the crude state, any syntagmatic chain must be regarded as having no meaning; either because no signification appears at the outset, or because we suppose we perceive a meaning but without knowing if it is the right one." The same gesture, which is the refusal to be content with the perceptible organization of a text, assumes different significations in these two cases: in the perspective of reading, each layer of the text has a meaning.

To simplify, I shall reduce the constitutive operations of reading to two, which I shall call superposition and figuration, and which I shall examine briefly on two contiguous and yet distinct levels, the intratextual and the intertextual.

Intratextual superposition is based on a principle we have stated earlier: the absence of impermeability between the work's linguistic levels, the possibility of immediate shift from one level to the other. Superposition will therefore have as its goal the establishment not only of classes of equivalence but of any describable relation: whether of resemblance (in the strict sense), opposition, gradation, or even of causality, conjunction, disjunction, exclusion. A remarkable example of such an endeavor is to be found in Boris Eikhenbaum's study, made fifty years ago, of the construction of Gogol's "Overcoat." A phonic analysis of proper and common nouns permits Eikhenbaum to analyze the tale's organization; a consideration of the rhythm of the sentences finds an immediate echo in the analysis of themes. In a study recently published in the French journal *Poétique*, Christiane Veschambre shows the way a narrative by Raymond Roussel is engendered by an anagrammatic analysis of the characters' names. These examples, both of which emphasize the graphic or phonic constitution of words, are not to be taken as the affirmation of a legitimate and universal dominance of the primary signifying layer over all the others. To suppose so would be once again to privilege one part of the text in relation to the others (and therefore to re-establish the form/content opposition, with all it implies); it would be to forget that all the levels of the work are signifiers, though in different ways. Such anagrammatic analyses have a value as examples rather than as a universal law for the structure of texts.

I shall take as an example of the second operation, which I call *figuration*, another work by Eikhenbaum (still remaining on the *intratextual* level). In his study of the Russian poet Anna Akhmatova, he first notes the frequence of oxymoronic constructions of the type—"she grieves gaily, decked out in her nakedness" or again "the vernal autumn"—to arrive at the hypothesis that on every level this poetic *oeuvre* obeys the figure of the oxymoron, that we will find in it "a special style whose base is oxymorism, the surprise of connections; this is reflected not only in stylistic details, but also in the subject." Thus we have it on the level of composition: "Often the strophe is subdivided into two parts between which there is no semantic link." "A poem will continue along two parallels, so that it can be divided into two, uniting all the strophes' first and second halves." Similarly for the organizing thematic element of the whole, the "lyric I" in Akhmatova's poetry—"Here there already begins to form the image of the paradoxical heroine in her duplicity (more exactly in her oxymoron): sometimes a sinner of tempestuous passions, sometimes a nun of the poor to whom God will grant forgiveness." "Akhmatova's heroine, who unites in herself the entire sequence of events, scenes, or sensations, is an oxymoron incarnate, the lyrical narrative whose center she occupies moves by antitheses, paradoxes, it avoids psychological formulations; it becomes strange by the incoherence of moods. The image becomes enigmatic, disturbing, it doubles, multiplies. The moving and the sublime occur alongside the terrifying, the terrestrial; simplicity is juxtaposed to complexity; sincerity to cunning and coquetry; kindness to anger; monastic humility to passion and jealousy."

Once again, we must not take the example for a universal rule. The figure Eikhenbaum describes happens to be an oxymoron, which is a familiar figure of rhetoric. But we must give the term *figure* a larger extension, especially since the figures are nothing but linguistic relations we can perceive and designate: it is the denominative act which gives birth to the figure. The figure which we read through the different levels of the work may very well not be found in the repertory of classical rhetorics. In studying the tales of Henry James, I found myself up against such a "figure in the carpet"; by schematizing, we may reduce it to this formula: "the essence is absent, the presence is unessential." This same "figure" organizes James's themes as well as his syntax, the composition of the story quite as much as the "points of view" in the narrative. We cannot a

priori grant a "first" or "original" status to any of these levels
(the others then being its manifestation or expression); on the
other hand, within a particular text we can discover a hierarchy
of this kind. We see at the same time that there is no break between superposition and figuration: the latter extends and elaborates the former.

Just as the meaning of a part of the work is not exhausted in
itself, but is revealed in its relations with the other parts, a work
in its entirety can never be read in a satisfactory and enlighten-
ing fashion if we do not put it in relation with other works,
previous and contemporary. In a certain sense, all texts can be
considered as parts of a single text which has been in the writing since the beginning of time. Without being unaware of the
difference between relations established *in presentia* (intratextual relations), and those established *in absentia* (intertextual relations), we must also not underestimate the presence of
other texts within the text.

On this level we recognize the two preceding (though modified) operations. *Figuration* can occur between one work and
another by the same author. It is here that this problematic notion, "an author's *oeuvre*," may regain a pertinence. Different
texts by an author appear as so many variations of each other,
they comment upon and enlighten each other. In a nonsystem-
atic way, this kind of reading has appeared in criticism from its
very inception; the Russian Formalists (Eikhenbaum, Jakobson) were able to give the intertextual figure a much greater
degree of precision. In France, it is in Charles Mauron's studies
that we first encounter a tendency to read the text system-
atically as a palimpsest, as a transformation of and commentary
upon an earlier text by the same author: here the figure becomes an "obsessive metaphor." This does not mean we must
follow Mauron when he extrapolates from an author's works an
ideal entity which would be anterior to them de jure and de
facto, "the personal myth": it is not necessary to postulate the
existence of an original in order to consider the individual texts
as its transformations; the text is always the transformation of
another transformation.

Figuration is only one of the possible relations among texts;

we can observe it only within an individual *oeuvre;* among texts by different authors, we should be invoking plagiarism, an activity penalized by our culture. But the relations of works between themselves (even of the works of a single author) can be different, and here we return to the operation of *superposition.* Let us first distinguish, within the works of a single author, relations of a paradigmatic type (in which the other text is absent and does not function reciprocally) from syntagmatic relations (in which the second text reacts actively). In the first case, depending on whether the new work confirms or invalidates the properties of the previous one, we will be dealing with phenomena of stylization or of parody. Yuri Tynianov, who is the first to have theorized this problematics, already noted in 1921: "Stylization is close to parody. Both live a double life: beyond the work, there is a second level, parodied or stylized. But in parody, the two levels must be necessarily discordant, out of phase; the parody of a tragedy will be a comedy (it is of little importance whether this is by exaggerating the tragic, or by substituting the comic for each of its elements); the parody of a comedy can be a tragedy. But when there is stylization, there is no longer this same discordance, but quite the contrary, a concordance of the two levels: that of the *stylizer* and that of the *stylized* which appears through it."

In the case of syntagmatic relations, the external text is not a simple model which can be imitated or mocked, it provokes or modifies the present discourse; the formula is that of the question/answer pair, and we habitually designate this relation as a concealed polemic. One of the last Formalists, Mikhail Bakhtin, describes this phenomenon as it occurs in Dostoyevsky, and offers a first—and for the moment the only—theory of intertextual relations. His merit is to have recognized the importance of an aspect of the work which had previously been treated with condescension. Yet as Bakhtin writes, "all literary discourse senses, more or less intensely, its auditor, reader, critic, and reflects his potential objections, appreciations, points of view." Thus what had been hitherto regarded as a secondary feature, affecting a limited number of works, is entirely revalued; at the same time, Bakhtin affirms that the text always refers, positively or negatively, to the prevailing literary tradition: "Every style possesses an internal element of polemic, the difference is only of degree or kind."

How to read? In attempting to answer this question, we have been led to characterize several types of critical discourse—projection, commentary, poetics, reading. Different as they are among themselves, these discourses also share one feature: they are all heterogeneous to literary discourse itself. What is the cost of this choice to read one language through another, one symbolic system by the intermediary of another? Freud has remarked that the dream cannot say "no"; might not literature, in its turn, have certain elements which ordinary language cannot say?

No doubt there is an *untheorizable* element in literature, as Michel Deguy calls it, if theory presupposes scientific language. One function of literature is the subversion of this very language; hence it is extremely rash to claim we can read it exhaustively with the help of that very language it calls into question. To do so is equivalent to postulating the failure of literature. At the same time, this dilemma is much too inclusive for us to be able to escape it: confronted with a poem, we can only resign ourselves to the impoverishment caused by a different language, or else (a factitious solution) write another poem. Factitious because this second text will be a new work which still awaits its reading: an entire autonomy deprives criticism of its raison d'être, just as a submission to ordinary language affects it with a certain sterility. There remains, of course, a third solution which is silence: we cannot speak of that.

Since the metaphor of the itinerary is particularly current in any description of reading, let us say that one of the possible paths leads us beyond the text; another leaves us on this side of it (the third solution consists in not setting out). To bring the two paths as close to each other as possible: does this not already hold out the hope that they will someday converge?

1969

Appendix

The Methodological Heritage of Formalism

The structural method, developed first in linguistics, has a growing number of partisans in all the human sciences, including the study of literature. This development seems particularly justified since, among the relations between human speech and the various forms of expression, those which unite speech to literature are profound and numerous. Nor is the study of such a connection an especially recent development. The "Prague Circle," one of the first schools of structural linguistics, is an offshoot of the literary studies conducted in Russia from 1915 to 1930 and known as "Russian Formalism." The relation between the two movements is incontestable; it is established by those who participated in both, simultaneously or successively (Jakobson, Tomashevsky, Bogatyrev), as evidently as by the Formalist publications, known to the Prague Circle. It would be an exaggeration to assert that structural linguistics has borrowed its ideas from Russian Formalism, for the field of study and the objectives of the two disciplines are not the same; nonetheless, traces of "Formalist" influence are to be found among the structuralists, in certain techniques of analysis as well as in general principles. Hence it is natural and necessary to review, in the light of today's growing interest in the structural study of literature, the Formalists' chief methodological achievements, and to compare them with those of contemporary linguistics.

Before undertaking such a comparison, it is important to establish some basic principles of the Formalist doctrine. Though frequently used, the expression "formal method" is imprecise, both the noun and the adjective being debatable. The method, far from being unique, comprehends a group of devices and techniques for describing the literary work, but also for making scientific investigations of very different kinds. In essence, we may say that the method will consider the work itself, the literary text, as an immanent system; obviously this is no more than its point of departure, not its detailed exposition. As for the term "formal," it has become no more than a convenient label rather than a precise designation, and the Formalists themselves avoid it. Form, for them, includes all aspects, all parts of the work, but it exists only as a relationship of the elements among themselves, of the elements to the work as a whole, of the work to its national literature, and so forth; in short, form is a set of functions. The strictly literary study, which today we call structural, is characterized by the viewpoint the observer chooses and not by his object which, from another viewpoint, could lend itself to a psychological, psychoanalytic, linguistic, or some other analysis. Jakobson's assertion—"The object of literary study is not literature but literariness (*literaturnost'*), that is, what makes a given work a literary work"—must be interpreted at the level of the investigation and not of its object.

Every study, when it attempts to be scientific, confronts problems of terminology. Yet most investigators deny literary studies the right to a well-defined, precise terminology, on the grounds that the categories of literary phenomena change according to period and nation. The fact that form and function, those two faces of the sign, can vary independently of each other, rules out any absolute classification. Any static classification must keep one of these faces the same, whatever the other's variations. It follows that (a) each term must be defined in relation to the others and not in relation to the phenomena (literary works) it designates; (b) any system of terms is valid for a given synchronic section, whose postulated limits are arbitrary. Tynianov raises the problem in his preface to the anthology "Russian Prose" and illustrates it by the classification of genres in his essays "The Literary Fact" and "On Literary Evolution." According to Tynianov, "the study of isolated genres is impossible outside the system in and with which they are in correlation." The static definitions of genres in current use take account of the signifier alone. A contemporary novel, for instance, should be related, from the viewpoint of its function, to ancient epic, but we relate it to the Greek romance because of the common prose form. "What was the distinctive feature of the 'poem' in the eighteenth century was no longer so in the nineteenth. Similarly, since the function of literature is correlative to other cultural series of the same period, the same phenomenon can be a literary fact or an extraliterary one."

The goal of investigation is the description of the functioning of the literary system, the analysis of its constituent elements, and the discovery of its laws, or, in a narrower sense, the scientific description of a literary text and, beginning there, the establishment of relations among its elements. The main difficulty comes from the heterogeneous and stratified character of the literary work. In order to describe a poem exhaustively, we must take successive positions on different levels—phonic, phonological, metrical, intonational, morphological, syntactical, lexical, symbolic—and take account of their interdependent relations. Further, the literary code, contrary to the linguistic code, has no strictly binding character, and we are obliged to deduce it from each individual text, or at least to correct its previous formulation in each new instance. We must therefore effect a certain number of transformations in order to obtain a model which, alone, will lend itself to a structural analysis. Yet contrary to the study of myth, for example, attention must be paid as much or more to the character of these transformations than to their result, since our rules of decoding are analogous to the rules of encoding employed by the author. If this were not the case, we should risk reducing entirely different works to the same model, thereby destroying their specific character.

The critical examination of the methods employed requires that we make explicit several basic propositions assumed in Formalist studies. These propositions are adopted a priori and their discussion is not within the realm of literary studies.

Literature is a system of signs, a code analogous to other signifying systems such as natural language, the plastic arts, mythologies, dreams, and so forth. Further, and here literature is distinguished from the other arts, it is constructed with the help of a prior structure, that is, language; it is therefore a second-degree signifying system, in other words a connotative system. At the same time language, which serves as the raw material for the formation of the units of the literary system, and which therefore belongs, in Hjelmslev's terminology, to the level of expression, does not lose its own signification, its content. We must further take account of the different possible functions of a message and not reduce its meaning to its referential and emotive functions. The notion of a poetic or esthetic function which bears on the message itself—a notion introduced by Jakubinsky, developed by Jakobson and Mukařovsky, and integrated into the notional system of linguistics by Jakobson—has a place in the system of literature as well as in the system of language, and creates a complex equilibrium of functions. Let us note that the two systems, often analogous, are not thereby identical; further, literature employs social codes whose analysis does not pertain to a literary study.

Every element present in the work bears a signification which can be interpreted according to the literary code. For Shklovsky, "the work is entirely constructed. Its entire substance is organized." The organization is internal to the literary system and is not related to any referent. Thus Eikhenbaum writes: "No single sentence of the literary work *can* be, in itself, a direct 'expression' of the author's personal sentiments; rather, it is always a construction, a form of play." Hence we must also take into account the various functions of the message, for "organization" can be manifested on several different levels. This observation permits a clear distinction between literature and folklore; folklore tolerates a much greater independence among its elements.

The systematic character of the relations among the elements stems from the very essence of language. These relations constitute the object of true literary investigation. Tynianov formulates these ideas, fundamental to structural linguistics, as follows: "The work represents a system of correlative factors. The correlation of each factor with the others is its function with respect to the system. . . . The system is not a cooperation based on the equality of all the elements, it presupposes an emphasis on one group of elements (the 'dominant') and the distortion of others." An observation of Eikhenbaum's affords an example of this; he remarks that when descriptions are dominated by the author's interventions, "it is chiefly the dialogue which manifests the argument and the style." To isolate one element in the course of the analysis is therefore merely a working method; its signification is to be found in its relations with the others.

The inequality of the constituent elements imposes another rule: no one element is directly linked with any other, the relation is established according to a hierarchy of planes (or strata) and of levels (or ranks), along the axis of substitutions and the axis of connections. As Tynianov notes, "The element enters simultaneously into relation with the series of similar elements belonging to other systems or works, even to other series, and further with the other elements of the same system (it has an auto-function and a syn-function)." The different *levels* are defined by the dimensions of their parts. The problem of the smallest significant unit will be discussed below; as for the largest, it is, in the context of literary studies, the whole of literature. The number of levels is theoretically unlimited, but in practice three are generally considered: that of the constituent elements, that of the work, that of a national literature. This does not rule out, in certain cases, emphasizing an intermediary level—for example, a cycle of poems—or else the works of a genre or of a given period. The distinction of various *planes* requires more logical rigor, and this becomes our first task. The Formalists have dealt essentially with the analysis of poems in which they distinguish phonic and phonological; metrical, intonational, and prosodic; morphological and syntactical planes. For their classification, Hjelmslev's distinction between form and substance can be quite useful. Shklovsky shows, apropos of prose texts, that this distinction is equally valid on the plane of narrative, where the compositional methods can be separated from the content of events. It is obvious that the actual arrangement of levels and planes in any text does not necessarily coincide with the arrangement employed in the course of analysis, which is why analysis often begins by treating the work as a whole: it is here that the structural relations are most clearly shown.

Let us first consider several methods, already suggested by the work of the Formalists but subsequently refined by the linguists. For instance, analysis into distinctive features: this appears quite clearly in the very first Formalist writings on phonetics by Jakubinsky and Osip Brik. Later, some of the Formalists participated in the attempts of the Prague structuralists to define the notions of phoneme, distinctive feature, redundant feature, and so forth (see, among others, the studies by Bernstein). The importance of these ideas for literary analysis has been indicated by Brik, apropos of the description of a poem, in which the distribution of phonemes and distinctive features may serve to form or to reinforce its structure. Brik defines the simplest link of repetition as "one in which we do not distinguish the palatalized or nonpalatalized character of the consonants, but in which voiced and unvoiced sounds are represented as different."

The validity of this type of analysis is confirmed as much by its success in contemporary phonology as by its theoretical basis, which derives from the previously mentioned principles: the relational definition is the only valid one, for the notions cannot be defined by relation to a substance which is alien to them. As Tynianov observes, "The function of each work is in its correlation with others. . . . It is a differential sign." But the application of this method can be considerably enlarged if we accept the hypothesis of the profound analogy between the two faces of the sign. Here again, Tynianov attempts to analyze the signification of a "word," in the same way one might analyze its signifying face ("the notion of fundamental feature in semantics is analogous to the notion of phoneme in phonetics"), by decomposing it into its constituent elements: "We must not begin with the word as an indivisible element of literary art, treating it as the brick with which we build our structure. The word can be split into much finer 'verbal elements.' " This analogy was not developed or refined then on account of the psychological definition of the phoneme prevalent at the time. But today this principle is increasingly applied in studies of structural semantics.

Last, we may try to apply this method to the analysis of significant units of the literary system, that is, to the content of the connotative system. The first step in this direction would consist in studying the characters of a narrative and their relationships. The numerous remarks by authors, or even a superficial glance at any narrative, show that certain characters are placed in opposition to others. Yet an immediate opposition of the characters would simplify these relations without coming any closer to our goal. It would serve our purpose better to decompose each image into distinctive features and to put these in a relation of opposition or identity with the distinctive features of other characters in the same narrative. We would thereby obtain a reduced number of axes of opposition whose various combinations would regroup these features into representative clusters of characters. The same procedure would define the characteristic semantic field of the work in question. At first, the denomination of these axes would depend, essentially, on the investigator's personal intuition, but the comparison of similar analyses would permit the establishment of more or less "objective" outlines of an author or even of a given period of a national literature.

This same principle engenders another method, of very broad application in descriptive linguistics: the definition of an element by its distributional possibilities.

Tomashevsky used this method to characterize the various types of metrical schema, thereby establishing a definition by substitution: "We must call iambic tetrameter any combination of sounds which can replace any iambic tetrameter line in a poem." Propp uses the same method in a semantic analysis of the utterance.

The method of analysis into immediate constituents is also employed in descriptive linguistics. It is often applied by the Formalists. Tomashevsky discusses it apropos of the notion of "theme": "The work as a whole can have its theme and at the same time each part of the work possesses its theme. . . . With the help of this decomposition of the work into thematic units, we finally reach the *undecomposable* parts, the smallest particles of the thematic material. . . . The theme of this undecomposable part of the work is called a *motif.* Ultimately, each proposition has its own motif." If the usefulness of such a principle seems obvious, its concrete application raises problems. First of all, we must refrain from identifying motif and proposition, for the two categories derive from different notional series. Contemporary semantics avoids the difficulty by introducing two distinct notions: lexeme (or morpheme) and sememe. As Propp has noted, a sentence may contain more than one motif (his example contains four); it is just as easy to find examples of the opposite case. Propp himself maintains a more prudent and nuanced attitude: each motif comprises several functions, which exist at the lowest level, and whose signification is not immediate within the work; their meaning must first be integrated at a higher level. "By function we mean the action of a character, defined from the viewpoint of its signification for the development of the plot." The insistence on functional signification is important here as well, for the same actions very often have a different role in different narratives. For Propp these functions are constant, limited in number (thirty-one in Russian fairy tales), and can be defined a priori. Without discussing here their validity for his analysis of folklore material, we can say that an a priori definition does not seem useful to literary analysis. For literary analysis as for linguistics, it would seem, rather, that the success of such decomposition depends on the order adopted in the procedure. But its formalization raises still more complex problems for literary analysis, where the correspondence between signifier and signified is more difficult to follow than in linguistics. The verbal dimensions of a "motif" do not define the level on which it is linked to other motifs. Hence a chapter is as likely to be constituted by several pages as by a single phrase. Consequently the identification of the semantic levels where the motifs become meaningful constitutes the indispensable premise of this kind of analysis. It is clear, moreover, that this minimal unit can be analyzed into its constituents,[1] but these no longer belong to the connotative code: the double articulation is manifest, here as in linguistics.

The diversity of the material can be considerably reduced by certain operations of transformation. Propp introduces this notion of transformation in the process of comparing paradigmatic classes. Once the tales are decomposed into parts and functions, it becomes clear that the parts which play the same syntactical role can be regarded as deriving from the same prototype, by means of a rule of transformation applied to the primary form. This paradigmatic comparison (a comparison by "vertical rubrics") shows that their common function allows us to relate forms apparently quite different: "We often take secondary formations for new objects; yet these subjects are descendents of former ones, the result of a certain transformation, a certain metamorphosis. . . . By grouping the *données* of each rubric, we may determine all the types, or more exactly all the species of the transformation. . . . It is not only the attributive elements which are subject to the laws of transformation, but also the functions." Thus Propp assumes that we can work our way back to the primary tale, from which the others have proceeded.

Two preliminary considerations come to mind. In applying Propp's techniques to literature, we must take account of the differences between the kind of creation characteristic of folklore and individual creation (Bogatyrev and Jakobson have written an article on precisely this subject). The specificity of literary material requires that we pay attention to the rules of transformation themselves and to the order of their application, rather than to the result obtained. Further, in literary analysis there is no justification for the search for a primary genetic schema. The simplest form, on the axis of connections or the axis of substitutions, grants our comparison the measure by which we may describe the character of the transformation.

Propp has made this notion explicit and proposed a classification in an article called "Fairy Tale Transformations." The

[1] As Charles Hockett, for instance, proposes: "A whole novel, evidently, possesses a kind of determined structure of immediate constituents; these immediate constituents consist, in turn, of smaller constituents, and so on, until we reach the individual morphemes."

transformations are divided into three large groups: changes, substitutions, and assimilations, the last being defined as "an incomplete replacement of one form by another, producing a fusion of the two forms into one." In order to group these transformations within each of the major types, Propp proceeds in two different ways.

In the first group he uses certain rhetorical figures and lists the following changes: (1) reduction, (2) amplification, (3) corruption, (4) reversal (replacement by the opposite), (5) intensification, (6) weakening. The last two modes of change concern chiefly actions.

In the other two groups, the origin of the new element furnishes the criterion of classification. Hence the assimilations might be: (15) internal (to the tale), (16) derived from life (tale + reality), (17) confessional (following religious changes), (18) derived from superstitions, (19) literary, (20) archaic.

Propp limits the total number of transformations to twenty. They are applicable at every level of narrative. "Whatever concerns the individual elements of the tale concerns the tales in general. If we add a superfluous element, we have an amplification; if we remove an element, a reduction."

Hence the problem of transformation, as crucial for contemporary linguistics as for the other branches of social anthropology, also arises in literary analysis; the analogy, of course, remains incomplete. Since Propp's attempt has not been followed by others of the same kind, a discussion of the rules of transformation—their definition, number, and utility—is not possible; it seems, nonetheless, that a grouping into rhetorical figures, redefined from a logical point of view, would produce the best results.

The problem of the typological classification of literary works gives rise in its turn to difficulties which also appear in linguistics. An elementary analysis of several literary works immediately reveals a large number of similarities and common features. An analogous observation gave rise to the scientific study of languages, and is also at the origin of the formal study of literature, as is shown by the endeavors of Veselovsky, the Russian Formalists' eminent predecessor. Similarly, in Germany,

Heinrich Wölfflin's typology in art history suggested a typology of literary forms (see for instance the work of Oskar Walzel, Fritz Strich, and Theodor Spoerri). But the value and significance of this discovery were not recognized. The Formalists approach this problem from two different principles, which it is not easy to coordinate. On the one hand, they recognize the same elements, the same processes throughout universal literary history, and in this recurrence they see a confirmation of their thesis that literature is a "pure form" with no (or almost no) relation to extraliterary reality, and therefore can be regarded as a "series" which derives its forms from itself. On the other hand, the Formalists know that the signification of each form is functional, that the same form may have various functions, which are all that matter in the comprehension of works, and that consequently to discover the resemblance between forms, far from advancing the knowledge of the literary work, would in fact be a distraction. The coexistence of these two principles among the Formalists derives in part from the absence of a consistent and exact terminology, in part from the fact that they are not used simultaneously by the same authors: the first principle is developed and defended primarily by Shklovsky, while the second is basic to works of Yuri Tynianov and V. V. Vinogradov, who are much more concerned to discover the motivation, the internal justification of one element or another within a work, than to note its recurrence elsewhere. Hence Tynianov writes: "I categorically reject the method of comparison by quotations, which suggests a *tradition* proceeding from one writer to another. According to this method, the constituent terms are abstracted from their functions, and ultimately we are faced with incommensurable units. Coincidences and convergences doubtless exist in literature, but they concern the functions of elements, the functional relations of a given element." It is obvious, in fact, that structural resemblances must be sought on the functional level; yet in literature the link between form and function is neither accidental nor arbitrary, since form too is significant—in another system, the system of language. Consequently the study of forms allows us to discover functional relationships.

At the same time, the study of isolated works, considered as so many closed systems, is insufficient. The changes the literary code undergoes from work to work do not mean that every literary text has its own code. We must avoid both extreme positions: supposing that there is a code common to all literature, supposing that each work engenders a different code. The exhaustive description of a phenomenon, without recourse to a general system which integrates that phenomenon, is impossible. Contemporary linguistics is well aware of this, for as Jakobson says: "It is as contradictory to describe isolated systems without including them in a taxonomy as it is to construct a taxonomy without descriptions of individual systems: each task implies the other." Only the inclusion of the system of internal relations which characterize a work in the most general system of genre or period, or in the context of a national literature, permit us to establish the different levels of abstraction in this code (the different levels of "form" and "substance" in Hjelmslev's terminology). Often the deciphering of such a code depends directly on external factors: hence Maupassant's tales "without ending" assume their meaning only in the context of the literature of the period, as Shklovsky remarks. Such a comparison also permits us to describe more accurately the code's functioning in its various manifestations. Nonetheless the precise description of an individual work is a necessary premise. As Vinogradov has noted: "To know a writer's individual style independently of any tradition, of any other contemporary work, and in its totality as a linguistic system, to know its esthetic organization—this task must precede all historical research."

The experience of the classifications attempted in linguistics and in literary history leads us to posit a few basic principles. First, the classification must be typological and not genetic, the structural resemblances are not to be sought in the direct "influence" of one work upon another. This principle, we may note, was discussed by Vinogradov in his article "On Literary Cycles." Next we must take into account the stratified character of the literary work. The principle defect of the typologies proposed in literary history under the influence of art history is that, though constructed on a single plane, they are nonetheless applied to whole works and even to entire periods.[2] On the other hand, linguistic typology confronts phonological, morphological, or syntactic systems without these various perspectives necessarily coinciding. Classification must therefore follow the stratification of the system into planes and not into levels (works). Last, structure can be as evident in relations between characters or in rhythm as in the various styles of narrative. Thus in Gogol's "Overcoat," the opposition is produced by the conflict of two different points of view, adopted successively by the author and reflected in lexical and syntactical differences (Eikhenbaum). The present state of linguistic studies on classification offers a good many suggestions as to this procedure of comparison and generalization.

Now let us consider the typology of simple narrative forms as sketched by Shklovsky and, in part, by Eikhenbaum. Such forms are chiefly represented in the tale; the novel is to be distinguished from them only by its greater complexity. Yet the novel's dimensions (its syntagmatic aspect) are related to the methods it utilizes (its paradigmatic aspect). Eikhenbaum remarks that the denouement of the novel and that of the tale follow different laws: "The end of a novel is a moment of weakening, and not of reinforcement; the culminating point of the main action must occur somewhere before the end. . . . This is why it is natural that an unexpected ending is a very rare phenomenon in the novel . . . whereas the tale tends precisely toward the surprise ending, in which all that precedes reaches its culmination. In the novel there must be a certain falling-away after the culminating point, whereas, in the tale it is more natural to stop at the high point once it is reached." Such considerations obviously concern only the "plot," the series of events as presented in the work. Shklovsky asserts that every subject answers to certain general conditions, outside of which a narrative has no subject, strictly speaking: "A simple image, a mere parallel, even the description of an event is not enough to

[2] Apparent exceptions, such as that of J. Petersen, who proposes ten binary oppositions on seven superimposed strata, are invalid because of the intuitive character of such oppositions—for instance, objective-subjective, vague-distinct, plastic-musical, and so forth.

give the impression that we are reading a story. . . . If no denouement is offered, we do not feel we are being given a plot." In order to construct a plot, the end must present the same terms as the beginning, although in a modified relation. We must not forget that all these analyses, which aim at articulating structural relationships, are exclusively concerned with the constructed model and not with the narrative as such.

Shklovsky's observations on the various ways of constructing the subject of a tale lead us to distinguish two forms which, as a matter of fact, coexist in most narratives: staircase construction and construction in a loop or circle. Staircase construction is an open form $(A_1 + A_2 + A_3 + ... A_4)$, in which the numbered terms always have some feature in common: for instance the analogous behavior of three brothers in folktales, or else the succession of adventures of one and the same character. Construction in a loop is a closed form $(A_1R_1A_2) ... (A_1R_2A_2)$ [3] which is based on an opposition. For example, the narrative begins with a prediction, which at the end comes true despite the characters' efforts. Or again, a father aspires to his daughter's love but realizes it only at the narrative's end. These two forms interlock in various ways; usually the tale as a whole describes a closed form, which accounts for the sense of completion it provokes in the reader. The open form is articulated in two main types, one of which is found in mystery novels and tales (Dickens), or in detective fiction. The other consists in the development of a parallelism, as in Tolstoy, for instance. The mystery narrative and the narrative with parallel developments are, in a sense, in opposition to each other, though they can coexist in the same story: the former unmasks illusory resemblances, shows the difference between two apparently similar phenomena. The latter, on the contrary, reveals the resemblance between two different and apparently independent phenomena. This summary is somewhat unfair to the subtle observations of a Shklovsky, who is never concerned to systematize his findings nor to avoid contradictions. The material he assembles to support his theses is considerable, elicited from classical and modern literature alike;

[3] A_1, A_2 . . . designate the paradigmatic units; R_1, R_2 . . . the relations between them.

yet he remains so general that he fails to be convincing. Such a study should be undertaken, at least initially, within the limits of a single national literature and of a given period. Here again the field of investigation remains unexplored.

One problem which has always preoccupied theoreticians of literature is that of the relations between literary reality and the reality to which literature refers. The Formalists have made a considerable effort to elucidate these relations. This problem, which arises in every field of knowledge, is fundamental to semiological study, for it puts questions of meaning in the foreground. Let us recall its formulation in linguistics, where we are concerned with the very object of semantics. According to C. S. Peirce's definition, the meaning of a symbol is its translation into other symbols. This translation can operate on three different levels. It can remain intralingual, when the meaning of a term is formulated with the help of other terms from the same language; in this case we must study the axis of substitutions in a language. It can be interlingual, as Hjelmslev shows when he compares terms designating kinship systems or color systems in various languages. Finally, it can be intersemiotic, when the linguistic perspective is compared with the perspective created by some other system of signs (in the broad sense of the term). As Hjelmslev says, "Semantic description must therefore consist primarily in comparing language with other social institutions, and in providing contact between linguistics and the other branches of social anthropology." None of these three levels necessitates the intervention of the "things" designated. For instance, the linguistic signification of the word "yellow" is not established by reference to yellow objects but by opposition to the words "red," "green," "white," and so on, in the English linguistic system, or by reference to the words "jaune," "gelb," "zholtyj," and so on, or else by reference to the scale of light-wave lengths, established by physics and also representing a system of conventional signs.

Syntax, according to the logicians, should be concerned with the relations among signs. As a matter of fact, it has limited its domain to the syntagmatic axis (the axis of connections) in language. Semantics, for the most part, studies the relations between language and the systems of nonlinguistic signs. The study of the paradigmatic axis (the axis of substitutions) has been neglected. Further, the existence of signs whose chief function is syntactic somewhat obscures the problem. In any natural language, these signs serve exclusively to establish relations among other signs, for instance, certain prepositions, the possessive and relative pronouns, the copula. Obviously such signs exist in literature as well as in language; they afford the agreement, the connection between the various episodes or fragments. This logical distinction must not be confused with the linguistic distinction between grammatical signification and lexical signification, between form and substance of the content, although the two often coincide. In language, for instance, inflection indicating number often belongs to "grammatical signification," but its function is semantic. Thus in literature, "syntactic" signs do not necessarily participate in a work's compositional rules (what corresponds to the grammar of a natural language). The exposition of a narrative does not necessarily occur at the beginning, or the denouement at the end.

The interaction between (syntactic) relations and (semantic) functions are quite complex. The Formalists chiefly studied them in transitions, where their role appears more clearly. For the Formalists, one of the chief factors of literary evolution is the way certain procedures or certain situations manage to appear automatically, thereby losing their "semantic" role and performing only a linking role. In a substitution—a frequent phenomenon in folklore—the new sign can play the same syntactic role as the one it displaced without having the slightest relationship with the "plausibility" of the narrative, which explains the presence, in folk songs for instance, of certain elements whose "meaning" remains totally alien to the rest. Conversely, elements with a dominant semantic function can be modified without changing the syntactic signs of the narrative. Skaftymov, who dealt with this problem in his study of Russian epic poetry, gives some convincing examples: "Even where, because of changes which have occurred in other parts of the epic, disguise is quite unnecessary and even contradictory, it is re-

ained despite all the disadvantages and absurdities it engenders.

The problem which most preoccupied the Formalists concerns the relation between the constraints imposed upon narrative by its internal (paradigmatic) necessities and those which
derive from its necessary agreement with other sign systems
bearing on the same subject. The presence of any particular element in a work is justified by what they call its "motivation."
Tomashevsky distinguishes three types of motivation: compositional, which corresponds to essentially syntactic signs; realistic, which concerns relations with other sign systems; and
esthetic, which shows how all the elements belong to the same
paradigmatic system. The first two types of motivation are generally incompatible, while the third concerns all the signs of the
work. The relation between the last two types is more interesting since their requirements are not on the same level and are
not contradictory. Skaftymov suggests characterizing this phenomenon as follows: "Even in the case of a direct orientation to
reality, the realm of reality envisaged, even if limited to a particular fact, will have a context and a focus from which it receives
its organization. . . . The effective reality is given only in its
broad outlines, the event appears exclusively in the design of
the canvas as a whole, and only insofar as it is necessary to the
reproduction of the basic psychological situation. Though the
effective reality is reproduced by a crude approximation, it is
this approximation which represents the direct and immediate
object of esthetic interest, that is, of expression, reproduction
and interpretation; and the singer's consciousness is subordi-
nated to it. The concrete substitutions in the body of the narrative are not indifferent to him, for they are controlled not only by
a general emotional expressivity but also by the requirements of
the song's object, that is, by criteria of reproduction and resemblance." Tomashevsky sees the relations between the two mo-
tivations in a quasi-statistical perspective: "We require an elementary *illusion* of each work. . . . In this sense, each motif
must be introduced as a *probable* motif for the given situation.
But since the laws of the subject's composition have nothing to

do with probability, each introduction of motifs is a compromise between this objective probability and literary tradition."

For the most part, the Formalists attempted to analyze esthetic motivation, though without ignoring "realistic" motivation. The study of esthetic motivation is more justified since we generally have no means of establishing the other kind. Our habitual procedure, which re-establishes reality according to the work and attempts an explanation of the work by means of this restored reality, constitutes a kind of vicious circle. It is true that the literary perspective can sometimes be compared to other perspectives given either by the author himself or by other documents concerning the same period or the same characters, if historical personages are involved. This is the case of the Russian epic poems which reflect a historical reality known by other means; the characters are frequently princes or Russian boyars. Studying these relationships, Skaftymov writes: "The tragic conclusion of the epic poem is probably suggested by its historic or legendary source, but the motivation of Sukhomanty's disgrace . . . is not justified by any historical reality. Nor is any moral tendency at work here. There remains only the esthetic orientation, which alone gives its meaning to the origin of this scene and justifies it." By comparing the various characters in the poems with historical personages, Skaftymov comes to the following conclusion: "The degree of realism of the various elements in the epic poem varies according to their importance in the general organization of the whole. . . . The relation between the characters of the epic poem and their historical prototypes is determined by their function in the general conception of the narrative."

Now that linguists are using mathematical procedures more and more frequently, we may recall that the Formalists were the first to attempt to do so: Tomashevsky applies Markoff's chain-theory to the study of prosody. This effort deserves our attention when "qualitative" mathematics is being widely used in linguistics. Tomashevsky not only left a valuable study of Pushkin's rhythm but also could see that quantitative study should not be rejected when the nature of the facts justifies its use, notably when it concerns statistical laws. Answering the many objecions provoked by his study, Tomashevsky writes: "Science must not be forbidden the use of any method. . . . Number, formula, and graph are symbols of thought just as words are, and they are comprehensible only to those who master this system of symbols. . . . Numbers decide nothing, they do not interpret, they are merely a way of establishing and describing facts. If numbers and graphs have been misused, the method itself is not to blame—the guilty party is whoever has misused them, not the object of this misuse." Abuses are much more frequent than the successful attempts, and Tomashevsky constantly warns us against premature simplifications: "Calculations often aim at establishing a coefficient capable of authorizing an immediate judgment as to the quality of the fact under analysis. . . . All such 'coefficients' are disastrous to the cause of a philological 'statistics.' . . . We must not forget that even in the case of a correct calculation, the figure obtained characterizes only the frequency of a phenomenon's appearance, but offers no enlightenment as to its quality."

Tomashevsky applies statistical procedures to the study of Pushkin's verse. As he himself has said, "All statistics must be preceded by a study which seeks out the real differentiation of phenomena." This study leads him to distinguish, in approaching the study of meter, three different levels—on one hand, a schema of obligatory character, though not specifying the qualities of the verse, for instance, iambic pentameter; on the other, "usage," that is the individual line of verse; between the two occurs the rhythmic impulse or norm (what Jakobson calls the "model of execution"). This norm can be established for a work or for an author when statistical method is applied to the material selected. Thus the last accented syllable in Pushkin coincides with the metrical stress in 100 percent of the cases, the first in 85 percent, the penultimate in 40 percent, and so forth.

Once again we find the notions of literary analysis approaching those of linguistics. Indeed we recall that for Hjelmslev, who establishes a distinction between usage, norm, and schema in language, "norm is merely an abstraction drawn from usage by an artifice of method. At most it constitutes a useful corollary for a context in which usage can be described." For Tomashevsky, the study of the norm is restricted to "the observation of typical variants within the limits of works united by the identity of rhythmic form (for instance, the trochee in Pushkin's tales of the 1830s); the establishment of the degree of their frequency; the observation of deviations from the type; the observation of the system of the various phonic aspects of the phenomenon being studied (the so-called secondary features of verse such as sonority, syntax, vocabulary); the definition of the constructive functions of these deviations (rhythmic figures); and the interpretation of these observations." This broad program is illustrated by exhaustive analyses of Pushkin's iambic tetrameter and pentameter, compared simultaneously with the norms of other poets or of other works by Pushkin.

This method is even more applicable to realms where the obligatory context is not precisely defined. This is the case for free verse and especially for prose, where no schema exists. Hence for free verse, "which is constructed as a violation of tradition, it is pointless to seek out a rigorous law which admits of no exceptions. We must seek only the norm, and study the range of deviations in relation to it." Similarly for prose "the average form and the amplitude of oscillations are the only objects of investigation. . . . The rhythm of prose must in principle be studied by means of a statistical method."

The conclusion is that we must not apply such methods either to the study of a particular example, that is, to the interpretation of one work, or to the study of laws and constants which control the major units of the literary system. We may thereby deduce that the distribution of literary units (of the connotative system) follows no statistical law, but that the distribution of linguistic elements (of the denotative system) within these units obeys a norm of probability. This would justify the many and brilliant stylistic studies of the Formalists (those, for instance, of Skaftymov and Vinogradov) which observe the accumulation of certain syntactic forms or lexical strata around paradigmatic units (for instance, characters) or syntagmatic units (episodes) in a literary system. It is obvious that what is being dealt with here is a norm and not an obligatory rule. The relations of these major units remain purely "qualitative" and generate a structure which cannot be studied by statistical methods. This explains the varying success of such methods when they are applied to the study of style, that is, to the distribution of linguistic forms within a work. The basic defect of such studies is that they ignore the existence of two different systems of signification (denotative and connotative) and attempt to interpret a work directly from the linguistic system.

This conclusion could doubtless be extended to literary systems of large dimensions. The formal development of a national literature, for instance, obeys certain nonmechanical laws. According to Tynianov, it must be subdivided into the following stages: "(1) a stereotyped principle of construction dialectically evokes a contrary principle of construction; (2) this principle is applied in its easiest form; (3) it extends to the majority of phenomena; (4) it becomes stereotyped and evokes in its turn contrary principles of construction." These stages could never be delimited and defined except in terms of statistical accumulation, according to the general requirements of epistemology, which teaches us that only the temporary states of phenomena obey the laws of probability. In this fashion the application of certain mathematical procedures to literary studies might be better founded than they have been to the present time.

1964

A Note on Translations of the Formalists

Two anthologies contain most of the studies quoted here (as well as some others): L. Lemon, M. Reis, eds., *Russian Formalist Criticism: Four Essays* (Lincoln: University of Nebraska Press, 1965); L. Matejka, K. Pomorska, eds., *Readings in Russian Poetics: Formalist and Structuralist Views* (Cambridge: MIT Press, 1971). Similar anthologies exist in French and German. The basic study of the Formalist movement remains that of Victor Erlich, *Russian Formalism, History—Doctrine* (The Hague: Mouton, 2d ed., 1965).